SAGE was founded in 1965 by Sara Miller McCune to support the dissemination of usable knowledge by publishing innovative and high-quality research and teaching content. Today, we publish over 900 journals, including those of more than 400 learned societies, more than 800 new books per year, and a growing range of library products including archives, data, case studies, reports, and video. SAGE remains majority-owned by our founder, and after Sara's lifetime will become owned by a charitable trust that secures our continued independence.

Los Angeles | London | New Delhi | Singapore | Washington DC | Melbourne

Advance Praise

A refreshing set of real-world experiences with excellent insights on the issues faced by organisations makes this book an essential read for HR professionals. I am sure young HR professionals or those wishing to pursue HR will be fortunate if they have chanced upon this book. The robust experience of the authors comes shining through!

Harsh Goenka
Chairman, RPG Enterprises

The tragedy of the HR profession is that everyone in the corporate world, be it a junior executive or a CEO, believes that they are 'HR experts'! This book brings together numerous concepts in a very structured manner, offers pragmatic perspectives and nudges a sense of urgency to address them for corporate excellence. This should convincingly get HR a seat at the table of strategic thrust in corporates. Finally, I have read a book written by three strong HR professionals that makes concepts simple and directions practical.

Suresh Narayanan
Chairman and Managing Director, Nestle India Ltd

HR should not just be in service of the business, but at the centre of it—HR should shift from filling the cracks to laying the road.

As a function, we look after the greatest asset of the business—our People—and we have the responsibility to better the business and the world. This book helps readers truly understand how to amplify the impact of HR and I highly recommend this to HR and non-HR practitioners alike.

Leena Nair
Chief Human Resources Officer, Unilever

HR Here and Now is written by HR leaders who have worked across different organisations as HR leaders. They have brought their ideas to shape several students of HR in B-schools and are sought-after advisors to companies. The result is a must-read book to understand the potential of HR in today's Digital Tsunami.

Abhijit Bhaduri
Author, Columnist and Leadership Development Coach

The authors have beautifully re-imagined the role of HR team and HR leadership that is needed for an organisation in this age of young employees, competitive talent market, how millennials think about purpose of work and how an organisation's culture can be the competitive differentiation in today's world. With pointed examples and case studies from different kinds of organisations ranging from hospitals to technology companies, this book will give good insights to aspiring students and young professionals on what they can expect when they enter into the people function, how the role of HR is transforming into a strategic business function and the mindset they would need for them to be successful in modern organisations.

Girish Mathrubootham
Founder and CEO, Freshworks Inc.

HR Here and Now is a refreshing perspective on the multiplier effect that human resources plays in building organisational capacity and enabling strategy delivery when combined effectively with individual competence, credibility and selfless service. The authors integrate their decades of experience with emerging trends and case studies for leveraging human capital as a distinct source of business sustainability and competitive advantage. *HR Here and Now* has valuable insight for all business leaders and HR practitioners.

Sandeep Bakhshi
MD and CEO, ICICI Prudential Life

Three veterans have created a compelling road map for all those who want to gain sharper and a nuanced insight into people dynamics in contemporary organisations and use the same to unleash the energy of their colleagues and associates. The distilled wisdom of experience and the pragmatism of practitioners come alive in every page.

Santrupt B. Misra
Chief Executive Officer, Carbon Black Business and Director, Group HR, Aditya Birla Management Corporation Pvt Ltd

HR HERE AND NOW

HR HERE AND NOW

THE MAKING OF THE QUINTESSENTIAL PEOPLE CHAMPION

GANESH CHELLA   **HARISH DEVARAJAN**   **V. J. RAO**

SAGE | Response Business Books

Los Angeles I London I New Delhi
Singapore I Washington DC I Melbourne

First published in 2018 by

SAGE Publications India Pvt Ltd
B1/I-1 Mohan Cooperative Industrial Area
Mathura Road, New Delhi 110 044, India
www.sagepub.in

SAGE Publications Inc
2455 Teller Road
Thousand Oaks, California 91320, USA

SAGE Publications Ltd
1 Oliver's Yard, 55 City Road
London EC1Y 1SP, United Kingdom

SAGE Publications Asia-Pacific Pte Ltd
3 Church Street
#10-04 Samsung Hub
Singapore 049483

Published by Vivek Mehra for SAGE Publications India Pvt Ltd, typeset in 11/14 pts Adobe Caslon Pro by Fidus Design Pvt. Ltd., Chandigarh and printed at Chaman Enterprises, New Delhi.

Library of Congress Cataloging-in-Publication Data
Names: Chella, Ganesh, author. | Devarajan, Harish, author. | Rao, V. J., author.
Title: HR here and now: the making of the quintessential people champion / Ganesh Chella, Harish Devarajan and V.J. Rao.
Description: Thousand Oaks : SAGE Publications India Pvt Ltd, [2018]
Identifiers: LCCN 2018007730| ISBN 9789352806935 (print (pb)) | ISBN 9789352806942 (e-pub) | ISBN 9789352806959 (web)
Subjects: LCSH: Personnel management.
Classification: LCC HF5549 .C44465 2018 | DDC 658.3—dc23
LC record available at https://lccn.loc.gov/2018007730

ISBN: 978-93-528-0693-5 (PB)

SAGE Team: Manisha Mathews, Priya Arora and Shaonli Deb

To Sudha, my wife, who has been the quintessential people champion at home.

—*Ganesh Chella*

To Vijaya, my wife, for her constant support, understanding and patience.

—*V. J. Rao*

To my highly talented wife, Nandini, who has been the anchor in our home, but for whose selfless support much of what I have achieved would have remained just a dream.

—*Harish Devarajan*

Thank you for choosing a SAGE product!
If you have any comment, observation or feedback,
I would like to personally hear from you.

Please write to me at **contactceo@sagepub.in**

Vivek Mehra, Managing Director and CEO, SAGE India.

Bulk Sales

SAGE India offers special discounts
for purchase of books in bulk.
We also make available special imprints
and excerpts from our books on demand.

For orders and enquiries, write to us at

Marketing Department
SAGE Publications India Pvt Ltd
B1/I-1, Mohan Cooperative Industrial Area
Mathura Road, Post Bag 7
New Delhi 110044, India

E-mail us at **marketing@sagepub.in**

Get to know more about SAGE

Be invited to SAGE events, get on our mailing list.
Write today to **marketing@sagepub.in**

This book is also available as an e-book.

Contents

List of Abbreviations   ix
Preface   xiii
Acknowledgements   xv
Introduction   xvii
Contributing Organisations and Leaders   xxiii

Part 1. HR Refreshed   **1**
   1. Through the Eyes of the Beholder   3
   2. New Meanings   11
   3. Evolving Expectations   29
   4. The Doing, Feeling and Thinking Paradigm   42

Part 2. Bringing People on Board   **49**
   5. Planning in Uncertain Times   51
   6. Remaining Attractive   69
   7. Choosing Right   81

Part 3. Managing People   **97**
   8. The Spectrum of Relationships   99
   9. Learning, the New Way   106
  10. Beyond Managing Performance   121
  11. Money and Beyond   143
  12. Managing the Moments of Truth   168

Part 4. Management and Leadership Development   179
     13. Aspirations and Needs   181
     14. Channelising Aspirations   184
     15. Institutionalising the Process   200
     16. Developing Managers and Leaders   220

Part 5. Making the Organisation Effective   241
     17. Leading Change   243
     18. Designing Organisations   258
     19. Contributing to Leadership Effectiveness   275
     20. Shaping the Way Organisations Work   285

Part 6. Managing the Relationship with Employees   299
     21. Boundaries Redefined   301
     22. What Really Matters   313
     23. Towards Progressive Employee Relations   327

**Part 7. The Making of the Quintessential People
Champion   347**
     24. Advancing in HR   349
     25. The Young HR Professional's Readiness
         to Serve   356
     26. The CEO's Schooling as a People Champion   362

Epilogue   366
About the Authors   371

List of Abbreviations

4Ps	price, product, promotion and place
ABG	Aditya Birla Group
AI	artificial intelligence
AMB	Airtel Management Board
ASAL	Automotive Stampings and Assemblies Limited
AV	audiovisual
B2C	business-to-consumer
BPO	business process outsourcing
BUs	business units
C&B	compensation and benefits
C4G	Connected4Growth
CAB	Corporate Advisory Board
CAP	change acceleration process
CCBTs	country category business teams
CCL	The Center for Creative Leadership
CDCs	community development centres
CFI	Coaching Foundation India
CFO	chief financial officer
CHRO	chief human resources officer
CIBIL	Credit Information Bureau (India) Limited
CMO	chief marketing officer
COD	charter of demands
CoEs	centres of excellence

CSR	corporate social responsibility
CTC	conversations that count
DDU-GKY	Deen Dayal Upadhyay Gram Kaushalya Yojana
EBIT	earnings before interest and taxes
EC	executive committee
EE	employee engagement
EPC	engineering, procurement and construction
EQ	emotional quotient
ER	employee relations
EU	European Union
EVP	employee value proposition
GET	graduate engineering trainee
HIPO	high potential
HRBPs	HR business partners
HRIS	Human Resource Information System
HUL	Hindustan Unilever
IDP	individual development plan
IMD	International Institute for Management Development
IP	intellectual property
IR	industrial relations
ITeS	information technology-enabled services
KPOs	knowledge process outsourcing
KRA	key result area
L&D	learning and development
L&T IPM	L&T Institute of Project Management
L&T	Larsen & Toubro
L.I.M.E.	Lessons in Marketing Excellence
M&A	merger and acquisition
MC	management committee
MD	managing director
MDA	my development aim
MDP	my development plan
MI	machine learning
MIS	management information system

MP	managing performance
MRO	maintenance, repair and operations
NBFCs	non-banking financial companies
NSDL	National Securities Depository Limited
NTTF	Nettur Technical Training Foundation
OB	organisational behaviour
OD	organisation development
P&L	profit and loss
PCMM	People Capability Maturity Model
PRP	people review process
QWL	quality of work life
ROI	return on investment
SAS	Scandinavian Airlines System
SCM	supply chain management
SF	Sundaram Finance
SLAs	service-level agreements
SMT	self-managed teams
SOPs	standard operating procedures
SVP	senior vice-president
SWP	strategic workforce planning
TACO	Tata AutoComp Systems
THSL	TACO Hendrickson Suspensions Pvt Ltd
TI	Texas Instruments
TQM	total quality management
TSNA	The Sankara Nethralaya Academy
ULIP	Unilever Leadership Internship Programme
UFLP	Unilever Future Leaders Programme
USPL	Universal Sportsbiz Pvt Ltd
VC	venture capital
VDA	variable dearness allowance
VRS	Voluntary Retirement Scheme
VUCA	volatility, uncertainty, complexity and ambiguity
WHO	World Health Organization
WWA	Wipro Wide Approach

Preface

Why did we decide to team up and write this book? What was our motivation?

There were three clear reasons for investing the last several months in writing this book.

In the early days of our work as HR professionals, all three of us have encountered internal stakeholders who asked us some very difficult and uncomfortable questions about our work, our contribution and the reason for our existence.

These interactions impacted us quite deeply and fuelled in us not just a sense of anger but also a sense of pride and a burning desire to establish, in our own small way, a positive impression and perception of what an HR professional can do. As we look back, we have left many who have engaged with us, convinced about the value that this profession and its practitioners can deliver. We see this book as a great way of passing on not just our insights and experiences but also our sense of hope, optimism and pride about who we are and what we can do.

In the past few years, we have been working with hundreds of HR professionals to enhance their capabilities through bespoke in-house programmes as well as public programmes. The experience of conceptualising, designing and delivering these programmes over these years has given us a rich repository of insights and perspectives. Equally, the process of thinking about HR has only contributed to our own clarity on a number of issues that are of relevance to the HR community. We felt that this book could be a great platform to share some of these insights.

Organisations in India have done a lot of innovative work in the field of HR, but they have been too modest to talk about it. As a result, there is a continued reliance on experiences reported from other countries to tell us what is right and what is not. It is time that we in India craft our own theories and ideas. This book is a modest attempt in that direction.

This book is meant for anyone who is a people champion—managers, leaders and of course HR professionals—who have or would like to champion any aspect of people management. This book is especially targeted at the young HR professionals. It is our firm belief that the perspectives and views these young HR professionals subscribe to will eventually determine their attitudes and orientations to the function.

It is our hope that this book would help any people champion to:

- Develop a more balanced view about the function, including a sense of pride about what has been accomplished and optimism about what the function can aspire to achieve.
- Embrace a contemporary view of the function that is appreciative and contextually relevant but also grounded in reality.
- Understand the real needs, issues and challenges of the function and respond in a way that makes sense for today and tomorrow.
- Bring focus on the competencies that need to be developed keeping in mind current as well as future needs and demands.
- Understand, apply and practise the science and art of HR in developing solutions to contemporary issues.

This is the very purpose of the book.

With our collective experience and continuing engagement with businesses and the HR function, we would like to put forth our insights and perspectives in the hope that it will be of some value to HR professionals who are either starting off or are in the midst of their amazing career journey.

Having worked in HR and been HR professionals all our lives, we don't just feel competent but also passionate about doing this for the future generation of HR leaders. This is our inspiration.

Acknowledgements

This book is not just the result of what the three of us did over the past two years but it is also the result of what the three of us were beneficiaries of for the past three or four decades.

Our alma maters, some of our teachers, our managers, our mentors, the organisations we worked with, have all positively shaped us and have contributed to our growth. Some of them need special mention.

Tata Institute of Social Sciences (TISS) and XLRI, Jamshedpur, are two great institutes we studied at. But for these iconic institutions, we would not be here in HR.

Cadbury's, Hindustan Unilever, RPG Group, Tata Group and TVS Group would feature as organisations that shaped us and touched our lives in remarkable ways.

Legendary HR leaders such as R. R. Nair, Late Tarun Seth, Pravin Dave and Aroon Joshi would deserve special mention for the role they played in mentoring us. We remain ever grateful to them.

The hundreds of client organisations that we worked with as consultants, coaches and HR educators served as rich grounds for our learning and experimentation. As much as we made a difference, we learnt too. Our thanks to them for giving us these wonderful opportunities to contribute and learn.

All three of us were fortunate to have been surrounded by an extremely wide, vibrant and value-adding network of highly accomplished professionals with whom we could spar, exchange ideas and learn. We thank each one of them for enriching our professional lives.

Through the inevitable highs and lows of our professional lives, it has been our families that have been around, been our cheer leaders and supporters. We can never thank them all enough.

It is never easy when three authors with different thinking and writing styles come together on a book-writing project. Integrating our efforts, creating multiple drafts of manuscripts, making endless corrections, living through computer crashes and of course sticking to deadlines was all possible, thanks to the tireless efforts and support of Sumathi Mohan, our project manager and documentation expert. We compliment and thank her for the patience, keen interest and the diligence she demonstrated.

It was our dream that this book should strike a fine balance between our professional perspectives and current organisational practices. The overwhelming support received from organisations which were so willing to share their experiences made this dream a reality. For this, we remain ever grateful to them.

SAGE has always been extremely efficient in their interactions with us, and it has been truly a pleasure working with the SAGE team.

Introduction

So much is happening in the world of HR every single day. There are new needs and problems cropping from all corners of the business. Business leaders, HR leaders and thought leaders are coming up with new ideas and solutions to address these needs and problems without losing time. Obviously, therefore, there is so much to think, talk and write about in HR.

So when the three of us decided to write a book on HR, we had to do a lot of thinking—what slant to give, what slice to explore and what message to deliver.

After a lot of deliberation, our choice popped up for us. We'd like to explain our choice using an analogy. If today's HR was a game of cricket, the three of us could choose to be giving a running commentary—ball by ball, describing what was happening, deeply immersed in the details—or we could step back, look at the game from a distance and offer our expert comments on a few things that catch our fancy. Both have their place and their value. One would deliver knowledge and the other perspective.

This book is about perspectives on HR here and now. Perspectives from where we stand. It is not our intention to elaborate the science or practices or to offer tools and techniques.

The vision of this book is to engage you in a debate and discussion about how we see HR as a function and profession here and now—how we see the practice and the practitioner. The intent is to reflect on what we are seeing, hearing and experiencing about the function in an inclusive fashion. You will find us going back in time not to glorify the past but to learn a bit from history. We will of course dash back to the present to interpret current realities and occurrences and learn from it too. As we do this, what is good will be acknowledged because there is indeed a lot that is good. The things that concern us will be called out. Where appropriate, some suggestions based on what seems to work for others would be shared. Of course, there will be an attempt to look into the future, where we are able to see it.

Some of you may not necessarily agree with our views—that is the nature of expert comments. It will not be a commentary of facts but some sparring with transparency and openness which can generate some fresh thinking.

Through all this, we would like to influence the current and future generations of managers and leaders who are responsible for and passionate about anything to do with people in organisations— the 'people champions' as we call them.

How the Book Is Organised

Given that we have approached the subject from three vantage points—the function, the demands placed on it and the professional—the book is organised on similar lines.

In the first section, we take a fresh look at HR in ways that have not been explored too often before. In the first chapter of this section, we look at the function through the eyes of its beholders. Given that the function and the functionary trigger strong emotions, we have explored what lies behind these perceptions using a simple model.

In the second chapter, we have presented a potential system of classification across various dimensions—a classification system or taxonomy that most comprehensively captures the new meaning that HR holds for all of us.

In the third chapter, the realities around the function and functionary on the ground are explored—what seem to be the expectations, how the function has fared, what progressive changes have taken place, what measures matter and finally what the future might look like. This chapter is based on a survey that was undertaken among some stakeholder segments of the function.

We end the first section by offering a new paradigm to look at the function through the three well-accepted domains of doing, feeling and thinking.

As a part of our research and the taxonomy system that we have proposed, five areas have been identified where businesses will expect results from HR in the coming days. We call these the five demands on HR.

In the five sections that follow, specific themes under each of these demands focusing on what needs attention, what progressive practices exist and what concerns the practitioners most in these areas are explored.

In all, 16 specific themes or areas within the HR function are elaborated under the five broad demands. Here is a snapshot:

1. Bringing people on board
   i. Planning in uncertain times
   ii. Remaining attractive
   iii. Choosing right

2. Managing people
   iv. Learning, the new way
   v. Beyond managing performance
   vi. Money and beyond
   vii. Managing the moments of truth

3. Management and leadership development
   viii. Channelising aspirations
   ix. Institutionalising the process
   x. Developing managers and leaders

4. Making the organisation effective
   xi. Leading change
   xii. Designing organisations

xiii. Contributing to leadership effectiveness
xiv. Shaping the way organisations work

5. Managing relationship with employees
xv. What really matters
xvi. Towards progressive employee relations

Organisational Practices

Each chapter contains two critical elements: (a) our views, opinions and perspectives on the specific theme and (b) one or more real-life organisational practices that are related to the theme. Here is how we went about choosing the featured organisational practices.

Certain organisational practices are very well documented and widely publicised. We therefore felt that it would be redundant for us to reproduce them here. These have been left out. Certain other practices seemed relevant only to a certain industry or cultural context and did not offer the possibility of appropriate adoption across a wider context. These have been left out too.

We then chose those organisational practices (after obtaining prior permission) which passed the following criteria:

- The practice reflects a certain level of innovation or novelty and is worthy of study and emulation.
- The practice has positively impacted business results or organisational effectiveness.
- The practice or experience has some sustainable and enduring value.

The objective of sharing these organisational experience and practices is not to prescribe but to balance our narrative of issues and challenges with a strong dose of organisational reality, so that you as readers are introduced to solutions that have been attempted by organisations to address many of the current HR challenges.

These chapters are intended to bring to sharp focus the issues that really seem to matter and should therefore figure in the agenda of HR functions and its practitioners.

The last section focuses on the making of the quintessential people champions. In this section, we focus on what it will take to advance in HR. We have dedicated one chapter to explore the young HR professional's readiness to serve. The final chapter in this section examines how CEOs get schooled in people championship.

As has been said in the beginning, this is not a running commentary—a treatise about HR. It is not a textbook about the theories and sciences contributing to the practice. It is a book that offers expert comments—a look at HR here and now—which can provide its readers a scaffold that can help them successfully scale the challenges that the function presents. It is intended to open up possibilities for looking at the function through modern and contemporary lenses.

Throughout the book, care has been taken to ensure that whenever there are references to the HR professional or the employee, both women and men are mentioned. In fact, we recognise that the HR profession attracts more women than men and that is a great development. If in some places we have referred to the HR professional or the employee as his or he, please read it as including her or she!

While we have not attempted to predict the future, we are mindful of the uncertainty surrounding the emerging directions and the tectonic shifts that are potentially possible. We have referred to some of these in our epilogue where we have also expressed our confidence about the ability of the function and its functionaries to reinvent as appropriate to sail the waves of the times.

Contributing Organisations and Leaders

It was our dream that this book should tell a story and not read like a textbook. It was our network of business and HR leaders who supported us spontaneously with their ideas and their organisational experiences which helped us realise our dream.

As authors and researchers, we recognise that it is never easy to document and share what an organisation does. There are always heightened concerns when one puts oneself out there in the public domain. However, these organisations and their business and HR leaders took the leap of faith purely in the interest of promoting learning and for this we remain ever grateful to them.

We present here in alphabetical order the names of the contributing organisations and the business and HR leaders who supported us with the documentation and approval process.

Accel

Accel is a leading venture capital firm that invests in people and their companies from the earliest days through all phases of private company growth. The firm seeks to understand entrepreneurs as individuals, appreciate their originality and play to their strengths, because greatness doesn't have a stereotype.

Mahendran Balachandran, Narayan R. Thammaiah

Aditya Birla Group

The Aditya Birla Group is a US $41-billion Indian multinational conglomerate, headquartered in Mumbai, India. It is a premium global corporation with more than 120,000 employees world-wide belonging to 42 nationalities and is part of the League of Fortune 500.

Santrupt Misra, Ajay Soni

Airtel

Bharti Airtel Limited is a global telecommunications services company headquartered in New Delhi. Airtel is the world's no. 3 mobile operator in terms of customer base. It operates in 17 countries including India and Sri Lanka and 15 countries in Africa. The Airtel brand has been consistently rated amongst the top 3 in India.

Srikanth Balachandran, Papiya Banerjee, Shilpi Garg, Ritika Chadha

Amazon India

Amazon India (www.amazon.in) is an affiliate of Amazon.com, Inc. (NASDAQ: AMZN). Amazon.in seeks to build the most customer-centric online destination for customers to find and discover virtually anything they want to buy online by giving them more of what they want—vast selection, low prices, fast and reliable delivery and a trusted and convenient experience, and provide sellers with a world-class e-commerce marketplace.

Raj Raghavan

Automotive Stampings and Assemblies Limited

Automotive Stampings and Assemblies Limited (ASAL) is a Tata AutoComp Systems Limited (TACO) group company and manufacturer and supplier of sheet metal components, welded assemblies and modules for automobiles.

G. D. More

Asian Paints

Asian Paints is India's leading paint company and ranked among the top ten coating companies in the world. The company operates in 16 countries and offers paint and décor solutions. Asian Paints is recognised as one of the most valuable brands in India and has received several accolades including being ranked as 8th amongst 'Top 100 Most Innovative Companies in the World' by Forbes (August 2017).

Emrana Sheikh, Bindu Subramani, Sachin Singh

Beroe Consulting (I) Pvt Ltd

Beroe is a premier global provider of customised procurement services specialising in sourcing, supply chain visibility, financial risk analysis, and environmental impact.

Anand Narayanan

Brakes India Private Limited

Brakes India Private Limited is a joint venture company of TVS/ Sundaram Group. It was founded in the year 1962 as a joint venture with Lucas Industries of the United Kingdom. Brakes India Pvt Ltd. is a leader in India in braking systems. They are also manufacturers of ferrous castings and polymers. With an annual revenue of over ₹3,600 crores, over 6 manufacturing sites in India and over 7,000 employees, Brakes India is a market leader with a focus on technology, quality and operational excellence.

N. Ravindran

Café Coffee Day

Cafe Coffee Day Global Limited is a Chikkamagaluru-based business and is the largest producer of Arabica beans in Asia and runs the chain, Café Coffee Day, popularly called CCD, a favourite hangout for coffee and conversations with over 1,500 outlets across 28 states.

N. Balachandar, Shyamala Deshpande, Rahul Nayar

Hindustan Unilever

Hindustan Unilever Limited (HUL) is India's largest fast moving consumer goods company with a heritage of over 80 years in India. The company has about 18,000 employees and has a net sales of ₹33,895 crores (financial year 2016–2017). HUL is a subsidiary of Unilever, one of the world's leading suppliers of food, home care, personal care and refreshment products.

B. P. Biddappa, Aakriti Chandra, Anand Tripathi, Ankush Punj, Boishakhi Khan, Navashree Bharadwaj, Neeta Dubey

ICICI Prudential Life

ICICI Prudential Life Insurance is a joint venture between ICICI Bank and Prudential Corporation Holdings Limited. The company offers products across the categories of protection, savings and investments that fulfil the different life-stage needs of customers. The company, as on 30 September 2017, had an AUM of 1,305.91 billion.

Judajit Das

Larsen & Toubro

Headquartered in Mumbai, Larsen & Toubro (L&T) is one of the largest and most respected companies in India's private sector. With over 75 years of a strong, customer-focused approach and a continuous quest for world-class quality, L&T has unmatched capabilities across technology, engineering, construction and manufacturing and maintains a leadership in all its major lines of business.

Yogi Sriram

Murugappa Group

Founded in 1900, the ₹300-billion Murugappa Group ranks among India's most admired corporate houses. The group has 28 businesses including eight listed companies. The group has a rich history of building sustainable and successful businesses based on a strong foundation of corporate governance, business and people practices.

Shyam C. Raman

Rivigo

Founded in 2014, Rivigo is a technology-enabled logistics company that aims to deliver reliability through its well-established network and its unique operational model and cutting-edge technology while improving the quality of life of its delivery people.

Deepak Garg

Sundaram Finance

Sundaram Finance Ltd (SFL) is the flagship company of the T. S. Santhanam arm of the TVS Group. One of the most respected names in financial services, SFL and its subsidiaries offer a range of retail financial services such as commercial vehicle and car loans, home loans, deposits, mutual funds, general insurance and a variety of working capital products.

T. T. Srinivasaraghavan

Texas Instruments

Texas Instruments (TI) is a global semiconductor design and manufacturing company. TI India, established in 1985, was the first development centre of any technology company in India. From its inception, TI India has focused on innovation through product and cost differentiation. Today, there is hardly any chip produced by TI that is not touched by the engineers at TI India.

Sanjay Bhan, Shubhra Bhandari

Thermax Group

Thermax Group is a Pune, India headquartered global company providing a range of engineering solutions to the energy and environment sectors, operating globally through 33 international offices and 13 manufacturing facilities, 7 of which are in India and 6 overseas.

Sharad Gangal

TVS Logistics

TVS Logistics Services Ltd is a group company of the US $8-billion TVS Group. It is among the best third-party logistics companies in India and provides integrated supply chain solutions to customers across the world in diverse sectors such as automobile, distribution, electronics, discrete components manufacturing, defence, engineering, retail and FMCG business segments.

E. Balaji

Wipro

Wipro Limited is a leading global information technology, consulting and business-process services company. A company recognised globally for its comprehensive portfolio of services, strong commitment to sustainability and good corporate citizenship, Wipro has over 160,000 dedicated employees serving clients across six continents.

Saurabh Govil, Vishal Singh

HR AND HERE NOW

PART 1
HR Refreshed

1

Through the Eyes of the Beholder

Produced by General Electric Theatre and aired in 1953 was the episode 'The Eye of the Beholder',[1] starring Richard Conte and Martha Vickers.

Containing all of the drama of a murder mystery, this video portrays how five people perceive Michael Gerard, a painter, during a 12-hour period. One sees him as a 'lady's man', another as a 'good boy', the third as insane, the fourth as a gangster and the fifth as a murderer.

Produced as a television serial, this has perhaps emerged as the single most powerful, popular and educative video to illustrate the subject of perception and more specifically how our perceptions can easily be influenced by our beliefs based on our past experiences, fears and expectations. This classic also illustrates the dangers of judgement, projection, prejudice, predisposition and preoccupation.

What is true for Michael Gerard is certainly true for HR!

Type the phrase 'Why we love HR?' and Google will return a million search results. Type the phrase 'Why we hate HR?' and

---

[1] 'The Eye of the Beholder' was the 13th episode of Season 2 of a television series produced by General Electric Theatre and Broadcast by CBS Radio and television in 1953.

Google will return another million search results. That tells us something about what might have been in the minds of the beholders.

When the *Harvard Business Review*[2] carried a cover story titled 'It's Time to Blow Up HR and Build Something New', it certainly created a stir. So what did the beholders have in their mind?

When stand-up comedians pick on HR to evoke laughter or when young employees routinely rant about HR on social media, there is an underlying message.

When business leaders routinely confess that leadership and people agendas concern them the most, it tells us something about their expectations.

When organisations commit significantly higher budgets every successive year to staff HR functions and fund HR programmes, it tells us something about what they value.

When more and more students choose HR as their profession, their choice tells us something.

When you learn that the engagement scores of HR teams itself is very low, it tells us something about how they feel.

Like in the case of Michael Gerard, the value and place of HR is in the eyes of the beholder, and that can be quite hard to understand and accept, especially for its practitioners.

In fact, no other profession evokes as many varied views, expectations and emotions as the HR profession does.

To understand this uniqueness better, it might be useful to draw a distinction between the HR function and its practitioners.

The Functional Perspective

The manner in which HR as a function is perceived is in good measure influenced by the role expectations placed on it by leadership—*in other words, how HR is positioned within the*

---

[2] 'Time to Blowup HR and Build Something New' is the cover story of the July–August 2015 issue of the *Harvard Business Review*.

organisation. How much does HR as a function count in the way the organisation is managed?

Our experience across a wide range of organisations suggests that the functional positioning ranges from a high level of centrality to a moderate level of centrality and further to a low level of centrality.

High centrality	Moderate centrality	Low centrality

Such positioning in many ways determines what is expected from the function. This gets demonstrated in how much the function is included, valued and consulted in all employee- and organisation-related decision-making.

Where the centrality is very high, the function ends up having a say in everything that is important and significant within the organisation. Such inclusion goes beyond HR matters. When the centrality is moderate, the inclusion and the consultation is restricted to functional aspects. However, within the functional domain, there is a high level of inclusion and consultation. The position is as an expert function. When the centrality is low, the function does not get included or consulted even in HR matters.

The Practitioner Perspective

The manner in which the practitioners or the HR professionals are perceived is in good measure influenced by the role expectations placed on them by their diverse stakeholders and of course the manner in which these expectations are perceived to have been fulfilled. *In other words, what was my experience of interacting, engaging with and depending on the HR professional?*

In our experience, the perceptions of how helpful HR professionals were when approached for any kind of assistance ranges from being seen as *extremely helpful* at one end to being seen as *least helpful* at the other end. The perception of helping and not helping is from the vantage point of how much the employees sees the HR professional is seen as furthering their goals.

Extremely helpful   Moderately helpful   Least helpful

← ————————————————————————————————

When the role expectations from the function are combined with the actual experiences with the professional, you will end up seeing several possible emotions being triggered about the function and the professional.

High centrality   Moderate centrality   Low centrality

← ————————————————

Extremely helpful	*Delighted*	*Pleased*	*Surprised*
Moderately helpful	*Satisfied*	*'OK'*	*Indifferent*
Least helpful	*Angry*	*Unhappy*	*Frustrated*

When the function is positioned as highly central and the professionals are seen as extremely helpful, recipients are delighted. On the other hand, when the centrality is low and the professionals are also not helpful, it leads to a feeling of frustration. When the function is given its place of prominence but its functionaries are not helpful, it does lead to a sense of anger. Finally, when the centrality is not very high but the professionals are doing their best to help in whatever manner possible, at least the moments of truth are positive and there is a sense of being surprised.

Like the story of Michael Gerard, all of this does not take into account the aspirations, dreams and expectations of the practitioners themselves.

So the next time one encounters a perception about HR, it might be useful to see the vantage point from which it emanates. What is important to recognise is that there is a distinction between the function and the functionaries. The positioning of the function is attributable to the culture of the organisation whereas the perception of the functionaries is attributable to the capabilities and behaviours of individuals. It is important that one does not confuse the function with the functionary.

Positioning of HR: The Contextually Evolving Story

The positioning of HR, in many ways, seems to be a function of the buoyancy in the economy. Organisations in rapidly developing countries like India have seen a very strong reliance on their HR function to realise their growth aspirations.

If Indian businesses have grown dramatically in the last two-and-a-half decades, at least some of that is thanks to HR as a function reinventing itself constantly to meet the growing role expectations. If Indian businesses have gotten better at the art and science of adding hundreds of thousands to their workforce and developing and nurturing them, it is thanks to HR transforming itself. If Indian businesses have been doing a reasonable job of growing talent from within, at least some of that is thanks to HR contribution!

Contrary to common perceptions, the HR function in India has been hugely innovative and has constantly and continuously evolved itself to meet business needs.

Be it the innovative Voluntary Retirement Scheme (VRS) in the 1990s, designed and implemented to reduce costs, or the productivity-based wage settlements, or the use of total quality management (TQM) to build employee engagement and commitment, or the adoption of supply chain models to scale up in recruitment or the use of People Capability Maturity Model (PCMM) in IT and engagement practices in information technology-enabled services (ITeS), the use of technology to automate and enhance employee experiences in the delivery of HR services, or the smart adoption of e-learning solutions, or the constant innovations in leader development, we see more and more instances of HR across businesses moving along the continuum from being positioned as peripheral to being positioned as central.

Looking at the positioning of HR from a role expectation perspective is not complete without recognising the conflicting expectations. In other words, whose needs and expectations is HR expected to fulfil and are there indeed conflicting expectations?

For example, employees may want HR to take a strong stand with leadership on issues that impact them. Employees also expect HR to influence the way they are treated by their managers. Employees demonstrate a market-oriented approach when they are hired but expect special consideration when the business needs to restructure. Leaders and managers want HR to demonstrate empathy but also take tough actions. Leaders and managers want the freedom and flexibility to take reward decisions, but HR is also expected to ensure fairness and equity. Depending on how HR responds to these varying expectations and depending on whom you ask, you will get a different view about HR. However, all of these perceptions are indicative of the centrality of HR in the minds of people, and that is good news. It is just that, given the fact that it touches everyone's life, each of them feels qualified to have a view or opinion on how HR should be run.

Professional Capabilities: A Mixed Bag

If we begin to recognize that there is an increasing tendency to accord a more central status to the HR function, at least in rapidly growing and competitive economies with equally competitive labour markets, it follows that the expectations of the professional—the face of the function—is growing quite rapidly.

Be it feeling angry or feeling frustrated, it is evident that HR professionals evoke strong emotions when they are perceived to be hindering the goal achievement of employees.

The large-scale addition of numbers to the profession with little training and preparation is certainly adding to the poor perception of at least a good number of HR professionals. Clearly, HR professionals can do a lot more to enhance the way they are experienced by those who engage with them.

That indeed is both a challenge and an opportunity. With the right capability, which includes functional competencies, human skills and mindsets, the perception of HR professionals can change quite dramatically. Having facilitated hundreds of HR professionals in their capability-development journey, we have hope and significant optimism on this count.

Who is HR?

This brings us to the rather mysterious question—who is HR? Is impactful HR work done only by those donning the HR hat or also by all those who lead the business—promoters, leaders and other professionals?

Strangely, many of the policies, practices and decisions that employees like or dislike are in fact shaped or taken by business leaders, founders and CEOs, and more often than not, HR might only be the face that implements them. HR professionals are constantly battling with business to be positioned more centrally so that they can better influence the decisions impacting employee experiences and then be rightfully expected to own the consequences of what is done. However, promoters and business leaders are constantly telling their HR teams that unless they generate more confidence and are experienced as helpful, they will not grant them a more central positioning. Until that gets resolved, most of the impactful HR work will continue to be done by business leaders and senior managers themselves.

Diverse Beholders

The variations in perceptions is not just within organisations but also across industries. The manner in which the function and the professionals are experienced in the IT and ITeS industry seems different from the experience and perception of the function and professionals in the manufacturing industry. The experiences in large organisations seem different from those in smaller organisations.

Incidentally, the experiences in India seem different from those in the United States, Europe or China.

Some countries place shareholder returns ahead of employees' needs. Some labour markets are not competitive or operate in environments that are highly legislated. In some countries, economic growth is not high and things are predictable. In all such cases, the experiences could be seen differently.

Closing Reflections

The moot question is certainly not about the relevance and centrality of HR as a function. It is about when and how the expectations will become clearer and better understood. It is about how HR will balance between the conflicting role demands placed on it. It is also about how HR can independently assess the context and evolve appropriate responses. The goal for HR professionals is to become Aware, Acquire (capabilities), Act (appropriately) and Achieve (trust/credibility).

The purpose of this book is to trigger the quest towards these four A's through our perspectives on the issues and challenges and our research about current practices.

With the right capabilities, the function and its functionaries will be able to discern expectations, balance conflicting demands, appreciate the context and respond with competence, and through that be perceived well. It is this exciting agenda that this book attempts to further.

2
New Meanings

Think of a *phone* and we would think of talking to someone. Today, the phone means very different things—often far removed from the traditional notion of talking to someone!

Think of a *mall* and we would think of shopping. Today, we go to a mall to watch a movie or eat a meal but we still call it a mall.

Think of Amazon, and, well, by the time this book is out, its meaning to us would have expanded further!

Think *marketing* and we were schooled to think of the 4Ps (price, product, promotion and place). A multitude of forces have led to the redefinition of this profession and function in unimaginable ways.

Things, places and even professions change and evolve to keep pace with the changing demands and expectations of its users and patrons. So too HR as a profession has changed very significantly within the world of organisations. For each of us it means so many different things, and when you try and put it together it is often a confusing maze.

To navigate our journey through the new HR profession, we need a map—just the way we need a map to navigate our way through a website or a city or a complex profession. In fact, every mature profession works to create a system of classification to help its users find out what is where and what belongs where. This is what the world calls a system of taxonomy—the science of classification. The field of medicine is a good example. The field has seen the evolution of a complex system of specialisations, sub-specialisations, diseases, disorders and so on. Taxonomy in this field is not rigid and fixed but is capable of modification as well as absorption of the new advancements that take place.

As we begin our exploration of what is contemporary in HR today, it would be useful to be armed with a commonly understood system of classification or taxonomy. We call it *new meanings* and will keep relying on and referring to this all through the book. While the taxonomy of HR has evolved over the years, our current focus is on the new and emerging taxonomy in HR.

As this system of classification was put together, it became clear that none of the elements in the system are mutually exclusive. There are inevitable overlaps, connections and dilemmas. What is also clear is that this may not be the only way to reclassify HR.

So let's get started.

The classification of contemporary HR is presented under the following five broad dimensions:

1. Professional origins and influences
2. Specialisations
3. HR functions and HR roles
4. HR competencies
5. The demands on HR

What Is HR?

Before getting started with the classification system, it would be useful to agree to a contemporary definition of HR or agree to what HR is, today.

HR can be seen as a multidisciplinary field with its scope including everything that touches the employee, the organisation, its leadership, its performance, its culture and its sustainability.

While HR is a function within organisations it is also a philosophy and approach to managing people.

The practice of HR is not restricted to HR professionals. Nor are all HR practitioners trained in HR. This by itself is one of the critical challenges that the function faces.

While the term 'HRD' was intended to be different from the term 'personnel management' and 'employee relations' or 'industrial relations', today, HR in most organisations includes all of these and more.

The term 'talent management' needs some explanation. The word 'talent', which was popularised by the book *The War for Talent*,[1] led to many organisations referring to their employees as talent and prefixing the term 'talent' to many of their HR processes—talent acquisition, talent management, talent engagement, talent transformation and so on.

Some organisations even use 'talent management' in a generic way to refer to most of the HR functions while others use talent management to specifically refer to the process of identifying, developing and retaining highly valued employees. While this aspect will be covered in detail in this book, in our system of taxonomy, it will be our endeavour to refrain from using the term 'talent' in a generic fashion because it causes a lot of confusion.

Professional Origins and Influences

HR as a profession drew its know-how from several allied sciences and disciplines. Its work has also been shaped by several fields over a period of time. This is what makes HR truly multidisciplinary.

Psychological Literacy

The influence of psychology on HR work is perhaps very well understood. It is well known that many of the HR practices such as selection, potential assessment, performance management, employee engagement, leadership development, career

---

[1] Ed Michaels, Helen Handfield-Jones, and Beth Axelrod, *The War for Talent* (Boston, MA: Harvard Business Review Press, 2001).

development, job analysis and job design, occupational stress, work–life balance, diversity, organisational change and culture have their origins and roots in one or more branches of psychology.

As one looks ahead, it appears that HR practitioners will depend even more heavily on the field of psychology to gain fresh perspectives and find solutions to needs around human motivation, adult learning and development including leader development, teamwork and collaboration, cultural intelligence (using a convergence of psychology, sociology, anthropology and neurosciences), psychological well-being and so on.

Sociological Literacy

Given that organisations and their employees represent a slice of society and the fact that issues and problems in the larger society tend to find their way into organisations, understanding social behaviours, societal trends, social issues such as class, inequality, mobility, stratification, inclusions, exclusions and the state of social institutions has been key to HR work.

In the days to come, HR professionals will look to sociologists and social researchers to find new insights into social phenomena such as income disparities, unemployment, diversity, generational differences, the impact of social media, the changing face of collective action, urban migration and the changing meaning of work, social institutions, societal values and work values.

Economic Literacy

As organisations become increasingly market oriented in their HR policies and practices (the philosophy where the customer and therefore the competitive forces form the basis for all decisions), external events and developments will have a huge bearing on HR policies and practices. Be it the election of Donald Trump as the President of the United States, UK's decision to exit from the European Union (EU), the slowdown in China, India's demonetisation drive or the introduction of GST in India—all of these developments have a significant impact on business and people.

More and more HR practitioners are expected to develop this larger understanding of the economic and market context.

Interestingly, with the increasing dominance of market-oriented practices, the erstwhile importance placed on full compliance with labour laws seems to have lost the holy cow status, albeit, only in some areas.

Embracing Technology

Needless to say, technology has impacted HR work in unimaginable ways. From automation to shared services to analytics to learning, technology has significantly altered the way in which HR work is done and delivered.

Going forward, success in HR will depend not only on developing literacy in and actively leveraging applied psychology, sociology and economics. It will also depend on one's ability to embrace technology. HR will be much more multidisciplinary in its approach to addressing people and organisational challenges tapping into the latest from all of the aforementioned areas as well as newer ones such as artificial intelligence and neurosciences.

Specialisations

The evolution and maturity of any profession can be measured by the growth of specialisations within the profession.

As we explore a contemporary meaning for the function and a forward-looking system of classification, the all-important question that needs to be answered is this: What are the current streams of specialisations within the HR profession? What qualifies as a specialist field? What are the streams within the profession where one will and can acquire specific specialist qualifications based on training and practice to distinguish oneself and excel in one's work?

The truth is that HR is no longer a generic, blanket, all-encompassing profession.

There are at least seven well-delineated specialisations that are currently evident in HR and widespread amongst companies across different segments. Some of them are old and well established, some new and evolving. Since different organisations use different terminologies to describe the incumbent specialisations, broad and generic terms are being used to merely describe these specialisation streams. In reality, they might be known as or called by different names.

1. HR operations and services
2. Staffing, recruitment and selection
3. Employee relations
4. Compensation and benefits
5. Management and leadership development
6. Organisation development
7. Learning and development

Let us explore each of these in brief in order to establish a common understanding.

HR Operations and Services

This is one of the earliest areas of focus in the function, though it neither got accorded the status of a specialisation nor the respect it deserves.

What started as a set of clerical tasks within the function (maintenance of employee attendance and records, processing payroll and administering benefits) has now evolved into a serious specialisation, thanks to the advent of automation, shared services and outsourcing. The growing expectations of employees for superior and consistent quality in these services has probably been the single most important reason for this progression into a specialisation.

In the days of yore, there were clerical staff proficient in maintaining records with numerical skills employed in the time office and payroll operations. Today, HR operations is a significant component of the business process outsourcing (BPO) industry which attracts young graduates who have considerable quantitative, analytical, systems and communication skills. The positioning of this industry and its employees has gained global recognition.

Simply put, HR operations and services as a specialisation is responsible for managing the millions of moments of truth along the entire life cycle of service for an employee starting from joining right through to separation.

This includes information management, interface management, processing, administration and of course controls.

The advent of self-help portals, mobile technologies, shared services and outsourcing has made the function extremely complex and mission critical, especially for large and geographically distributed businesses.

While some parts of this function used to reside in the accounting department and some others in the personnel department, now with increasing scale, automation and service expectations this has become a fairly independent specialist function and therefore a specialisation.

Staffing, Recruitment and Selection

It is our sense that this specialisation employs the largest number of people within HR today. Many estimate that close to 50 per cent of the people employed in HR do work relating to staffing, recruitment and selection.

From a time when staffing was one of the many things that an HR person did, it has rapidly evolved into the largest professional stream within HR and it is the only thing many HR professionals do!

The growth of the IT industry and other manpower intensive businesses on one side and competitive labour market conditions on the other side has contributed to the explosion of numbers in this professional stream. The labour-intensive industries have also been the reason for increasing focus on efficiencies and reliability in this area. This specialisation could reside within organisations or in professional services firm.

Simply put, staffing, recruitment and selection as a specialisation is responsible for planning the staffing strategies and models and bringing people on board.

Staffing, recruitment and selection as a specialisation consists of a wide variety of roles including planners, recruiters, campus-hiring champions, lateral hiring champions, specialist skill-hiring champions and so on. There are also recruitment operations roles that are responsible for the workflow management within the function. There are people responsible for campus relationships, employer branding and so on. Behind them are outsourced teams working on sourcing CVs and conducting background verification. There are also search firms, placement companies and staffing-services companies providing people (including temps) or services.

Some argue that staffing, recruitment and selection is now not even a part of HR, at least the technical hiring bit, especially in BPOs, knowledge process outsourcing (KPOs) and IT companies.

Employee Relations

As old as HR operations is employee relations (ER) as a key specialization within the HR function.

Also called labour relations, union relations and industrial relations, this specialisation and its accompanying roles were traditionally responsible for employee welfare, employee terms and conditions and of course managing union relationships. It also included understanding and managing the government machinery associated with unions, discipline, collective bargaining and compliance.

As long as the unionisation rate remained robust, the expertise of managing employee relationships in the face of unions was nurtured and promoted.

Simply put, ER as a specialisation is responsible for defining and managing the boundaries of the relationship between the organisation and its employees, both individually and collectively, keeping in mind the legal, social, psychological, economic and philosophical dimensions.

The specialisation has also been facing a certain crisis of identity given that several of its elements are performed by others in the function who do not wish to be labelled as employee relations professionals, given certain negative imagery of this role from the past.

ER as a specialisation deals with a wide variety of tasks and demands including union relations, compliance with labour legislations, employee wellness, diversity and inclusion, occupational health and safety, security, grievance redressal, dispute resolution, discipline, employee engagement, employee communication, employee assistance, employment structuring and employment contracts, employment conditions, wage and long-term settlements with unions.

Compensation and Benefits

Compensation and Benefits (C&B) (also called by many other names) emerged as a specialisation only after 1991, when the Indian economy opened up and global corporations re-entered India and our employees and their compensation began to be structured and managed in a systematic and professional manner.

Simply put, C&B as a specialisation is responsible for all aspects of pay and benefits keeping in mind internal and external equity as well as the business model, cost and labour market considerations.

C&B as a specialisation deals with a wide variety of tasks and demands including external benchmarking, internal analysis, setting up pay structures, designing benefits programmes, running annual pay increase programmes, designing and implementing long-term and short-term incentive plans as well as employee stock option plans.

   Given the need for numerical and analytical skills, significant financial acumen, the need for confidentiality and, above all, many years it takes to gain mastery in the area, this has rapidly developed into a super specialist function where its practitioners, once in, seldom move out. Also, given the dependence on external service providers for market data and other C&B solutions, this has remained a small function with perhaps one or two professionals within the organisation.

Organisation Development

Organisation development (OD) has always existed as a distinct discipline and professional practice which focuses on organisational effectiveness and change facilitation agendas. It has been offered as a professional service by external consultants trained typically in human process consulting at the individual, group and organisational level.

   Given the growing complexities within organisations, a new breed of HR professionals has been acquiring formal OD capabilities and offering it within their organisations as internal consultants.

   Simply put, OD as a specialisation is responsible for helping the organisation remain or become more effective by identifying areas within the organisation that need progressive change and then using a range of planned methodologies to design and implement such change and learn from it.

   OD specialists within organisations seem to be involved in diagnosing and then intervening into various organisational processes in order to enhance organisational effectiveness. This could include performance, team effectiveness, employee engagement, learning, leadership effectiveness and so on.

   While the use of OD specialists within organisations is not yet widespread, there are clear signs of organisations recognising the need for internal consulting capabilities and the effort to build the same within organisations, either among OD specialists or among other role holders.

At the very least, any critical and special project within HR that does not fall within any of the specialisations seems to be called an OD project and handed over to one of the more senior role holders. Increasingly, HR business partners (HRBPs) are also expected to possess this capability and fulfil this need with the support of specialists from within or outside.

Learning and Development

Training departments have existed as a part of HR functions for an extremely long time, perhaps as long as the function has existed, in one form or the other.

With greater insight into how people learn and innovations to empower the learners and the attempt to shift the onus from the employer to the employee, training has morphed into learning.

Simply put, learning and development (L&D) as a specialisation is responsible for conceptualising, designing and implementing strategies, plans, programmes and solutions to address the L&D needs of employees within the organisation.

L&D as a specialisation deals with a wide variety of tasks and demands including definition of competencies, need identification, development planning, learning design and delivery through a range of strategies and effectiveness management and measurement.

What is unique about L&D as a specialisation is that it attracts to its fold professionals with a strong passion for academic pursuit and learning. As a result, like C&B specialists, most learning specialists tend to remain learning specialists. That of course brings with it a set of associated problems which will be explored later in this book. Today, this function is looked upon from the perspective of overall capability building within the organisation and includes technical and functional learning.

Emerging Specialisations

We see the following two specialisations emerging in the coming years:

HR Analytics

HR analytics or workforce analytics or evidence-based HR is all about using analysis to ensure that HR interventions lead to the right business outcomes. Analytics goes beyond opinions, guesses and correlations and uses data to validate carefully crafted hypotheses about what kind of HR interventions will lead to what kind of outcomes.

HR analytics is slowly emerging as a specialisation at least among large global organisations which have access to data as well as the capability to run analytics projects to improve the quality of their people decisions.

It will, however, be a while before a significant number of HR professionals and line managers give up a gut feel and opinion-based approach and embrace an analytics approach to decision-making on people issues. Not all HR decisions can be based on analytics, there will always be preference for human judgement!

Management and Leadership Development

While a distinction has always been made between technical/functional training and management/leadership training, the distinction and separation has become even more pronounced today.

Given the mission critical urgency of growing managers and leaders from within, the complex tasks of managing the internal mobility, development and growth of employees across functions and levels to build management and leadership depth while catering to the aspirations of employees are receiving sharp focus today.

Traditionally, such efforts were handled under the umbrella of management development and tended to cover all employees in the management cadre. More recently, the proponents of talent management have been suggesting that such efforts be directed only towards those having high potential or of significant value to the organisation. As a result, the process of identifying employees with high potential has gained significance and has become one part of this specialist function.

The other equally important aspect of this specialist function is the design and implementation of programmes to develop leaders across levels—building the leadership pipeline as it is popularly referred to.

In our view, management and leadership development as a specialisation includes the following:

1. Designing career tracks for various professional streams and roles and implementing policies for mobility within and across career tracks and roles.
2. Championing career and succession planning programmes as part of strategic workforce planning (SWP).
3. Implementing specialised programmes to identify and manage those with high potential or unique value to the organisation.
4. Running leadership development programmes to build functional and business leaders across levels.
5. Promoting mobility of resources across functions and divisions in the interest of the employee and the organisation.

The Doubtful Ones

There are important disciplines within HR which have very significant business impact and value but have not yet emerged as specialisations in our reckoning.

Organisation Design

Organisation design as a specialisation is neither well understood nor well established.

In most organisations, while this capability is beginning to be recognised, structurally it is played by different roles and functions. The task of job design which is an integral element of the science of organisation design is often performed by the staffing, recruitment and selection specialists, albeit, inelegantly.

The task of evaluating jobs, defining pay points and work levels—yet another essential ingredient of organisation design—is performed by C&B professionals.

Similarly, the task of creating and offering a range of career paths is performed either by HRBPs or other OD specialists.

Finally, the task of making structural choices for the organisation is often performed by the CEO or other business leaders with the help of external strategic consultants and the involvement of the chief human resources officer (CHRO) given its strategic implications.

Therefore, while organisation design as a science and discipline is invaluable, its practice is fragmented and distributed across roles and other functional specialisations.

Performance Management

The task of managing organisational performance and as a consequence individual performance has grown in complexity and sophistication over the years. With increasing pressures on CEOs to sustainably deliver short-term financial results and enhance shareholder value, execution has become their number one priority. As a consequence, CEOs and their leadership team members rely on performance management as a strategic business tool to achieve results.

Similarly, CEOs use the balanced scorecard or TQM-led methodologies to cascade organisational goals into individual performance measures. Years of effort to remove subjectivity in the performance planning and measurement process has led to businesses taking a far higher role in putting in place clear performance metrics. As a result of all of this, performance management is no longer something that HR does as a functional intervention. Managing performance is what leaders are expected to do. Having said this, HR plays a role in designing a framework and process that is fair and transparent, creating the capability and clarity around goal-setting, ensuring process adherence, moderating assessment, evaluation and decision-making, upholding the values of fairness, transparency and meritocracy as well as automating the workflow and enhancing the employee experience.

While the design elements are centrally driven, the deployment is mostly handled by the HRBPs within the businesses.

Given this evolution, we see performance management as a business process rather than as an area of specialist HR know-how.

HR Function and HR Roles

Our journey of discovering the emerging HR taxonomy brings us to the manner in which the HR function is being organised and as a consequence the manner in which the HR roles are classified.

The HR function is today broadly organised in three parts:

1. Those who do specialist kind of work (centres of expertise)
2. Those who do the operational or transactional kind of work (shared services)
3. Those who engage with employees and business to address their specific needs (HR partners)

These three groups have always existed in one form or the other. For instance, the time office or the payroll team always existed. Today, it is called shared services.

Similarly, Learning or Compensation specialists always existed. Today, they are called centres of excellence (CoEs).

There always existed site or corporate business HR teams called by various titles. They are now called HR partners.

Arising out of this, HR roles are today classified as:

1. Specialist roles
2. Operational roles
3. Business/employee partner roles
4. HR generalists
5. Leadership roles

Specialist roles are played by functional specialists within each of the functional streams in HR.

Operational roles are played by people who ensure a high degree of efficiency/accuracy in the implementation of the operational tasks.

Partner roles are played by those within businesses. They are called HRBPs or employee partners.

In smaller companies, these distinctions do not exist and they are rolled into a single role—HR generalists.

Those in leadership roles lead HR for a significant business or unit or lead the operational arm of HR or the function for the organisation as a whole.

HR Competencies

Being effective in HR calls for a wide range of skills and competencies and of course several years of disciplined application.

For the purposes of our exploration of a classification system, the universe of HR competencies has been grouped into three themes:

1. Functional competencies that provide the required functional fundamentals in all the seven areas of specialisation to all HR practitioners and functional depth for the specialists in a chosen area.
2. Managerial and leadership competencies that will help all HR professionals perform their roles effectively. These competencies would include the basics like planning and

problem-solving and help the HR leaders think strategically and enhance overall effectiveness.

3. Partnership competencies which includes the range of consulting skills that will help HR professionals engage with employees and business and dialogue effectively to understand their need, and on that basis develop appropriate solutions and implement them effectively.

Beyond these three themes, it would be important for all HR professionals to uphold certain values and standards of professional excellence which are unique to the HR profession. This includes the most basic ones such as ensuring fairness to the more complex ones such as displaying diligence or committing to continuing professional development.

The Demands on HR

Having presented the various dimensions of the emerging HR taxonomy, let us look at what we see as the five demands being placed on HR today. Transcending the scientific origins, the specialisations, roles and competencies, these five demands represent our understanding of what business expects from HR. In other words, this is a rather non-technical, simple outside-in view of what is demanded of HR.

Business expects HR to:

1. Bring people on board (staffing, recruitment and selection).
2. Manage people (performance, rewards, L&D, life-cycle management, retention).
3. Develop managers and leaders (career paths, potential identification, leader development, internal mobility).
4. Make organisations effective (organisation design, culture, values, leadership effectiveness, productivity).
5. Manage relationship with employees (ER, engagement, well-being).

It is through these five filters that contemporary HR will be explored through the rest of this book.

Closing Reflections

As you walked along with us through this journey of exploring the new meanings of HR, it must have occurred to you that the profession has indeed come a long way. The know-how required to solve many of the emerging problems in organisations seems to exist.

How effective are practitioners in leveraging this to make a difference is the real question.

3
Evolving Expectations

The day an HR professional stops reporting to a functional manager and starts reporting to a business manager, she or he comes of age, in a manner of speaking.

From that moment, what the person knows, or how much that person knows stops mattering. All that matters is whether the person can help take the business forward.

It will happen to all of us, at various stages in our careers—for some earlier and for some later. And when it does happen, it can be quite challenging.

Business leaders will ask us to cut to the chase—ask us to be focused. They will ask us to show them evidence. They will tell us if something is working or not. They couldn't be bothered with functional details or processes that HR professionals are so excited about, but will have a lot of time for things that matter to the business and organisation.

So following the chapter on the subject of perceptions and meanings is an 'on the ground' assessment of HR as seen through the eyes of business leaders. Our survey asked them what they expected, how they thought HR was faring, what measures mattered to them, what progressive changes they were noticing and what suggestions they had for the profession and the professional.

Of course, these same questions were posed to CHROs and other senior HR professionals too.

Our respondents were drawn from both the private and public sectors, multinational and home-grown Indian companies, medium-sized organisations and large conglomerates.

For the sake of consistency, our findings are presented using the terms and classifications that have been outlined in the 'New Meanings' chapter.

So here is what it looks like, on the ground!

Expectations

The first piece of good news is that there appears to be complete congruence between what business leaders expect and what the CHROs and senior HR professionals experience as the ask from business.

So it is fair to conclude that HR professionals by and large get it!

The survey then looked at whether the expectations were about doing new things or doing existing things in new ways or just continuing to do existing things.

The second piece of good news is that most of the priority expectations were about doing new things and existing things in new ways!

New Things	Existing Things in New Ways
Making the organisation effective • Develop organisational capabilities • Shaping organisational culture • Facilitating change	*Employee relations* • Employee engagement *Managing people* • Making it contemporary *Bringing people on board* • Hiring quality

These expectations are explained further in some detail.

Develop Organisational Capabilities

With the fast changing business context and the highly competitive market environment, the number one expectation seems to be around development of capabilities in the organisation. This requires HR to go beyond training and development and look at ways in which the organisation is able to equip itself with capabilities to meet the new demands placed on it. An organisation's capabilities translate into the organisation's ability to do new and different things well. This could include new functional and domain expertise as well as greater management and leadership depth and competence. It could also be about doing things faster, being more customer centric, embracing technology better, being more innovative or just having better governance.

Shaping Organisational Culture

The term 'culture' needs some explaining. Culture can be seen as an outcome and the culmination of many values and principles practised actively by the people in the organisation.

It is so heartening to find that a majority of business leaders are today not only aware of the role of culture for organisation's success but are also demanding that this becomes a priority focus area for their HR teams.

It must be clarified that while organisations are very protective about their enduring core values or their DNA and do not want to change that, they are very mindful about the need for the adaptive exterior to change. This adaptive exterior includes values that the organisation might reinterpret to meet the needs of today, workplace principles that it might incorporate or change in response to changing demands.

It may be driven by external demands or internal decisions. It may also be driven by the styles of new leaders in organisations.

Making the deliberate choice between what to retain and what to change and rallying the organisation around such a change is part of the HR agenda and ask. Equally, it is the task of HR to manage the inevitable conflicts between the adaptive exterior and the enduring core.

Facilitating Change

Despite all that is written and spoken about the inevitability of change, organisations struggle with the human and emotional consequences of change. Little wonder then that facilitating change is among the top few things for which business leaders expect HR support. These could be planned change to embrace new capabilities, culture or unplanned change thrust upon the organisation from the environment.

All of these are welcome developments for two reasons: First, it signals the recognition of need for help; second, it also signals the willingness to look towards their HR colleagues for help in these areas.

Employee Engagement

It isn't surprising that among the existing things that are required to be done in new ways, employee engagement features right on top.

More and more business leaders seem to recognise that in the current difficult times, engaged employees can contribute significantly to business turnaround. Given the turbulent business environment, organisations have had to take several hard decisions on pay, rewards and progression in addition to resorting to some level of rationalisation.

Through all of these trying times, businesses are turning to HR to monitor and maintain the positive climate in the organisation. With the absence of trade unions, the onus seems to fall squarely on HR to be proactive.

Once again, this is a significant expectation to be placed on the function.

Managing People

The tasks of managing performance, rewards, learning and employee life-cycle events have been considered core to HR work and tend to receive a lot of time and attention from the HR teams.

Our survey confirms the fact that this area is indeed receiving attention. However, the expectation seems to be around ensuring that the practices in these areas are current, appropriate and efficient.

Bringing People on Board

In this area, the expectation is not so much around the availability of numbers. The chase for numbers seems to be replaced with the pursuit of quality and competence; herein lies the value-adding opportunity for HR. There is recognition that while the supply in absolute terms outstrips demand, the demand for the highly competent and talented people is much higher than the supply! This is where business leaders are expecting HR to add value.

This list of six expectations—three in new and strategic areas and three in existing areas to be done in new ways—in some way sets the tone for what needs to be the focus of HR professionals in the near future so that their contribution is aligned with emerging business realities and is valued by their business colleagues.

It is interesting that many of the operational tasks being performed by HR did not even figure highly in the expectations such as HR basics or containing employee attrition. Our take is that they are being considered as part of the course and hence not being flagged as priority expectations. They are often referred to as table stakes or hygiene stuff—'necessary but not sufficient for success'.

We must, however, hasten to add that this may not necessarily be what all business leaders expect from HR and the way all HR professionals experience their business stakeholders. The more central the position of the function, the more evolved the expectations. Where there is a variance from this enlightened perspective, the onus is on the HR leader to make efforts to create awareness of the possibility to leverage HR in a strategic way to help enhance business success.

How Is HR Faring?

In trying to understand how HR is faring, in the eyes of its stakeholders, the seven functional specialisations were used as the basis to gather feedback. To get more granular feedback, a few more practice areas were added:

1. HR operations and services
2. Staffing, recruitment and selection
3. Employee engagement
4. Industrial relations
5. Managing performance
6. Compensation and benefits
7. Learning and development
8. Management and leadership development
9. Organisation development

Against these areas, the opinions of respondents in terms of how they currently experienced and evaluated the performance of HR were elicited.

Dimensions	Business View	HR View
HR operations and services	Meets expectations	Exceeds expectations
Staffing, recruitment and selection	Meets expectations	
Employee engagement	Meets expectations	Exceeds expectations
Industrial relations	Exceeds expectations	
Managing performance	Inconsistent	Exceeds expectations

Dimensions	Business View	HR View
Compensation and benefits	Meets expectations	Exceeds expectations
Learning and development	Meets expectations	Exceeds expectations
Management and leadership development	Inconsistent	Exceeds expectations
Organisation development	Inconsistent	Meets expectations

Business leaders in organisations with a blue-collared workforce seemed very happy with how HR was delivering in the area of industrial relations. HR professionals themselves were also extremely positive about how they were seen to be contributing in this area. Obviously, this is a niche skill demonstrated in a certain set of contexts.

In the areas of C&B, HR operations, staffing, recruitment and selection, L&D and employee engagement, business leaders seem to be of the opinion that HR is clearly meeting expectations.

HR professionals seem to be far more liberal in their self-assessment in these areas. Except in the areas of staffing, recruitment and selection, where they see themselves as meeting expectations, in other areas they believe that they exceed expectations.

In the areas of managing performance, OD and management and leadership development, business leaders seem unhappy and rate HR as inconsistent in its delivery in all three areas.

HR professionals, on the other hand, see themselves as exceeding expectations in the areas of managing performance and management and leadership development and as meeting expectations in the area of OD.

Clearly, there is a perception gap between how the business leaders rate HR and how HR professionals rate themselves.

Are HR professionals listening to their stakeholders and devising ways of receiving feedback? Are business leaders giving consistent and regular feedback? What are the organisational costs of misalignment in expectations on a prolonged basis?

These are questions that need to be answered if effectiveness on the ground needs to be improved.

Progressive Changes

Beyond all the noise and perceptions, there are some very clear markers of progressive change in the HR function. There is no denying it.

This came through not just in our survey but in all our discussions and all through our research efforts.

Well-staffed

First and foremost, HR functions are far better staffed today than ever before. HR leaders seem to have liberated themselves from self-imposed frugality and asked for and obtained budgets to hire more people. This has resulted in the functional specialisations receiving the attention and focus that they require. From a time when a single person wore multiple hats, the HR function in many organisations has come a long way. The fact that they are getting the budgets to hire and staff their function also speaks of the perceived value of the function and of course the expectations of it.

Process Orientation

Thanks to the demands of scale, geographical spread and the use of technology, the HR function in many organisations has been forced to establish strong processes in most areas. As a result, most of the basic work—be it hiring, onboarding, pay and benefits administration or learning—there are processes in place and a certain level of maturity and predictability around it. This is great.

Visible

More and more HR professionals are out there in the field, on the floor and in factories, in generalist or partner roles. This has enhanced their visibility in the eyes of employees. It has also helped them connect with employees and managers a lot better.

Most importantly, they are able to get closer to the business and its issues and challenges. HR professionals are travelling a lot more, making sales calls, meeting clients and having scheduled meetings with employees.

Almost all medium to large organisations have an HR leader in the top team.

Business Appreciation

Business literacy has become important for everyone in the organisation, irrespective of level or position. For HR it has become paramount. Thankfully, there is now an increasing number of HR professionals comfortable with seeking and understanding business-related information. Going beyond the numbers, they are beginning to get comfortable with understanding the impact of business on HR and vice versa. This is helping them focus on what matters to the business. The evolution of the HRBP role has helped hugely in this.

Clearly, these are huge gains and augur well for the function and the professional. However, while expectations are high and the progressive changes are many, the gaps in performance are still yawning.

Measures That Matter

How is HR's performance and contribution measured? Can views about HR's performance go beyond perceptions and opinions?

Our respondents seem to believe that there are quite a few process efficiency measures to track turnaround time and costs, attrition levels, days in training, participant-reaction feedback and such like in many of the HR processes.

Clearly, the expectation is that there should be a greater number of outcome measures to evaluate the impact from HR processes, policies and programmes.

While one does get to see some outcome measures such as employee engagement or the number of open positions filled from within, these appear to be few and far in between.

From our survey, it appears that there are a limited number of tangible and reliable measures to assess HR effectiveness. The few that are used need further refinement and regular use to enhance its popularity. There is a need to develop more appropriate measures to help the function establish its credibility better.

Suggestions for the Professional

We closed our survey by inviting our respondents to share with us specific suggestions for the professional—*ways in which they can make a more impactful and credible contribution.*

The following five clear suggestions emerged:

Style or Approach

The style and approach that HR will need to adopt towards employees will require serious rethinking.

With the change in demographics of employees at the work place as well as the fast-paced context in which the businesses find themselves, the old ways of doing things (controlling or policing) are ill-suited. What seems to be more acceptable and in demand is the facilitative approach. Such an approach must also be reflected in the policies that are framed and implemented.

HR professionals need to be honest, open, clear and to the point in their communication. This mirrors the style of today's young leaders and younger employees.

Having said this, HR professionals also need to be sensitive to the context while communicating. This may call for maintaining confidentiality, diplomacy or just human sensitivity. Prudence and judgement in these matters is paramount.

It is also recommended that HR professionals act in more pro-active ways and not wait to be asked or told. This may call for a certain level of empathy and anticipation of needs and expectations.

Finally, business leaders would like HR professionals to remain focused, do fewer things but do them well and offer only what is practical, effective and simple.

Business Partnership

Business leaders would like HR professionals to act as true partners of the business.

This calls for them to sit with business, become part of the business teams and therefore interact very closely with them and their issues leading to an enhanced understanding of the context as well as the challenges. With proximity and greater understanding, they will be able to join hands in enhancing business performance.

Armed with credibility, trust and competence, HRBPs are also expected to play the role of a coach and counsellor to team members (across levels). They need to support line managers as they deal with emerging people issues and ensure they uphold organisational values and role-model the key cultural characteristics.

With the average age of leaders coming down, there is a heightened need to hand-hold and mentor them as they engage with their own team members, thereby enhancing their confidence and leadership capabilities.

Learning and Leveraging

HR is expected to leverage technology, improve the speed and quality of delivery and thereby reduce the cost of its services. Wherever appropriate HR should explore outsourcing to improve the productivity of its resources. Benchmarking with other organisations to learn of the latest trends and be able to adopt what is appropriate for them is considered key.

It is also recommended that HR professionals become far more technology and data driven in all their actions and decisions. They must use analytics to enhance the quality of their diagnosis and insights, thereby improving the quality of their decision-making.

Employee Connect

HR professionals are expected to be most familiar with the pulse of the employees. It requires them to maintain a very close and trusting relationship with employees, know them and be fully familiar with their contexts (both personal and professional) on an ongoing basis. This calls for regular interaction with employees at an individual level and demonstrating interest and support for their professional and personal growth.

HR professionals should also become the trusted friends of all employees, across levels. This requires a high level of credibility which is built over time. They should be seen and experienced as fair and objective. This has to be demonstrated by their stance and actions with people at all levels (without fear or favour). It is this that will earn them credibility and trust with employees.

In-house Expert

The HR professional has to be the well-regarded in-house expert in their line of work. This regard has to be earned by the sheer dint of their knowledge, experience and demonstration of their competence. Much of HR will and must be practiced by all people managers in the organisation, but they will all require a go-to person who will be able to guide and mentor them. They will however go to this person only if they have a high regard for his or her counsel.

Qualifications (education) would provide access to accumulated knowledge and some amount of skill. Repeated practise and exposure to different situations makes one skilful and experienced. Willing and appropriate sharing of their knowledge and skill is what will make them a 'go to expert'.

Closing Reflections

As we synthesised all that we heard, a few possible future trends and opportunities seem to emerge.

1. The quality of expectations being placed on HR augurs well for the function and the professional. HR is clearly seen as fundamental and a key enabler for business success. There is a desire for HR professionals to have a skin in the game.

The shift from being an administrative provider to being a trusted business partner and soon a business leader is palpable and evident.

2. The survey clearly points to the fact that the process and transactional aspects of the function have been mastered. These will eventually get even more automated and outsourced. This may not even be a part of HR going forward. Functional specialization and adequate staffing have certainly helped.

3. Line managers will embrace and adopt most of the people processes and employee interface aspects as part of their roles.

4. There is a clear organisational need for help in the areas of culture, change and capability-building. There is also a need for building the conscience of the organisation as it evolves from being just a money-making institution to one that serves a larger societal purpose. Who will fulfil these emergent HR needs is the question. Will the new generation of HR professionals rise up to this challenge? Will budding business leaders be attracted to such work in the HR domain? Maybe so. This space will need to be watched closely.

5. The gap between what the function can deliver and what its practitioners are perceived to be delivering is still wide. While there will be a tendency to throw the baby out with the bathwater, those joining the profession should be optimistic about the possibilities and the enormous scope for adding value to the different stakeholders.

The function is certainly on a firm footing and so are many of the functionaries. Of course, as Robert Frost said,

The woods are lovely, dark and deep.
But I have promises to keep,
And miles to go before I sleep,
And miles to go before I sleep.

4

The Doing, Feeling and Thinking Paradigm

I am sure many of us have come across this typical exchange in the selection interview of young and aspiring HR professionals from B-schools. The candidate is asked this fateful question by the senior HR leader, 'Why do you want to be in HR? What attracted you to HR?', and the young student says, 'Sir, I chose HR because I have a natural flair for people, I really like interacting with people', to which the candidate gets a dismissive look from the interviewer. The interviewer might want to retort that if she wants to interact with people, she should work in a retail store!

The truth is that many enter the profession with the assumption that the profession calls for a lot of human interface and offers a place for people who are interpersonally effective and empathetic. There is a fond hope that their gifts on the human side will be put to great use.

They of course get a rude shock when they realise that many of them spend 90 per cent of their time in front of laptops and on phones and not with people. They soon realise that they are swamped by processes to manage, metrics to live by and transactions to complete.

On the other hand, employees often complain that their HR colleagues do not 'care' enough for their needs and problems. Even business leaders complain that HR professionals are losing touch with employees and are not caring enough.

You ask some of the more senior HR professionals and they will tell you that they really wish to get out of transaction mode and do more strategic stuff. In fact, when organisations began outsourcing a lot of their transactional stuff to specialist firms, their main argument and business case was not just cost—their argument was that it would free up time for the HR folks to do strategic stuff. Yet, after more than a decade of HR outsourcing, one finds many HR professionals still stuck with doing operational stuff.

Listening to all of these situations, we are often left wondering if HR professionals are expected *to do* or *feel* or *think?* Which of the three modalities of doing, feeling and thinking matters most?

What Do These Three Modalities Mean?

The terms 'doing', 'feeling' and 'thinking' are being used here with a 'technical meaning' rather than a dictionary meaning in mind.

The term 'doing' refers to those HR tasks and functions that call for an action and execution bias, for administrative efficiency, diligence, the ability to get things done well, the ability to deliver results and, in general, taking pleasure in completing tasks.

The term 'feeling' refers to those HR tasks and functions that call for the demonstration of empathy, care, concern for people and their welfare; the optimism and interest in their development; the courage to stand up for what is right; to speak and advocate; the ability to connect with people with ease; understand their feelings and motives and build and nurture strong supportive relationships.

The term 'thinking' refers to those HR tasks and functions that call for strategic orientation, detailed planning, problem-solving approach, the insight and advisory focus, and transformational vision, including thinking of novel and productive ways.

Using this working definition, let's explore some of the dilemmas, constraints and limitations across the three modalities.

Doing and Thinking

So who in HR does the thinking and who does the doing?

In many global organisations, global headquarters typically does the thinking and brings out standardised policies, programmes and practices. Local teams are expected to 'roll out' these programmes.

In large and small Indian businesses, a lot of the thinking typically gets done either by the promoters or by those in corporate HR. The business partners are expected to implement these policies and programmes.

In the last two decades, a large number of professional services firms took birth to help organisations cope with the demand for specialised products, services and solutions. In the interest of embracing global models and best practices, many organisations signed up with these firms for their solutions. So be it an engagement survey or a compensation survey or an assessment and development centre, these firms do the thinking as well as the doing.

Certain large organisations also created CoE roles which were expected to do the thinking. The generalists or HRBPs were expected to implement their ideas.

For businesses, there is a lot at stake as far as the thinking modality is concerned. Businesses will never hand it over to HR on a platter nor should they. This modality will always be jointly owned by business and HR. Where HR is positioned as central and the HR professional is seen as helping, the thinking modality will be shared and HR will have a strong role to play in it. Where HR is positioned as peripheral, businesses will do most of the thinking and will only call in HR for the doing.

However, seasoned and mature HR professionals realise that they will have to earn the right to be included in the thinking modality and work towards it.

Doing and Feeling

It might appear from the narration that doing is not as exciting. Not really. It must be stated with great pride that an entire generation of HR professionals has mastered the fine art of doing things well. The doing has taken the form of speed, scale, automation, process orientation, service-level agreements (SLAs), metrics, strong performance measures and so on. In many ways, many parts of HR are no longer what was referred to as a staff function. They are as much a line function as manufacturing and sales. It is only through this relentless focus on doing that HR teams have helped businesses achieve scale and manage growth. It is only through this focus on doing that HR teams are able to manage a global workforce in a seamless manner.

The fact that HR has achieved a certain level of maturity in delivering predictable outcomes on the operational aspects, has led to businesses placing higher order demands on HR. It is the doing modality which earns HR professionals their right to be heard.

The biggest casuality of scale, growth and the preoccupation with *doing* has unfortunately been the feeling modality. Organisations and HR teams seem to have lost their connect with employees. Human sensitivity which is supposed to be the hallmark of HR professionals is also largely missing.

Organisations and HR teams are beginning to be perceived as cold and business-like. Even the so-called employee engagement activities are executed in a *doing* mode!

Over a period of time, HR teams and business leaders have been appealing to line managers to perform some of the people management functions that HR was traditionally expected to perform and as a result take on the feeling modality from HR. Has this robbed HR of the opportunity to feel?

We see this differently. We do not believe that anyone does or will prevent an HR person from engaging with the feeling modality. It is a choice that HR professionals have to make for themselves. They need to believe that it is possible to do and feel at the same time, that it is possible to uphold the human and emotional dimension even as one manages transactions and tasks.

Look around and spot HR professionals who have been successful, or ask business leaders about the qualities they expect in HR professionals and the feeling modality almost always comes right on top.

Thinking and Feeling

'Culture eats strategy for breakfast' is a famous quotation attributed to the late business management guru Peter Drucker.

What that really means is that many great strategies created by business leaders can end up being implemented very poorly because the cultural realities were ignored.

While more and more HR leaders are being invited to play a strategic role and partner with business to conceive and drive strategic HR initiatives to take the business forward, the uncomfortable question that remains to be answered is this—how many of these great strategic ideas actually see the light of day? If they fail, what causes the failure?

While HR leaders take great pride in being seen as strategic, true benefits will accrue only when strategic thoughts are combined with a deep humanistic connect and appreciation. In other words, thinking without feeling can led to unsustainable outcomes.

Be it change management efforts or other programmes that touch people, it becomes important to take an empathetic view in addition to a cognitive and strategic view.

Be it a restructuring project or a merger and acquisition (M&A) project, business insights need to be combined with human insights.

Be it a great leadership development programme or a technical or functional development programme—the conceptualisation of the contents should be married with a deep understanding of why and how people learn.

Closing Reflections

It will be evident by now that HR professionals need to respect, value and be competent in all the three modalities. All of them have their place.

Going by current trends, it is evident that more and more of the doing modalities will be automated or outsourced by many organisations or will be performed by someone outside of the function.

The growing significance placed on the HR business partnering role clearly demonstrates the need for a fine balance between the feeling, the thinking and the doing modalities. A successful HRBP must think, do and feel.

As technological advancement leads to disruptive changes, HR professionals will be called upon to look at and address the human implications and facilitate the change processes. This will call for feeling and thinking.

While on the surface it might appear that CoEs will need to think and can rely on others to do, that may not be so in the future. The CoEs will be expected to worry about the human implication as well as the implementation challenges in all their programmes and policies.

As far as the real strategic issues are concerned, business will want to play a role in the thinking process and will not leave it entirely to HR to do all the thinking. The right to think along with business will need to be earned.

The future belongs to those HR professionals who are able to cultivate all three modalities, demonstrate the right orientation at the right time with care and sensitivity. However, our view is that it is the feeling domain that must form the fulcrum around which the HR function and the HR professional need to revolve, for without that the person and the function and, therefore, the organisation will be soulless. This is our conviction.

HR AND HERE NOW

PART 2
Bringing People on Board

5

Planning in Uncertain Times

For a long time, many of us have been employing personal drivers to drive us and our families around. I am sure you agree that it has become increasingly hard to find and keep a personal driver. With the changing opportunity landscape and more flexible options available, many of us are having to rely on service providers who will give us 'Acting Drivers' or 'Drivers on Demand'. Similarly, the birth of hyper-local firms that thrive on an app have changed the landscape of local services. Be it a plumber or carpenter or a birthday party organiser, you can hire someone on demand without having to employ him or her.

Would the founders and promoters of many of the engineering colleges that mushroomed in recent times have imagined that they would need to shut them down for lack of demand?

Twenty years ago, would we have imagined that when the sales director of a global pharma company in some part of the United States wants to make a product-related decision, the background work including the presentation is done in a KPO in India and shipped to him?

Why is it that everyone is now talking about the 'Uberization' of their workforce? And what does that imply?

Futurologists from a variety of fields such as Alvin Toffler[1] and Charles Handy[2] have been writing about the future of work. Many have gone to the extent of predicting that jobs and organisations in the form that we have known will cease to exist.

While one might argue about the degree of change that has taken place, the reality is that the concept of how work gets done in organisations has indeed undergone very significant changes in the past few decades.

While organisations continue to rely on people to get their work done and they may do so for some more time (robots have started to share the work space with humans), the nature, the relationship in terms of the structure, tenure and other aspects are undergoing radical changes, mostly dictated by the changing and uncertain conditions in which businesses are operating as well as the changing values of people towards work and organisations.

The task of planning for people in these dynamic times can be hugely challenging and makes for an interesting exploration.

In our view, there are three dimensions to the task of planning for people in these times:

1. Managing the people portfolio
2. Managing the supply side
3. Managing the internal labour market

Managing the People Portfolio

Given the uncertainties and rapid changes, the various players in the labour market have helped create different segments within the market to meet the different needs of businesses.

Each segment represents a category in the portfolio of resources now available.

Organisations will need to take a decision on the mix in their people portfolio to get their work done. Such a decision will

---

[1] Alvin Toffler's famous books include *Future Shock* and *The Third Wave*.
[2] Charles Handy's famous book is *The Age of Unreason*.

have implications on cost, quality, risks, their relationship with employees and of course future sustainability.

Given the strategic significance of these portfolio management decisions, they are taken either by business managers or jointly between HR and business managers, depending on the positioning of the HR function in terms of its centrality.

Based on the emerging choices being made by organisations keeping in mind task demands and business preferences, we have abstracted a people portfolio model that most closely reflects current realities and future possibilities.

As you can see from the model (Figure 5.1), there are two drivers influencing the portfolio choices—task demands and business preferences.

Arising out of the combination of these two dimensions, there are four possible portfolio choices or employment models that seem to emerge:

S1 represents the entire pool of contingent workforce or what is also called contract labour or temporary staff. This segment meets the needs of transactional excellence while offering flexibility and cost advantages.

S2 represents the pool for full-time permanent workforce deployed in skilled roles that are critical for the organisation's competitive advantage. This segment meets the needs of transactional excellence while offering stability. These could be nurses in a hospital, skilled workmen in a factory, software engineers, those in KPOs and other skill-intensive roles.

S3 represents the pool of managerial and leadership employees in expert roles that are necessary to run the organisation. These are the very core of the organisation where professional excellence, cultural integration, depth, seasoning and complex competencies become critical. These are the highly paid elite group within an organisation.

S4 represents the expert pool of people with niche or hard-to-find professional skills who are required at critical times to solve specific problems. This segment offers professional excellence

Figure 5.1   The Emerging Segments in the People Portfolio Model

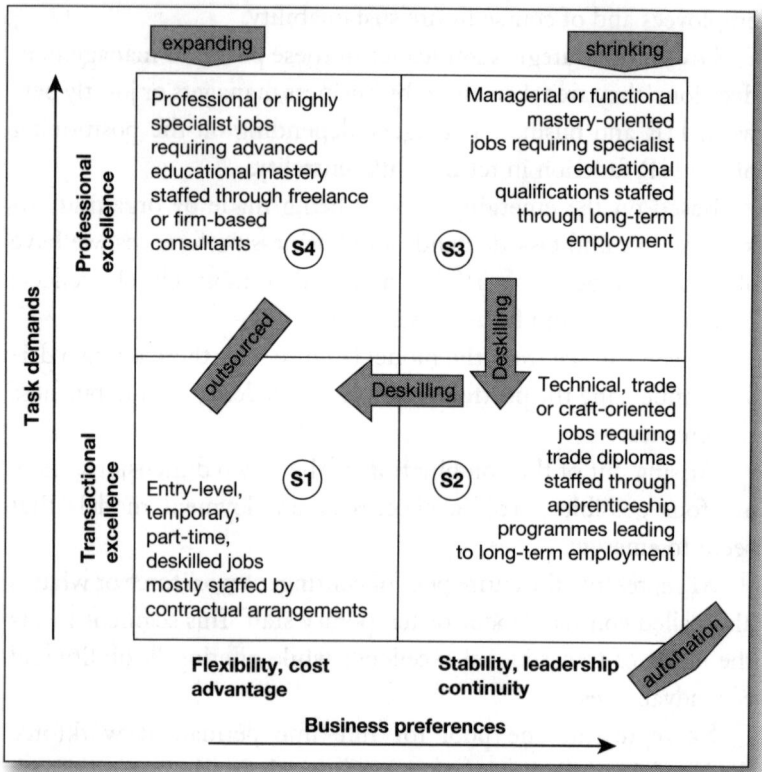

Source: Employment 2010, a totus consulting research project lead by Ganesh Chella in 2003.

along with flexibility and cost advantage. Those in the S4 segment are also referred to as fractional executives who could give a fraction of their time and mind space to a bunch of organisations. Today we have fractional CEOs, chief financial officers (CFOs), CHROs, chief marketing officers (CMOs) and so on. This segment in the labour market has become so large that is now referred to as the gig economy.

The people portfolio model is dynamic and is evolving all the time. In many of the start-ups where infant mortality (of the business) is very high, the portfolio is made up of employees on contract (S1/S4), even though they are highly qualified and core to the business. As the business stabilises the model changes and it starts to make many of these employees, who were on contract terms, permanent (S2/S3).

Employment on contract is no longer a bad proposition. It is preferred by both companies and prospective employees. In fact, in the world of projects in hyper-development geographies (like the Middle East) the predominant portfolio choice is employees on contract, irrespective of the nature of work and qualifications. The dominant factor is time cycle and flexibility.

Helping businesses make the right portfolio mix decisions can have far-reaching impact on the success and sustainability of the business, and therefore represents an extremely strategic contribution of the HR function.

India has been a net beneficiary of the decisions taken by leaders across the world about their people portfolio management in the form of millions of jobs flowing into our country.

Companies in India have now started doing what their clients did.

In a typical manufacturing facility, it is common to find all or a part of the plant being run by contingent workforce. In the same facility, you will find skilled technicians in the quality labs or in the engineering functions, who are on the permanent rolls. In addition to the managerial team, you will find hordes of consultants and free agents working on a variety of time-bound projects.

Take the case of a super specialty hospital. While the nursing staff might be full-time permanent employees and the heads of some of the medical and non-medical departments might be full-time permanent employees, many of the doctors might be employed as consultants. Much of the support services such as housekeeping and catering are also outsourced.

This is a dynamic context. The decision is not that of the organisation alone but that of the potential employee pool as well. The reason why hospitals have consultant doctors is not because the hospital wishes for it, but because the specialist doctor is in so much demand that he prefers to consult across many hospitals.

As traditional manufacturing businesses continue their fight to remain competitive, every rupee saved through smart management of their people portfolio is invaluable.

On the other hand, in the IT and ITeS industry, the changes today are even more radical. This is requiring them to go back to the drawing board and revisit their people portfolio. At the same time, many of their overseas clients who took decisions to engage people on contract based on their people portfolio preferences are also revisiting their decisions due to changing political and social demands.

It is our view that HR's role in many cases is restricted to execution of portfolio decisions unless the function and its functionaries are positioned as central to the functioning of the organisation.

With the advent of people portfolio management you can see the birth of businesses to support organisations implement such decisions—thousands of organisations that provide resources across various skills with the assurance of reliability and of course the attraction of flexibility and lower costs.

It must be clarified that irrespective of the portfolio mix, the line managers and even the HR functions are beginning to exercise greater oversight over all categories of employees from a governance, capability building and fair treatment point of view. In fact, organisations are assigning dedicated HR professionals to manage those especially in S1. They are even willing to spend money and pay attention towards engaging consultants and partner firms to professionally manage HR for these resources in S1.

Managing the Supply Side

Let's now shift our attention to the strategic planning that is currently going into managing the second and third segment—S2 and S3.

A large number of service businesses and manufacturing businesses continue to rely on a permanent workforce for many of their core tasks. These can either be for legacy, philosophical or pure business reasons. Let's explain this better. In some cases, if the organisation is old, it may find it difficult to change its portfolio given the demands and expectations of various stakeholders and may continue in that manner. In some cases, the promoters and management might strongly believe that they should operate a direct model. Finally, in many cases, it might make good business sense to have your own people.

Whatever might be the motivation, organisations need to plan for ways in which they are assured of a perennial source of supply.

Three Kinds of Organisations

When it comes to planning and providing for people, organisations could be classified into three distinct types:

1. Predators
2. Autonomous
3. Wellsprings

Predators

There are many organisations which almost perennially depend on the external labour market for their staffing needs. All their efforts end up adding to the existing demand in the labour market. These we refer to as 'predators'.

They may end up having a disparate workforce and culture but they might take a view that it is okay.

Autonomous

There are organisations that might start off as predators but quickly establish their own model of vitality hiring—hiring of employees straight out of campuses and training them while continuing to rely on the labour market for some of their needs. We call such organisations as 'autonomous'. In difficult times, these organisations struggle with staying committed to their vitality hiring strategy, especially because they might find it hard to protect their stock from the predators. In despair, many even abandon their autonomous plans and revert to becoming predators.

Then there are a few organisations with a visionary focus on building a robust supply of resources not just for themselves but for the industry. We refer to them as 'wellsprings'.

This model will be explored in greater detail because this is where HR can truly add value, not just for the organisation but for the industry.

Wellsprings

When Sankara Nethralaya, one of India's leading not-for-profit institution for complete eye care started their operations, they realised that there was an acute shortage of skilled resources in the field of eye care. To address this, they started The Sankara Nethralaya Academy (TSNA), which is a one-of-its-kind institution, that offers a distinctive series of educational programmes ranging from certificate to doctoral level programmes in various fields including allied health sciences such as ophthalmic nursing, operation theatre assistance, medical laboratory technology, medical records, optometry, ophthalmology, and undergraduate and postgraduate course in hospital management. The primary goal of the academy is to critically create a pool of comprehensive, well-trained health care professionals with the confidence and capability to meet the challenges in the health sector.

Similarly, the Elite School of Optometry in Chennai run by the Medical Research Foundation of Sankara Nethralaya in collaboration with SASTRA University, Thanjavur, India offers a four-year professional degree in optometry (BS Optometry). Students enrolled in the course undergo three years of academic training in the Elite School of Optometry and the final year of internship includes training in various specialties in all the branches of Sankara Nethralaya. Elite School of Optometry is a pioneer in the field of optometry education in India and is the first college to offer a four-year professional degree in optometry.

Thanks to their pioneering efforts, India has become a leading destination for eye care across the world and has helped prevent blindness for thousands of people.

When the Oberoi Hotels or ITC (earlier called the Welcomgroup) needed trained professionals to work in their hotels, they found that the institutes of hotel management were not adequate to meet their needs. They set up their own schools. While it created a captive supply source to meet their own needs, it also increased the supply for the industry as a whole.

ICICI Bank has taken the initiative to set up banking-related postgraduate courses in collaboration with a number of educational institutes/companies. Take, for instance, the Institute for Finance, Banking and Insurance, a vocational training institution set up by global talent development company NIIT in association with ICICI Bank. It offers a range of courses for those interested in entering the industry or for those already in the industry, it offers course for acquiring additional credentials. Manipal University offers a 1-year Post Graduate Diploma in Banking (PGDB) programme in partnership with ICICI Bank. It is a vocational training programme designed to develop a pool of first-level managers with banking knowledge and required skill sets to perform efficiently in their day-to-day activities.

When RPG set up its retail business back in 1995 it was creating an industry that did not exist. Instead of being a predator, it chose to be a well spring and set up the RPG Institute of Retail Management to create trained front-line retail employees.

Many conglomerates across the country have set up very high quality polytechnics to impart a range of diploma programmes to build engineering skills among the youth and make them employable. By playing host, they have helped increase the supply while taking care of their own needs.

The Tata group set up the Tata Management Training Centre in 1966 to not only develop managers and leaders for the Tata group but for the nation. Even today, the institute offers learning opportunities to the Indian Civil Services.

On the face of it, it might appear that being a wellspring (of talent) is expensive and even a distraction from the main business of the organisation. However, playing this role has several path-breaking advantages, especially if you are a player of significance within your industry. You can set new benchmarks, create perennial supply and of course make a larger contribution to the industry.

Managing the supply side is another area where HR has a huge opportunity to partner with business and make a landmark contribution and there are several examples of this all around us.

Managing the Internal Labour Market

Every organisation, especially with a large workforce resembles a labour market, albeit, internal. There are hundreds of transactions between the employer and employees within the organisation. These transactions are governed by the policies and decisions of the leaders and managers in the organisation.

The quality of these decisions can affect the efficiency with which the internal labour market is operated. By managing the internal labour market better, we can shape the workforce to meet our business needs.

On the contrary, if organisations fail to manage their internal labour market well, they can be susceptible to the predatory activities from the external labour market.

To put it simply, the HR professionals responsible for recruitment are constantly competing with the HR professionals responsible for talent management in other organisations.

In organisations that do not have an efficient internal labour market, employees who are talented might find it easier to find opportunities outside rather than inside. On the other hand, organisations that run an efficient internal labour market are able to facilitate growth and mobility with the same ease as the external labour market.

This is where organisations with very sound internal job posting schemes accompanied by ease of release policies score. Similarly, where organisations establish the norm that talent at a certain level and above belongs to the organisation and not the manager are able to make the internal labour market efficient. Several companies also insist on filling up positions of a certain level and above from internal resources only.

Closing Reflections

Planning for people in changing and uncertain times calls for strategic thought and action.

Such planning efforts will call for decisions and trade-offs in terms of the people portfolio for the organisation. It will also call for efforts to manage the supply side and of course pay attention to the internal labour market.

The compulsion of market forces has forced companies to treat this as a strategic differentiator both from a flexibility and cost perspectives. Today, therefore, the largest employers could be the staffing companies such as the TeamLeases and Addecos of the world and not necessarily the operating companies for which the employees of these staffing companies work.

All of these practices and accompanying challenges are discussed in greater detail in the chapters to follow.

The entry of women in large numbers into the industry and the need for diversity has also impacted planning in a significant way.

Organisational Experiences

Aditya Birla Group's Hiring Freeze as a Tool for Developing People Faster

With the objective of providing greater and faster opportunities to its employees and to reduce reliance on the external hiring for the talent requirement at the mid- to senior level, Aditya Birla Group (ABG) implemented a three-year hiring freeze at senior management levels starting January 2016. This freeze was applicable to the entire global operations of all group businesses. The only exception to this hiring freeze was key senior positions and new projects.

Significant time and effort was spent by each of the businesses to prepare for this initiative. The foundation of this preparation was the SWP (strategic workforce planning) exercise that each of the group businesses had done a year earlier. This exercise had been done role by role, forecasting the 'demand'—number of people required to man these roles on the basis of the business strategy—and also estimating the 'supply' through the exiting HR metrics. Thus, each company was able to establish, gaps both in terms of key roles and the key capabilities.

Learning and Development at the Core

Each business of the group used this information as the basis for creating robust learning and development plans, revisiting their hiring strategies and expanding the GET (Graduate Engineering Trainee) and management hiring programmes. Each of the businesses created journey programmes for accelerated development of the talent, the basis being their specific needs. Besides classroom events, these journey programmes included capstone projects, e-learnings, educational visits, and community learning. Hiring strategies were reworked upon to hire talent only at entry level and GET/ GMT programmes revamped to build the talent pipeline to support future business strategy.

For the developmental requirements that were common to many businesses, Gyanodaya (group centre for leadership learning) ramped up its operations. ALP (accelerated learning programmes) participations went up three times and overall nominations for Gyanodaya programmes have doubled in the past two years. A big thrust was put on technology-based learning at the group, including e-learning, videos and simulations, and consequently use of tech-based learning has gone up by 50 per cent.

Leverage Diversity of the Group to Build a Diverse Leadership Pipeline

Given the diverse nature of the group (the group has significant businesses both in services and manufacturing sectors), gaps in talent in one business could be fulfilled by high potential talent from the same or another business. New processes were created where the functional leaders from different companies come together and discuss the talent requirements and talent available. Many people movements as well as development decisions are made in these sessions.

All of the aforementioned has had some excellent outcomes. The group was able to create a vibrant internal talent market and encouraged mobility of people across locations, businesses and functions. The initiative accelerated focused development of internal talent, thereby building a culture of strategic people development. The cross-business movements of people have gone up by 150 per cent. The exposure of ABG employees to multiple businesses has gone up in an exponential manner. This not only is helping fill talent gaps, but is also helping create more knowledgeable and diverse leaders of future for the group.

Impact: A Leadership Pipeline for the Business and Career Development for the Employees

The hiring freeze at ABG was intended to be a *bold initiative to give bulk of the people's careers a big boost, and open up blocked career paths spurring them to avail of the learning and career development opportunities.* Clearly, this vision has begun to unfurl.

Skilling at Café Coffee Day

As we at Café Coffee Day (CCD, as it is popularly known) started with our retail presence in the cities, it made sense for us to provide opportunities to the rural youth in the coffee-growing areas—select them based on their attitude and groom them for the job skills of a Barista.

With growth, we recast our rural skilling initiative as a scalable model with twin objectives:

1. Provide employment: Job opportunities in Chikmagalur district were scarce and so we set up Yuva, a vocational training institute to train and upskill the local youth in Chikmagalur—we provide uniform, lodging and boarding and relocation support across CCD locations post training, including engaging with parents to get their support.
2. Provide a steady source of skilled manpower: As CCD was growing at 150–160 stores a year, we needed a continuous pipeline of skilled manpower for coffee-making and customer service, and a pipeline for operations leadership roles.

In 2005, we started Yuva (under the aegis of the SVGH educational trust) to offer a 6-month residential course in hospitality management, culinary skills, supply chain management (SCM) and store audit. This is followed by a 12-month internship at CCD.

We tap into a network of government schools and various NGOs which operate in districts of Karnataka to leverage their strength in the communities. We also depend on referrals from students and the communities where we have traditionally operated such as Chikmagalur, Hassan, Coorg and Shimoga districts of Karnataka to enrol students who have dropped out of the mainstream educational network.

We replicated the model in Eastern India, and started an association with Gram Tarang (part of Centurion University) in Odisha in the year 2012. Here we have access to students from rural parts of Odisha, Northeast and Eastern India. Similar to Yuva, skill training is conducted at residential campuses in Bhubaneswar, Guwahati and Chabua.

Coffee Day has also been selected as a champion employer by Ministry of Rural Development, Government of India in 2014. Students are trained under the Deen Dayal Upadhyay Gram Kaushalya Yojana (DDU-GKY) in states of Karnataka, Kerala, Bihar and Odisha.

By the agency of these interventions, we have trained approximately 7,500 students across all states.

These initiatives help in building a strong pipeline of trained resources who start as 'team member' at a tender age of 18 years and soon run a store P&L (profit and loss) independently, and the best performers in 5–6 years run an 'area' of 8–10 stores. Some have also become city managers. Every career transition is done carefully with detailed classroom sessions and shadowing of leaders to help them gain confidence to run larger markets. We have a much higher retention percentage which is in excess of 60 per cent after one year. About 70 per cent of the promotions are internal within CCD operations.

The programme has provided economic independence as well—while they all start with minimum wages and based on performance they progress to senior roles, from a compensation perspective in about five years earn about ₹4–6 lakhs per annum as first-time managers. These employees also excel at coffee-making events within Coffee Day as well as at all-India and international competitions hosted by the coffee trade. In the recent past, our star performer Poonam, a student from Bokaro district, Jharkhand, within 18 months of leaving her village, represented India at an international stage in Mexico. It's a true story of 'Zero to Hero' as most start with academic credentials of school drop-out level and transform to front-line leadership roles, even before they become 25 years of age!

While those with ambition, learnability and resilience have progressed all the way to middle management, several of them struggle to make the transition, and that is our challenge. Their inability stems from attitude to adjust to city-life, lack of support systems or just being recalled to the village to help the family. Women get equal opportunity in this programme and while we start with 35–40 per cent of them in the programme, many return back to their hometown for early marriage or to help ageing parents. It's a continuous effort to help them cope with challenges and succeed in life.

L&T's Institute of Project Management

('Stay Ahead–Stay Relevant–Stay Connected')

Genesis

The year 2008 was a milestone for Larsen & Toubro's (L&T) project-knowledge building initiative and its vision to groom project managers for the years to come. L&T Institute of Project Management also known as 'L&T IPM' was established in the year 2008 to cater to the project management capability-building efforts of L&T. The need for the IPM was realised as the organisation aspired to grow by taking up higher challenges through empowering its people with the required knowledge and skills to successfully execute complex Indian as well as international projects. Thus, the vision and mission for the institute envisions as follows:

Vision: *To develop a premier world-class education centre, for creating global project management professionals, thereby making Larsen & Toubro (L&T) a centre of excellence in project management.*

Mission: *To develop and deliver high-quality education and research in project management in consonance with the vision of L&T by providing state-of-the-art infrastructure and learner-friendly atmosphere with innovative pedagogy thereby creating a pool of world class and socially responsible project professionals.*

With more than 75 per cent of L&T's revenue from project business, the demand for project management professionals is significant. Even the business units that are focused on products have realised the need for constant injection of projects such as 'new product development'. With the growing size and complexity of projects, the need for enhancing project management capability has gained great importance. Project management education in L&T has gained further significance with the company aspiring to explore new geographies.

L&T has created a body of knowledge in conceiving, planning and executing mega-scale projects. Being a major player in engineering, procurement and construction (EPC) projects in India, the leadership team felt that there is a significant need and a great opportunity to create a knowledge repository for project management within L&T. L&T IPM's knowledge-building initiative also received great support from its senior leaders.

L&T IPM is committed to develop contemporary programmes to create a pool of well-trained project professionals and strengthen project management talent to meet the business aspirations. The L&D focus of L&T is to empower people with knowledge and skill that would enable employees to perform their roles better. The efforts in this direction led to grooming people not only in functional competencies but also in project management and business leadership.

Trinity of Talent Development

Developing 'L&T's three leadership archetypes' is one of the pioneering efforts of L&T's human resources department. This L&D initiative focuses on people and their professional growth and nurturing its synergy with the organisation's growth.

L&T's three leadership archetypes are:

- Functional leadership
- Project management
- Business leadership

L&T firmly believes that the aforementioned three capabilities delivered in the right mix are the means to enhance execution efficiency and optimise costs in a sustainable way within the organisation. To align with the said objective, L&T IPM has been developing project management curriculum to deliver a structured yet flexible framework for tackling a wide array of issues in a faster, better and more cost-effective manner.

6
Remaining Attractive

If you have watched the movie *Lion King*, you will certainly remember the famous words of the Hyenas—'Look at you guys, no wonder we are dangling at the bottom of the food chain.... You know if it weren't for the Lions, we'd be runnin' the joint'.

No organisation would like to find itself in the pitiable state like Shenzi—at the bottom of the food chain—unable to attract and retain people. In fact, everyone would like to be the Lion—walk away with the lion's share of the best resources. But then, everyone cannot be the lion!

In a competitive labour market where every organisation is competing to gain the attention of prospective employees and move up the food chain, there are some organisations that are constantly punching above their weight—with an image and reputation much beyond their true accomplishments—and there are some organisations that are punching below their weight—with an image and reputation which does not do justice to their accomplishments. So is modesty a bad thing when it comes to attracting people? Is branding important for HR?

This brings us naturally to the question of making it into at least one of the lists of so-called 'best employers' published by a clutch of consulting firms and media houses every year. As one might know, these lists are based on each firm's hypothesis or

definition of who is a 'best employer' and a research methodology
the firm adopts to validate that hypothesis or definition.

As one sees these lists, one has more questions than answers.
While one finds some familiar names there are surprise additions
and omissions, and then there appear to be many who did not even
participate.

All of these raise many questions about employee-value propositions (EVPs), engagement and the larger issue of branding.

1. Why branding? What is its relevance?
2. Is there one truth as to who the 'best' employer is? If an
   organisation does not appear on any of the lists, does that
   mean they are not a good employer? If an organisation is on
   the list, is it truly among the best employers? Is there life
   beyond these lists?
3. Should organisations work on building brands or are brands
   the outcome of other fundamental actions? What is the
   future of these branding efforts, especially given the power
   of social media?

Let's explore these and other questions.

Why branding? What is its relevance?

Every organisation which operates in a competitive business in
any case invests in building its brand. However, organisations
recognise that their brand as perceived by a consumer may not be
relevant and adequate for its prospective employees. In fact, the
brand as an employer often needs to have far greater depth given
the nature of the ensuing relationship.

Without going into the technical definition of what an
Employer Brand is, it would be adequate to say that it represents
the reputation and image of the organisation as an employer, in
relation to other employers in a similar industry or the same
geography or labour market.

An employer brand also needs to authentically generate recall of the value that it can provide and has been offering its various segments of employees in a consistent manner.

Let's look at a few examples.

For several decades now, the TVS Group in South India has had the reputation of being a great employer—offers lifetime employment, takes great care of its employees in a personalised way and offers its employees unmatched pride in the community. This is a reputation that was built through actions—not through advertisements or a Twitter handle or validated through a survey because none existed.

Think Taj Hotels in India, and you would immediately think of extremely well-trained hospitality professionals of global standing.

Think Asian Paints, Citibank, Hindustan Unilever or ITC and you immediately associate them with some of the best management trainee programmes.

Organisations with something valuable to offer to some segments of its employees became recognised and built a reputation around that.

In a competitive labour market where employees need to make quick decisions about joining an organisation and need to select from a wide array of options and have an overload of information and promises, it becomes necessary for employees to be able to pick up the signal from the buzz. They want to be able to zero in on the ones that are truly aspirational and attractive. Therefore, it is important that organisations not only have a credible reputation but are also able to present it in a way that catches the attention of prospective employees.

An employer brand cannot however be a marketing or public relations gimmick. It has to authentically reflect the greatness of the experience that exists within as might be relevant for a specific segment of the labour market. The importance of authenticity cannot be emphasised enough. False claims by wannabe best employers have a short lifespan—the attrition saga sets in soon!

Is there one truth to who the 'best' employer is? Is there life beyond these lists?

That brings us to the next important question: Is there only one truth about what your brand should stand for? Can the yardsticks that apply to a financial services company be applied to an auto ancillary company?

If two different organisations are dealing with two different segments of the labour market, how can they be compared?

In our view, there is no one-size-fits-all or one global model which can solve the reputation problems of every organisation. Even for a given company the brand proposition could change from time to time depending on the kind of roles and people it wishes to attract or target.

This is where having a compelling EVP becomes relevant. In our view, if an organisation has a compelling EVP and is able to deliver on that value proposition consistently, it will end up creating a reputation that is consistent with its enduring core.

Let's explore this further.

Value Proposition for Employees

The term 'value proposition' is used primarily in the field of marketing to denote the distinctive value that an organisation offers as perceived by its customers in comparison to competitive offerings. In other words, value proposition is the organisation's solution to the customer's problems. In the field of marketing, it is believed that every organisation must have a compelling value proposition that appeals to its *relevant target segment* when compared to competitive offerings. It is also understood that delivering the value proposition must be profitable for the firm.

Using the term 'value proposition' for employees is a clear acknowledgement of the fact that in an extremely competitive labour market, employees and customers are no different. The term 'employee-value proposition' refers to a firm's distinctive value offered to its target segment of employees in comparison to competitive offerings. EVP recognises the fact that, like customers, employees are making important choices and will stay committed as long as the value proposition is attractive. The term 'value proposition' clearly denotes a strong marketplace orientation to employee practices.

Value proposition presupposes that, like customers, there are different employee segments, and organisations must have the ability to segment their labour market and position their value proposition appropriate to the labour market segment that they want to operate in.

Value Proposition over Satisfaction

In a market-oriented world, the concept of value proposition seems far more relevant compared to the concept of satisfaction. Satisfaction leads an organisation to view all employees as one ubiquitous group and attempts to move the entire mass up on their aggregate satisfaction. The concept of satisfaction leads an organisation to try and do everything for everybody. This is further complicated by the fact that different consulting firms and external organisations attempt to use their models to influence how a particular organisation should define and measure engagement, satisfaction and reputation. As a result, satisfaction or engagement is inward-focused, too general and therefore very difficult to action in a market-oriented world.

On the other hand, organisations are constantly making choices and trade-offs and are responding to a rapidly changing market environment, especially in terms of their people portfolio. Organisations are forced to adopt policies and practices that will certainly impact one or other segments of their labour market positively or negatively. An EVP approach helps organisations to use their unique framework to guide and calibrate such actions.

Let's now use the same four segments in the people portfolio (refer Chapter 5) as the basis to map potential value proposition drivers for each segment (see Figure 6.1).

Figure 6.1   The Employee Value Proposition Drivers

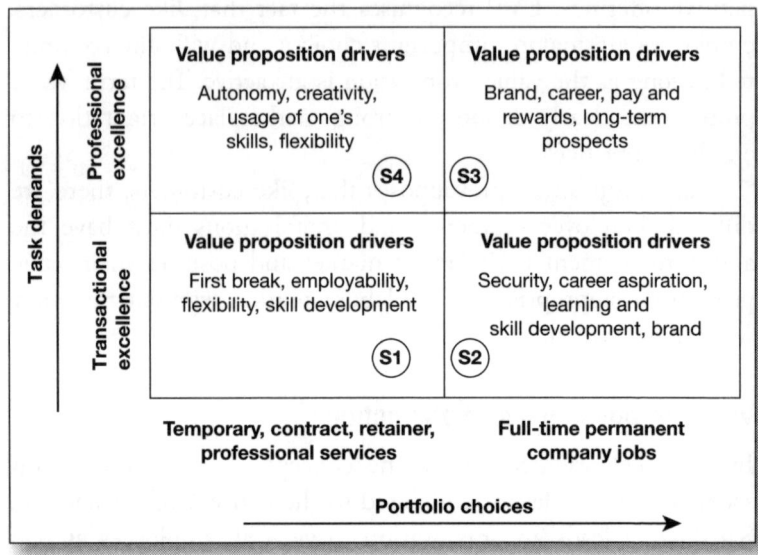

Source: Authors.

You will notice that each segment of employees have a different set of expectations depending on where they are in the people portfolio model or on Abraham Maslow's hierarchy of needs.

Organisations are indeed attempting to develop a deep understanding of what their current and prospective employees in each segment really expect, assess what they are currently being offered and seeing if and how they can bridge the gap.

At a time when food was in short supply and good food was unaffordable, any factory which offered a basic canteen was a big deal. Not any longer. Given the progress that the nation has made, most employees across socioeconomic segments are exposed to and even used to a range of dining options. In light of this change, any cafeteria will not do. There is need for variety, novelty and, of course, hygiene and great presentation at least among larger organisations of repute.

When jobs were in short supply, security was great. Today, a role change after 18 months seems to be critical.

In general, it is more challenging to offer a compelling value proposition for young employees in the 2–7-year-experience segment today because they seem to be wanting everything and are not sure of their priorities as yet. The mobility and attrition rate in this segment is very high because many of them are exploring and wanting to experience different organisations and cultures before they decide which is really appropriate for them.

Beyond that age group, employees seem to be a bit more conscious about the consequences of their choices and have moved into the next stage of their life. At this stage, other more important considerations come into play and they tend to take a much more pragmatic view of what they want.

For example, the same organisation which would never have been popular in the campus placement circuit of any of the B-schools may be considered a perfect choice for many of the graduates a few years later. The content of the job, the responsibilities, the job location and many other variables might be more relevant than whether the company was granted day-one status on campus or it figures on any best employers list.

It is interesting that companies have recognised the changing needs of the workforce and have therefore modified some of their people practices and the same are reflected in the value propositions offered. The focus is therefore much more specific rather than generic or broad based. For example, organisations are now emphasising job content and challenges, developmental opportunities and not necessarily life-long employment or pension schemes. Similarly, start-ups are offering a high risk–high return proposition.

In the same vein, organisations have recognised the need amongst the newer generations to be associated with socially responsible organisations and so they have started highlighting their contribution to the larger societal context and have also started including their philosophy towards the community as part of their employee value proposition.

Remaining Attractive in the World of Social Media

How does the advent of social media change things for the reputation of organisations and their ability to build and maintain their brand image?

Has the reputation of the Tata group or Infosys taken a beating after some of the board battles that they went through? With so much information out in the open about all the goings-on, little is left to the imagination of the young employee. What is reflected in a list or what an advertisement says is hardly going to matter in a world where real-time information about organisations, their policies and their people reach potential employees through their mobile phones on a daily basis.

When a young HR professional attempted to ask an employee to leave and the employee uploaded a recording of the conversation on WhatsApp, the reputation of the organisation took a beating, albeit, momentarily.

When any high-profile CEO is removed for certain alleged misdeeds, the whole world knows about it, in minutes.

Thanks to Glassdoor, Facebook, Twitter and WhatsApp, the power to make or mar the reputation of the mightiest of organisations is now in the hands of every employee.

Under these circumstances, organisations will need to pay attention to every moment of truth and cannot rely on the results of one good survey for the next 12 months.

Closing Reflections

Every organisation needs to think deeply about its current location in the food chain and then set itself a vision for where it would like to be. However, getting there is not the sole responsibility of the HR function.

We find progressive HR functions taking the lead in shaping their organisations' efforts to establish their reputation as good employers which is attractive for a chosen set of segments in the labour market. This is a hugely enduring contribution, if accomplished well.

This is why more and more HR leaders are concerned about the experience matching the promise. The consequences of not being so could be disastrous.

Organisational Experiences

HUL's Employer Brand

HUL's Brand Positioning

HUL's strong employer value proposition or brand positioning has always been rooted in its unique positioning as a school which builds leaders—offering big jobs early on in the career to groom for functional and leadership responsibilities.

With the 'School of CEO's' theme in place, we undertook an exercise to redesign our employer brand key and campus pitch in 2015 around the tagline 'Marketing is Business'. The emergence of e-commerce as a preferred sector in 2015 as per the Nielsen survey had led to a low preference for FMCG-sector jobs in the market. This was coupled with the fact that the millennial population in our target campuses were getting the impression that the job opportunities in HUL would be limited to only marketing and making ads. They felt it would not be about a real contribution to the business, which an opportunity with a general management company or a start-up could result in.

This brand key was developed by a special task force created by the combined forces of the marketing and employer brand teams after a comprehensive exercise of focused group discussions, interviews and surveys with internal employees, fresh recruits and campus students. It helped build the aspiration of students towards starting their careers with a sales role, which prior to the campaign, would not be regarded as highly as marketing roles on campus. It helped drive across the agenda of building general managers from the beginning of their careers.

Translating the Brand Key into Activations

After the proposition was developed, we ensured that all of our communication on campus revolved around reiterating this message. This was done in the following ways:

Pre-placement Talks

In the past, the brief given to speakers conducting their talks on campus was about communicating their leadership journeys at HUL to the students. This was made sharper and more structured by creating a brand key and an official campus pitch, based on the 'Marketing is Business' theme, which speakers would use for their talks. Additionally, an audiovisual (AV) was created to be played to students which was around the same theme and which spoke about the importance of having sales as their first job.

Unilever Unplugged

Unilever Unplugged was launched as a marketing workshop for first-year students which would help build their aspiration towards marketing as a sector. Earlier the manner in which the workshop was conducted emphasised marketing and making ads or commercials but with the refreshed proposition the format was changed to a business simulation game around the 6Ps of marketing which would provide a more holistic perspective to the students.

L.I.M.E.

L.I.M.E. or Lessons in Marketing Excellence is the biggest marketing case study challenge in India and is thus our flagship offering on campus. This year we have had nearly 4,000 teams register for the 9th season of the competition, across B-schools in India—the highest yet. In keeping with the 'marketing is business' proposition, we have chosen to have cases around the theme of 'newer marketing models' which had students thinking both about the marketing proposition and successful business models.

Retaining the Brand Promise

HUL offers a rigorous summer internship experience through the Unilever Leadership Internship Programme (ULIP). Interns go through an enriching learning experience by managing live projects that have a direct and huge impact on the business. Our flagship Unilever Future Leaders Programme (UFLP)—a programme highly sought after by fresh recruits and acknowledged within and outside Unilever as the best programme of its kind—is another key programme with a legacy of grooming leaders for over 60 years. The UFLP provides young managerial recruits an extensive functional and cross-functional experience through live projects and learning assignments, including rural and international exposure, within 12–15 months preparing them for bigger responsibilities very early in their careers. What makes the programme unique is the strong support system of senior leaders who act as tutors, coaches and mentors. This regular interaction along with a robust reverse feedback mechanism on effectiveness of the support system ensures the best grooming and inputs for the trainees.

After the completion of their management-training period, the trainees are compulsorily allocated the role of an area sales manager where they are responsible for the sales and distribution and management of their respective territories.

Measure of Success

As per the latest Nielsen Campus Track Business School Survey, for the sixth year in a row, HUL has emerged as the No. 1 Employer of Choice across all sectors for the 2016 graduating batch of B-school students, across functions. In addition, HUL retains the 'Dream Employer' status for the eighth year running and continues to be the top company considered for application by B-school students. HUL has also been ranked No. 1 for marketing as well as No. 1 FMCG in finance. HUL has been ranked significantly higher than other companies on all the employment drivers. This is the 17th year of the Nielsen Campus Track B-school study.

This achievement is a clear recognition by students of the consistent actions HUL has taken over the years to build mutually beneficial relationships and engagements with the student and academic community. HUL believes in a 365-day relationship with our campus audience, investing senior leadership time and effort in bringing alive our employer value proposition on campuses.

7
Choosing Right

In the entire 'value adding' chain of bringing people on board (staffing, recruitment and selection), it is the selection element which remains the weakest. Little wonder that in our survey business leaders pointed out that quality of hiring efforts was an area that needed attention.

Why is it that choosing right continues to be a challenge despite the fact that for years some of the greatest psychologists in the world have been researching and developing methods to select right? Why is it that despite so much being known about what it takes to select well, organisations and HR teams get it wrong?

The Fine Balance Between Service and Protection

All business-enabling functions such as finance, IT, legal, administration and HR have one thing in common—they need to strike the right balance between the service orientation that they demonstrate towards their internal customers and the vigilance they exercise to protect the interest of the organisation.

When the function scores very high on service, there could be a potential risk that some of the internal controls are being compromised, and the protect dimension is tending to be low.

Take the case of this typical conversation that a line manager is having with the HR manager.

> Ram, can you please issue an appointment letter to this person whose CV I have just emailed to you. He is a good guy. Have known him for a while—have seen him operate in the market and I know that he is a winner. I have offered him the same salary as Bala who left us. Same profile, you know. Please send him the letter and keep me informed.

If the HR manager does shoot out the letter immediately, the service levels would be rated as high but protection very low. On the other hand, when the focus is on protection, there could be a feeling that the service dimension is being ignored.

Take the case of another typical conversation that the HR manager is having with a line manager.

> Ashish, the onboarding will take time because I still don't have the manpower approval form signed by you and your director to hire that product executive, which is a new position. I also don't have a job description which is required. The candidate has to also take the psychometric test, which is as per policy. Of course, three rounds of interviews need to be done, then we need to do three reference checks and of course complete the internal parity check. Once all this is completed, we can proceed.

In the first chapter of the book, we had spoken about the extent of centrality that HR as a function enjoys within an organisation. Where HR's centrality is low, its practitioners end up playing an extremely procedural and servile role as far as selection is concerned. They find it hard to play their governance and protection role assertively. Even worse, they might end up exercising pseudo-controls which might add little value except causing irritation. On the other hand, line managers and promoters might take the decisions and use HR only to get the paper work done.

Where the centrality is moderate, HR might just do an adequate job on the service and control dimensions. Some aspects of control might be missing just as certain aspects of anticipating and understanding the service needs might also be missing.

It is only when HR is positioned centrally is the function able to balance service and protection. That is when HR ends up playing a truly supportive and strategic role in selection.

Taking a Segmented Approach

Before looking at the strategic role of HR in selection, it would be useful to clarify the segments in question as far as selection is concerned because each segment might require a different approach.

In the first chapter of this section, we had outlined four segments in the people portfolio. Of these S2 and S3 are the two segments where selection matters.

- S2 as a segment typically consists of two groups:
  - Semi-skilled employees
  - A wide variety of skilled employees
- S3 as a segment typically consists of two groups:
  - Employees who are hired into professional and managerial roles
  - Employees hired into executive leadership positions

The approaches and strategies that HR will need to adopt are likely to vary significantly across these segments.

Let's now examine the strategic role of HR in selection in three phases—*before, during and after.*

HR's Strategic Role in Selection: Before

One of the important metrics that successful organisations pride themselves with is the number of applications they receive for every open position. Some of the most admired employer brands in the world might receive upwards of 300 applications for every open position. That makes the selection process not just competitive but also meaningful because the organisation would have considered so many before making a final choice.

On the other hand, if the organisation has very few people to choose from, the whole concept of selection loses meaning. That is when organisations cynically declare that 'trespassers will be hired'.

Good selection therefore necessitates a good pool to choose from and that is a function of remaining attractive.

Organisations that attract, nurture and develop a good pool of potential resources are able to do a better job of selecting the right people. In fact, be it manufacturing or service businesses, they are able to use apprenticeship-like approaches to not only train employees to meet their needs but also give themselves the opportunity to observe them during this period before they make a final selection decision.

For example, we have seen garment export companies offer courses in tailoring and through that process pre-select their employees who show the aptitude for the job.

Many manufacturing companies also have extended traineeship programmes through which they afford themselves the opportunity to observe the employees well enough on the job and on that basis make a final choice.

Many BPO companies use their initial training phase as the most reliable platform to observe and select the ones that are likely to suit the job.

Hotels rely on the interns from catering colleges as do hospitals on interns from nursing colleges.

Several organisations use summer internships to observe and select their management trainees.

Companies also conduct fairs, competitions and talent spotting events in campuses to be able to identify those that they might wish to invite for a formal selection process.

In summary, right selection depends in good measure on what organisations do before they actually select. Those that have access to a larger pool of prospective candidates and also have had the opportunity to see them perform, stand a better chance of selecting right.

HR's Strategic Role in Selection: During

The *selection model* that the HR function deploys to manage the selection process will play a huge role in sustainable hiring results. So what do we mean by a selection model?

The best way to explain this is by drawing an analogy with the way a financial services institution works. Financial services institutions that lend funds have a lending team and a credit team. The lending team is interested in selling and mobilising maximum customers and the credit team is interested in ensuring the credit worthiness of the customer and thereby managing risk.

In the space of manpower hiring, we observe that invariably both HR and line managers are jointly responsible for quantity and quality of selection and when under pressure, you can imagine what gives way. A good selection model is one which is HR managed and not necessarily HR operated. In other words, if the quality of selection is incumbent upon HR interviewing each candidate, HR checking each piece of paper, HR being accountable for all outcomes, such a model will collapse sooner or later and will remain so on paper but get compromised in reality.

The Essential Ingredients of an HR-Managed Model

Following appear to be the essential ingredients of a sound HR-managed selection model:

1. In an HR-managed model, there will be a clear separation between the lending and credit process so to speak. In other words, the organisation must understand and accept the principle that those who source or shortlist should be different from those who interview and finally select.

2. The HRBP is responsible for the quality of the hire on time and (s)he ensures this through the development and adherence of proper processes rather than personally running around the country to source, shortlist and interview! In an HR-managed model, the basics to support distributed hiring would be in place. For example, there would be clear job descriptions, well-developed supply sources, well-established procedures for selection, training and certification for all those authorised to select, a system of audit to check at random for quality, selection aids such as tests and interview guides and so on. There will also be traceability of who or which panel or committee signed off on a hire along with their comments and recommendations.

3. In an HR-managed model, there is a shared ownership between line managers and HR for quality. Line managers do not expect HR to be the policemen. Nor do HR managers see line managers as offenders who must be apprehended.

4. In an HR-managed model, the two sides of the HR role are well established. It is well understood that HR has a front-end service dimension to their role. It is also understood that HR has a back-end control dimension to their role. They are never browbeaten to compromise on their control dimension by the CEO or senior leaders. On the other hand, HR leaders would also have earned their right through their track record and expertise to be able to stand up against potential violations.

   Such organisations will pay attention to completing selection interview forms because these forms will be reviewed independently and their judgement will be questioned for being flippant or hasty in the process. Similarly, there will be strict adherence to the various steps of the selection process, be it written tests or a specified number and nature of interviews.

   Given various other forms of concerns around security as well as falsifications by employees, verification of credentials and the employee's background is becoming an extremely critical control role for the function. The back-office processes of reading and verifying adherence to the various process steps including the interview outcomes will never be compromised.

5. Of course, an HR-managed model will have the flexibility to recognise special circumstances. There will be times when line managers will leverage their networks to spot good candidates and HR needs to encourage that. Of course, line managers must also recognise that just because they have spotted candidates, they cannot pass through a green channel.

6. In an HR-managed model, careful attention will be paid to the special needs of each of the segments we outlined earlier. For example, if the business requires hiring a large number of semi-skilled employees for front-line jobs, the organisation will go beyond the slogan of hiring for attitudes and training for skills and convert this slogan into reality. It will do a lot of research to define attitudes and even more importantly figure out how to spot good attitudes.

   Similarly, if the organisation wishes to use competencies for selection, its managers will be trained in behavioural evidence-based selection so that they know how to look for evidence of the right competencies.

7. In an HR-managed model, HR will spend a fair amount of time on action research to understand which of its hires are doing well, what competences in the selection process seem most deterministic, what life themes seem to matter the most and so on. This is no different from a good credit function in a financial services institution building its body of insights on what profile of customers are most credit-worthy based on analysis of credit history and performance.

8. Most importantly, in an HR-managed process, there would be a very strong culture of respect for process. It would be well established that it will not require the HR head to cry

foul each time there is a violation. There is a well-established culture that selection is an extremely sacred process and it is the joint responsibility of all managers and leaders to preserve it. Review meetings are not used in such organisations to threaten that revenues will not be achieved for lack of people and thereby paving the way for compromises. There are several rituals in these organisations that value the selection process. Such organisations, for instance, will delegate the selection decision upward rather than downward when in doubt. The senior leaders in these organisations will readily participate in selection discussions and not need endless chasing to set up interview meetings. Similarly, such organisations might encourage an independent pair of eyes to see a candidate—someone form a completely different function. They might even encourage peer involvement. Such organisations may be slow in deciding. They would have multiple rounds. They may insist on meeting face to face. But they hire right more often than not.

The Myth of the HR Interview

In many organisations, there is a commonly held belief that the HR person has special skills in assessing behaviours, reading human behaviour or looking for culture fit. This is a myth. Line managers who are hiring for their teams have a much deeper understanding of the kind of behaviours and orientations that are needed for success in the role. The ability to assess behaviours is trainable and HR is seldom the sole repository of such expertise. Given this reality, what is the meaning of the HR interview? Candidates often see it as a procedural necessity. HR practitioners themselves are nebulous about what they are looking for and what specific value they should add.

It is our view that every organisation should have managers at various levels trained in selection and the HR team should be part of that pool of trained resources. The value addition of HR goes well beyond the HR interview as we have seen now. It is a myth that only by being involved in interviews HR will act as a custodian of good hiring.

HR's Strategic Role in Selection: After

We have in our section on management and leadership development maintained that no leader is 100 per cent ready for a position. While this is true for internal mobility into leadership positions, outside hires are seldom accorded this benefit of doubt. Given their past success, high pay levels, reputation and high expectations from all the stakeholders that the new recruit should hit the road running, the transition can be stressful. What makes it most stressful is what was mentioned earlier—that people in many organisations are hostile to the new senior hires from outside making their transition anything but easy.

However, the reality is that even the brightest of outside hires will need help to fit in, to be assimilated.

Therefore, when a senior hire fails unfortunately, it may not always be possible to say whether it was a matter of competence or compatibility or a bit of both.

Our own research suggests that employees, especially at senior levels, experience at least six distinct transition challenges:

1. Gaining acceptance from and building trusting relationships with new colleagues who tend to see him as new competition.
2. Aligning with one's manager and other senior stakeholders while establishing a sound working relationship with the right balance between autonomy and inclusion.
3. Adapting to the cultural differences and changes in the new work environment and context.

4. Understanding the expectations and opportunities fully to be able to set the initial agenda for self and others.
5. Developing new skills and competencies to deal with some of the new demands.
6. Managing oneself, including the pressures to succeed, the stress from having to do a lot and the weight of expectations.

Even the most competent executives need support to make it through a transition. Such support can come from a senior HR leader, an internal mentor or an external coach. Being sensitive to such a need and providing access to the same is of course the task of HR.

Key Dilemmas in Selection

The discussion on HR's strategic role in selection will not be complete without exploring some of the emerging challenges in the selection process.

A Two-way Process

The traditional notion that it is the organisation that has the prerogative to choose the employee and the employee is simply chosen or not and is powerless in the process is now a thing of the past. It is not just organisations that choose employees. Employees choose organisations too.

For instance, when employees choose to change their jobs, they go shopping around for options and pick the one that hopefully best fits their needs. Similarly, even on campus (at least the good ones), students tend to have a wide array of companies to choose from. When it comes to hiring at very senior levels, most talented leaders have standing invitations from multiple organisations. In other words, if there is someone the organisation is keen on hiring, chances are high that the person has several options.

Once organisations recognise this reality, they will conduct themselves in a manner that truly endears them to prospective employees. This might include being authentic and candid about realities, being sensitive about the process and graceful about the negotiation dialogue.

The Dark Side

If there is one part of the HR profession which has been discredited the most with allegations of wrongdoings, it is the recruitment and selection function. During the days of high growth and rush for numbers, specifically in the IT industry, one read a lot of reports about collusions between those in charge of hiring and their eco system. Most company websites today carry disclaimers and warn prospective employees not to fall for those middlemen who claim to guarantee these aspirants jobs in their organisation.

While one part of the dark side has to do with the practitioners, the other part of the dark side is to do with candidates. Clearly, it takes two to tango.

There are a significant number of reports about employees falsifying their educational credentials, work credentials or not fully disclosing information about their background. This has led to the birth of the background verification industry. Global threats around data theft and data terrorism have further fuelled the fears of hiring employees without verifying their background.

With more and more automation and dependence on techno-logy, accompanying threats are also on the increase and all of them finally lead to asking ourselves if we have hired right.

In the coming decade, as the mad rush for numbers will be tem-pered by an emphasis on finding more competent and trustworthy employees, the premium on choosing right will only go up.

Closing Reflections

As you can see, the human effort involved in choosing right and then setting people up for success is not just important for the business but also for the individuals involved, and HR is privileged to be called upon to support this. However, HR needs to be clear about its role boundaries in selection. HR cannot believe that it is omnipresent and omnipotent in selection. At the same time, HR needs to understand that being service-oriented in selection does not mean being servile. HR is the custodian of the process and has to both serve and protect.

Organisational Experiences

Amazon: Hire and Develop the Best

One of Amazon's 14 leadership principles is 'Hire and develop the best'.

Our leadership principles aren't just a pretty, inspirational wall hanging. These principles work hard, just like we do. Amazonians use them, every day, whether they are discussing ideas for new projects, deciding on the best solution for a customer's problem, or interviewing candidates. It's just one of the things that makes Amazon peculiar. Hiring the right quality of people is without doubt a key business driver for us in Amazon India, along with customer obsession, selection, pricing and convenience.

To find candidates who can help the company grow, our interviewers must get to know candidates authentically during the interview process. Candidates go through an online assessment and a phone screening before their first in-person meeting. Interview questions can run the gamut, from behavioural and situational to technical and functional questions.

We focus on hard and soft skills to learn about candidates and how they operate in different situations. In our interviews, we focus on candidates' strengths, accomplishments and a demonstration of deep curiosity. Since the very beginning of our journey, one of the tenets we have held was whether or not the new hire creates a sense of 'wow' amongst his or her peers.

To do this time and again, Amazon follows a rigorous process for hiring and selection of the right people.

Amazon considers all its employees as owners and encourages them to think and act like one. As part of this ethos, its existing people are encouraged to refer those who they think would be a good addition to the Amazon India team. This is a sure way of ensuring some meaningful pre-selection.

So what qualities do you look for in every candidate?

There is no fit stereotype at Amazon or who you must be like in order to be successful here. We focus more on the actual content or substance of what we are talking about [in every interview]. We focus on a problem and how to solve it.

During our selection process, it is not unusual for a candidate to meet with 6–8 interviewers. We think that as much as Amazon interviews a candidate, this process helps the candidates interview us as well. Each of these are invariably independent meetings and each interviewer is trained and certified to interview in the Amazon way. The mandatory certification process includes attending the 'making great hiring decisions' course. The invitation to be part of the hiring process is considered as a prestige, and the interviewers show exceptional commitment to the process for bringing on board exceptional talent.

Each of the interviewers is expected to focus on and assess for demonstrated capability that may include one or two of our leadership principles. Our interviews are invariably a free-flowing conversation with the intention of getting to understand the proficiency and competence of the candidate in the focus area.

There is an automated tracking system ('HIRE') that aids the selection process and each interviewer is required to fill out their assessment of the candidate. This is in the form of a narrative which justifies their bottom-line recommendation —meeting/failing/exceeding the expected bar.

None of the interviewers will be privy to the views of the other panel interviewers until they have submitted their individual notes and decision. This ensures independence and objectivity in the decision-making process. The recruiter then calls for a quick interaction amongst the interviewers and at this meeting (mostly virtual) the final decision on hire is made.

One of the interviewers is nominated to play the role of a 'bar raiser'. This is a role that is assigned to someone who is neither the hiring manager nor the recruiter. This is a key role and one which ensures that the quality of the hire is a net positive differentiator to the existing quality of talent in the organisation/team at that specific level. To be nominated as a 'bar raiser' an interviewer should have demonstrated great level of interviewing skills and a deep understanding of the organisational expectations. They need to have had the opportunity to shadow an existing bar raiser on a number of occasions and have been mentored to do this role.

The adherence to the process is very high and it is normal for interviewers to receive feedback from the bar raiser, on their interviewing skills and demonstrated capabilities as part of the process. The bar raiser as well receives feedback from the other interviewers.

There is also a regular stream of feedback from the candidates about their experience of the process and this is attended to with utmost seriousness. Intentionally, there is a lot of feedback that is shared amongst all involved to keep the learning and improvement ongoing.

All of the preceding discussion is serious business and there is regular review to ensure that the quality of hire at Amazon India is constantly improving and based on these reviews the nature of tests, interview questions and focus is modified suitably.

Will Talocity's Bots Help Hire Better?

For ages, HR practitioners and line managers were credited with that special ability to identify and hire the right candidates. However, we all know that despite best efforts, results are not always positive.

Well, it is predicted that artificial intelligence (AI) and machine learning (ML) may be able to replace human beings in the onerous task of identifying, interviewing and selecting right!

Among the many technology companies who are trying to use AI and ML in the hiring process, Talocity, a start-up, has built a futuristic product, which is a video platform enabled with AI and ML. The company claims that the machine can scan through thousands of CVs using the many preconditions (AI) to pick the right profiles. It is believed that once the machine starts repeating the same task, the ML will kick in and, over a period, the machine will develop patterns by analysing the profiles of selected candidates. Soon the machine will be able to shortlist profiles which exactly meet the requirements of a role and the traits required by the company. The platform can also conduct online written tests in case that becomes necessary.

The shortlisted candidates are then put to one-way or two-way video interviews through an application which can be loaded on any smartphone. The hiring manager can chose the questions needed to be asked and a bot will ask those questions to the candidate verbally in a language the candidate understands (regional or even foreign). While the candidate is answering on the smartphone or PC, the video platform using AI observes the gesture, eyeball movement and words used by the candidate to analyse his or her personality based on the five-factor theory. The machine then makes a recommendation!

Here again the ML kicks in once the machine starts analysing more interviews for the same role and over a period of time, the machine hires exactly the way the hiring manager would have done or perhaps even better as machine does not suffer from any kind of biases!

It is believed that once the machine reads the personalities and CVs of high-performing and satisfied employees in a particular role in one organisation, it creates patterns of similar profiles by means of prediction, and then matches those in the process of hiring, thereby ensuring high quality and success.

For one of its clients in the BPO space, the company uploaded over 5,000 video interviews on their platform. The number of candidates recommended by the machine was around 600 and the number that the client finally selected was around 400—a 70 per cent selection rate! Also, the improvement in select rate with ML from the previous month was 15–18 per cent (just in one month).

The organisation claims a benefit of 60 to 80 man-years of effort saved for every 1,000 people hired.

Scary or exciting? You decide!

HR
HERE
AND
NOW

PART 3
Managing People

8

The Spectrum of Relationships

It is when organisations begin to manage people that the true nature of their relationship shows up. That is when the rubber really hits the road.

On one side are the preoccupations that organisations have about surviving, making money, maintaining their competitive edge, staying on the right side of law, protecting their reputation, making their business model future-proof if they can, adapting to the technology and fighting disruptive changes.

On the other side are the preoccupations about doing all this in a manner that their employees find acceptable or are willing to and capable of supporting.

What organisations pay attention to and what they do not in many ways shape the relationship between the two. History is replete with stories where organisations have been obsessively preoccupied with the needs of employees and have perished in the bargain. History is also replete with stories of organisations that have been able to find a great balance between the seemingly competing demands. History has also taught us that there are times when survival becomes so critical and doing what is exigent is the only viable option.

In essence, 'context' is king. The manner in which organisations act is at least in good measure dictated by the context in which they find themselves. Of course, their own value orientation can temper the nature of their responses to the context.

We would like to label the two ends of the spectrum of employer–employee relationships as business driven and values driven.

Business driven   **Values driven**

Business Driven

Organisations that are entirely business driven tend to focus mostly on the task at hand. For a start-up, the task could be about proving a business model and establishing a client base. For an old organisation in a struggling industry space, it could be about surviving. For an established organisation in the throes of radical technology or business model or environmental changes, it could be about reinventing itself.

These organisations will hire from the open market, invest in training only to get their employees job-ready, emphasise the credo of perform or perish, pay to attract and retain an anchor team of employees, and keep the frills to the minimum or even do away with the frills.

When the context demands a business-driven approach, it is unlikely that the organisation will want to worry about long-term implications, succession planning, developing a leadership pipeline or even pushing up the employee-engagement scores by a few points.

In our view, this stance is completely understandable.

Values Driven

On the other end, organisations which are well established, have a strong heritage and legacy, are reasonably stable and secure in businesses, are part of a conglomerate which has businesses that are able to support each other in tough times or have generations of families running it with a strong foundation of values, the value fabric becomes predominant.

Everything tends to be viewed through the filters of what sits well values-wise.

These could be small businesses in niche areas which are privately held, or large family businesses that are publically held and take moderate risks but fiercely protect their values fabric.

These organisations always prefer to grow from within; not cut back on development costs in the face of a bad quarter; take a more long-term view of performance and are more tolerant of performance shortcomings; consider internal equity before taking pay decisions, even if it means it cannot hire special talent or protect those under threat of leaving and try to maintain a certain level of hygiene and care when it comes to employee benefits and facilities.

When the context demands a business-driven approach, values-driven organisations don't find it easy to shift gears and struggle to take decisions that are purely business driven at the cost of their long-cherished values. They are likely to be weighed down by the long-term implications of their action even as they recognise the short-term challenges that they might have to encounter.

The Pulls and Pressures in the Relationship

The equilibrium in an organisation's relationship with its employees is impacted by certain inevitable pulls and pressures.

It has been our experience that no organisation can survive without being market oriented. Market orientation is a stark reality especially in today's environment.

Similarly, no organisation can continue to act in ways that ignore people orientation as a value.

It is the task of HR leaders and HR business partners to help businesses find an appropriate place in the spectrum which is contextually appropriate and sustainable. To manage people, HR will need to conceive of and propose policies and practices that do not compromise either business interests or people interests, in the overall scheme of things. This will call for strong relationships and deep conversations with all stakeholders.

Everyone understands that investing in learning is good, that the bell curve hurts, that paying well is a good idea, that contemporary HR policies and practices, flexible working hours, a great campus, a wonderful cafeteria, good medical benefits and responsive employee services will do a lot of good for engagement.

Knowing what can be done when, what makes sense for the business, when will the business be ready and knowing what it will take for the business to be ready is the nuanced competence of a great HR team.

Keeping this overarching context and spectrum in mind, we will now look at some of the contemporary needs, challenges and priorities in managing people.

The first chapter in this section looks at learning the new way. The second chapter looks at what lies beyond managing performance. The third chapter in this section looks at money and beyond. The last chapter focuses on the importance of managing the moments of truth.

Organisational Experiences

How Brakes India Lives in Harmony with the Community

TVS is a 100-year old group with a unique achievement—it has never faced a serious industrial unrest situation. The first company of the group, TVS & Sons, set up in 1911, has a strike-free record. So do most of the other 30-odd companies, including Sundaram Finance (started in 1954), Wheels India (1962), Sundram Fasteners (1966) and Sundaram Brake Linings (1975). Only four companies have faced one strike each. Sundaram Clayton, Lucas TVS and Brakes India were briefly hit by a strike in 1977, while TVS Motor Co.

shut down for a few days in 1992. This unique story of the Brakes India group will help us understand the secret behind this unique track record.

The year was 1977 and the city of Chennai witnessed one of its worst-ever period of industrial unrest. Brakes India Ltd, part of the TVS Group, was no exception. There was a strike followed by a lockout—the first and last-ever industrial unrest for this group company. During the strike, the organisation was concerned about meeting its customers' requirements and was wondering what it could do. Meanwhile, in the village of Sholinghur, about 100 kilometres from the city of Chennai, the transport operators who were all loyal and happy customers of the TVS Group company Sundaram Finance heard about this strike and wanted to help the company in some manner.

They told the company that they had a movie theatre that they could offer as a makeshift facility to house the assembly shop of the brakes division of Brakes India. In a few days the theatre seats were removed, the floor was levelled and a small factory came up! Within a year, the local community was keen to see if they could persuade the company to set up their factory in the village for good. Having experienced the organisation, they realised that their entry into the village would change the destiny and fortunes of their present and future generations in such a positive way. They invited Brakes India to set up their factory there and offered to organise for land. The company offered them not just fair compensation but also one job for each family, who sold land to the company. There are stories about how the first set of CNC machines and materials arrived by bullock carts to the site!

From thereon there was no looking back. In a few years, their foundry division came up following the same principle. A decade later, another group company Turbo Energy was set up to manufacture hi-tech turbo chargers.

What had started as a small makeshift facility in a small movie hall has now grown into a thriving industrial hub set within a community characterised by a symbiotic relationship.

Recognising the need for trade and technical skills, especially in tool- and dye-making, the group partnered with Nettur Technical Training Foundation (NTTF) to set up the Matrix Craftsmen Training Centre. Matrix imparts a course in tool- and dye-making with significant on-the-job training opportunities. Admissions are made purely on merit and is open to children from the local community. Matrix graduates are able to find job opportunities within the Brakes India group of companies in Sholinghur or in many of the industrial establishments around the area and are doing very well today.

The group set up Vidya Peetam, a CBSE school in the village in 1982 where 50 per cent of the seats are reserved for the locals. Today, there are over 1,000 students studying in the school and over 28 batches have completed class X and 24 batches class XII, and its alumni are well placed in jobs all over the world.

One of the Turbo Energy group companies in Sholinghur called Real Talent Engineering also launched a 'Learn and Earn' training programme. Under the programme, they recruit 60 students per year—50 per cent are boys and 50 per cent are girls. They should have completed 18 years of age and must have completed 12th standard or 10th standard. They are provided training for two years, five days a week. They are given an opportunity to work on the machine for four days and one day they are given vocational training in the classroom. This training programme is conducted by NTTF. At the end of two years, they get a manufacturing technician certificate. During the period of two years, they are paid a stipend of ₹4,750 per month for the first year and ₹5,000 per month for the second year, apart from paying ₹2,900 per month to NTTF for the classroom instructions. Apart from the stipend and fees to NTTF, they also provide the students uniforms, safety shoes and subsidised food.

This programme has been running for over three years and the response has been quite good. But for this programme, many of the girls would have been forced into marriage soon after completing 10th or 12th standard. Instead, they are qualified, earn some money and are a lot more confident of themselves.

In 2014, the group set up a 25-bed hospital in Sholinghur to offer high-quality health care for the local community.

More recently, the local community approached Turbo Energy with a special request. The government girls' school there had only until class VIII and had no budgets to build more classrooms to go until class twelve. This resulted in girls dropping out or having to travel a long distance. The villagers offered to give land and in return requested the companies to construct classrooms so that they could jointly request the government to extend classes from eight to twelve.

The Brakes India group of companies have managed to establish many manufacturing facilities in Sholinghur by leveraging the local community resources without compromising on meritocracy, discipline and productivity while also enriching and enhancing the living standards of the local community in an empowering way.

Sholinghur can consider itself blessed, not just because of its famous temples but also because of its collaborative relationship with a business group that has been able to think beyond money and enriched the local community.

9

Learning, the New Way

The training room is ready, lunch has been organised, the trainer has arrived but the participants are missing—at least many of them.

Ask any L&D professional and she will tell you that her biggest challenge is to get participants into the classroom.

Ask trainers and they will tell you that they have come to accept a 15–25 per cent dropout rate (the percentage of employees who do not attend a scheduled training programme that they have signed up for or have been nominated to).

Line managers across levels are seen as the villains of the piece—the ones who swear by learning at the executive council meetings and say 'yes' to programmes but are alleged to have pulled their team members out a day before or in the middle of the programme.

Employees find it hard to balance between the need to fulfil mandated training man-days and complete their unending work.

More and more organisations continue to commit higher financial resources towards training. Given that signing off training budgets is the politically right thing to do, most CEOs find it hard to say no to training budget proposals.

At the same time, we see remarkable innovations in the field of learning that hold the promise of transforming the way people learn.

Unfortunately, neither the money nor the emerging technologies seem to be contributing to effectiveness. In fact, the most prevalent problem among L&D professionals is 'training effectiveness'.

Rechristening the function as L&D has hardly solved the problem. Today's L&D professionals continue to feel challenged about making training deliver results.

So what are the emerging business realities that L&D professionals need to recognise and pay attention to, so that they can deliver greater effectiveness?

Business Realities

Given today's business conditions, it appears genuinely hard for people to get away from work for classroom training of any duration. Making the time to attend a two-day programme without interruption is now a Herculean task. L&D professionals continue to find it hard to accept this reality and that is hurting. Accepting this reality might open up other creative options. L&D functions will need to find ways in which people can learn at their workplace through skilled experts or on their own and not have to depend on classroom training for all needs. This is one area that will need radical rethinking.

Businesses across industry sectors are crying for help in strengthening their functional and technical competencies. In fact, we are in an era of diminishing technical and functional expertise. Similarly, businesses keep experiencing specific performance challenges arising out of skill and competency gaps. Addressing these needs is no simple task since there are not enough off-the-shelf programmes or generic solutions. Unfortunately, many L&D professionals seem so wedded to their specialisation that they conduct themselves like academicians. They do not do enough to engage with business, get under the skin of the key jobs in the organisation and understand the critical capability needs and design solutions to address the same.

In an outsourced world where the face of your organisation is not your employee, in a world where your employees are so geographically dispersed, the idea of everyone coming to a classroom physically to learn how to do their job better seems almost impossible. Take, for instance, a service technician or a salesperson or a check-out cashier in a retail store. They all need to be imparted training on job skills the day they join and cannot wait for a batch to be formed or travel to a training centre hundreds of miles away spending time and money to get job-ready.

Also, young employees in front-line jobs need to be given job-skill training in small chunks, just at the time that the skills are required of them. Overloading them with things that are of little value just because we got them out of their workplace once is futile.

So L&D professionals will need to find ways in which they can take learning to the workplace rather than expect the learner to leave the place of action and come elsewhere to learn. Several service businesses in the world ranging from pizza stores to hotels have mastered this fine art. In fact, it is only by taking learning to the learner's workplace can L&D professionals achieve their popular 70:20:10 rule (that 70 per cent of learning should be on the job, 20 per cent through developmental relationships and 10 per cent through formal learning events).

L&D professionals have been unable to wean businesses away from the process of measuring training man-days. Organisations continue to budget and measure the number of man-days of training as a metric for training investment while L&D functions swear by 70:20:10—quite a contradiction. They continue to ask participants to sign training attendance sheets and fill in post-training feedback forms despite the espoused theory that actual results are evident on the job. Many claim helplessness since it is perceived to be an ISO requirement. We have to move away from man-days which is an input measure and look at capability proficiency to meet job requirements which is an outcome measure.

For far too long, L&D professionals have over emphasised executive leadership. As a result, the task of functional excellence and functional leadership across levels has been neglected. More and more businesses find that the leadership models produced by their L&D teams are too generic and do not address the specific needs of their building functional leaders at all levels. We are beginning to see the welcome signs of some organisations launching functional academies to address this gap. This is a long and painful process but will yield great long-term results, provided the organisation is in a context where it can take such a long-term view.

Employees' Learning Styles and Preferences

A few years ago, if I wanted an employee to study the features and prices of his or her competitor's products, the person may have depended on the organisation's market research department to gather and share the information or might have needed time off to physically go and gather such information.

Thanks to the Internet and e-commerce sites, the employee can access the information in a few minutes.

There was a time when the organisation or the trainer had exclusive access to some invaluable data, information or videos. These helped the trainer look superior and create magic in the classroom.

Professional trainers confess that they can no longer compete with content online. They are no longer the ones who have access to never-seen-before videos or never-read-before quotes or articles or books. Most participants have seen so many videos and have read so many things already. Every five minutes employees are receiving some quote or video clip or pdf attachment about something of educational value.

Under these circumstances, the expectations that employees have from trainers has gone up several notches. They will refuse to listen to lectures or be subjected to boring slide presentations and this is entirely understandable. The days of using training programmes to deliver content are over and that is what employees are telling us by voting with their feet and staying away from classrooms. Employees want to see trainers who can engage them in conversations, share perspectives or impart critical skills.

Attention spans have become extremely short. Most employees, especially young employees, are subjected to so much of incessant sensory stimulation that it is hard for any trainer to hold their attention for two or three days. Add to this the presence of 25 smartphones and tablets and laptops in a classroom and you have absolute chaos. If people must be motivated to come to a classroom and stay there for a day or two, it has to be extremely stimulating, engaging and experientially rich.

Employees today openly question the contradictions between what is professed in the classroom in terms of desirable behaviours and what their own managers and leaders practise. At the same time, they value their managers and leaders leading training programmes to share functional and technical know-now and perspectives. In other words, the divide between real life and the classroom is becoming unacceptable. Training design that ensures good connect between reality and the learning content works and where it isn't, it just does not work.

More and more young employees are used to the do-it-yourself culture. Be it their banking or shopping transactions or travel bookings, they prefer to do it themselves.

So if they have a job-related question, they would like to find answers the moment they have the question—right at that moment. This is where online communities, peer forums and self-learning resources are becoming increasingly valuable. The L&D function will need to gain a deeper understanding of how today's and tomorrow's employees work and seek to solve problems and then align learning solutions to that new realisation.

It is also evident that employees are willing to seek help from others to learn and solve problems of living and working. Little wonder then that interventions such as coaching, mentoring, learning communities, peer learning forums and global online resources have been able to deliver outstanding value. For trade, technical and professional roles, learning through a system of apprenticeship (especially, the nuances and the tacit knowledge embedded in the heads of skilled seniors) has been well established. L&D functions are leveraging these developments to help employees learn from others.

Organisations often lament that employees are not taking ownership for learning and that their managers and L&D functions have to shepherd them into classrooms and make them learn. This conclusion does not appear to be entirely true. How does one then explain the fact that fitness centres, yoga classes, cookery classes, guitar classes, pottery classes and a whole host of other things that people fancy are very well attended? How do you explain the fact that more and more young people are spending their time and money learning to do things that they are passionate about—from mountain biking to releasing music videos? How do you explain the growing popularity of self-learning sites such as Coursera or Udemy? Clearly, everyone has an inherent desire to learn and progress. The motivation does exist.

For far too long, we have been patronising in our approach and as a result smothering the employee's inherent desire to learn. L&D professionals will need to spend a lot more time establishing the environment that will motivate employees to learn.

What Are the Emerging Trends?

Given the sweeping force of business realities on one side, the radical shifts in the learning styles and preferences of employees on the other side and the rapid advancements in the field of learning on yet another side, we are able to observe at least eight emerging trends as far as L&D is concerned.

1. The flipped classroom is slowly becoming a reality. Most job-skill learning will soon be delivered to the employee at

his workplace at a time when he or she needs it, not when L&D can mobilise a batch. Such training will be delivered in small doses, consumed when the learner is ready and needs it. Classroom training will be used only to impart specific skills, share perspectives and discuss practical issues and learn from peers. Participants will soon be expected to consume and digest all the content in advance.

2. Self-learning and learning through online resources, peer networks and developmental relationships are becoming even more popular. Given the power of social networks, online resources and pressure on time, people are keen to learn on the go, from peers and through seniors that they value. Once people know what they need to learn and they are convinced why they need to learn it, the how is something they will be able to figure out.

3. Leadership development is being addressed by offering a range of developmental experiences and moving away from learning event centricity. This includes receiving high-quality feedback, solving real-life problems, working with coaches and mentors, receiving support to manage critical job transitions and so on. By linking leadership development investments to talent management goals, organisations will be able to come up with fairly personalised solutions for individuals.

4. Organisations are showing keenness to invest in building functional academies to strengthen the functional pillars within the organisations in support of their ambition of grooming from within. Many of these academies will be led and managed by line managers rather than L&D professionals.

5. Given the easy access to high-quality online resources, individuals may finally begin to spend their own money and their private time to learn a skill or master a concept. They

will do it because they find value and it is available at the click of a button.

6. Trainers will reinvent themselves to earn the respect of participants. More line managers are being co-opted to share their experiences and impart skills alongside external trainers.

7. The currently useful 70:20:10 rule will get refined and redefined. The ratios might change and new dimensions might get added. People will learn not just from job experiences but life experiences too. In other words, people will place a premium on those skills and behaviours that will make them effective not only in their work life but also their personal life. Similarly, a new dimension—learning by oneself—will be added. In fact, this might become the most potent dimension.

8. Technology will help hold people accountable for learning and behaviour changes. There are new apps that remind people about things they need to do, prompting them with appropriate suggestions and ensuring that learning and change is made sustainable.

Closing Reflections

The role of the L&D professional will need to change. She must have the consulting skills to partner with businesses and cocreate solutions. She must have the business acumen to understand what business needs. She must also be able to develop the depth to be equally comfortable with functional learning needs as well as behavioural learning needs. They must be able to act as mentors and guides for people who would like to know what and how to learn. Most importantly, they must be role models when it comes to learning.

Organisational Experiences

Learn, Lead, Grow—Digital Way @ Airtel

For organisations to succeed today, they need an omni-channel approach to meeting all customer requirements. Airtel too is investing heavily to engage customers across all available channels—to provide them with a consistent, unique and refreshing experience. We incorporate this mindset in our approach to building capabilities in our employees as well. Our multigenerational employee base requires opportunities to learn whatever, however, wherever and whenever they want. To bring such customisation, ease of access and empowerment to life, we must leverage digital to the fullest. We offer a bouquet of services to our employees encouraging them to learn, lead and grow digitally.

Airtel 101

Learning Modules

Airtel 101 is a recently launched mobile learning platform, which through its byte-size learning modules, helps learners get an over view of the subject and it also provokes them to explore something of interest further. It allows us to share content with a 'light touch', that, is 'use at will'. The emphasis is to create these modules as small consumable capsules, ensure a hold on the learner's attention span and facilitate recall and retention. Its gamified experience and interactive interface make learning fun and engaging.

Modules typically consist of learning cards or videos, followed by Q&A cards. Each card has corresponding points which accrue to the learner, basis the number of attempts taken to answer correctly. The content is designed with levels—to build in progression and a sense of achievement for learners. They also earn credits after completing a course, with a certificate of completion.

To ensure learning is productive, a pre-read is provided prior to the questions. Each question is then followed by an instant feedback which not only provides interesting knowledge nuggets but also validates their understanding thereby creating a pull to move to succeeding modules. Questions are designed in various forms, namely, multiple-choice questions, multiple response questions, match the following, true/false and many more. Leaderboard showcases the learners' ranking and score in each module along with their peers'.

Fastest Finger First Contest

We also run a competition called Fastest Finger First on Airtel 101. It is played on a weekly basis and each contest contains questions around multiple facets of our business. Learners who answer maximum questions correctly in minimum possible time are the winners. Learners are able to participate on the go and results are declared in a matter of seconds. They are able to view self and peer rankings, time taken to respond and the correct answers.

Airtel 101 Platform

In addition to the learning application, there is an admin portal which allows easy and quick content creation, report generation and content testing.

Case Studies

Going forward, mini case studies will be made available to learners on Airtel 101. Theses case studies will include situations that employees experience every day. The cases will challenge and encourage the learner to explore, rethink and re-examine their ability to respond to situations differently and continuously learn to emerge as a more rounded professional.

Airtel 101 will soon host treasure hunts, jumble words and a lot more to keep the learner engaged and wanting to stay plugged in.

Game of Networks

Participants learn to carefully utilise the Capex by deploying telecom sites (2G/3G/4G) and fibre backhaul, depending on the number 2G, 3G and 4G customers respectively. Participants are able to view the leaderboard at the end of 12 rounds. The score at the end of each round is the Capex productivity till that round (incremental revenue from the total Capex invested so far).

Telsim

Telsim is Airtel's proprietary business simulation game that helps telecom professionals build general management expertise around pricing, channel planning, network planning and investment, customer experience, marketing and branding, manpower planning and so on. The game is a role play wherein participants act as the top management of a telecom company and compete against rival teams to win customers, market share and the like. Teams are able to view the leaderboards at the end of each round.

Career App

Career App is a mobile-based application which can help an employee craft his own unique career path within the organisation. One or more similar roles are mapped to role clusters, which have functional skills mapped to them. An employee can find out the functional skills which his destination role demands and plan future roles and learning interventions so as to acquire those skills.

Insights+

Insights+ is a 360-degree feedback application. The user can request for feedback on self—on 20 questions, aligned with our leadership competencies. The feedback report is generated instantaneously on a real-time basis and the responses remain completely confidential.

Mood-o-Meter

Mood-o-Meter is designed with a vision of enabling our employees to voice their opinions on an ongoing basis at the click of a few buttons on their mobile devices. The feedback report is generated instantaneously and the responses remain completely confidential.

Innovative Learning Practices at WIPRO Limited

Leadership Development Journey

The Wipro learning team designed a leadership development initiative that entails a combination of classroom education, online modules, business projects, mentoring and offline learning capsules for a set of handpicked leaders.

One of the innovative practices was the use of Twitter during classroom sessions. Participants were encouraged to tweet their responses to a case question or reflections from a session. The core principle of tweeting was to shape clarity of thought in order to synthesise within 140 characters.

Additionally, participants were required to create specific videos (e.g., video resume, introducing a digital product) in order to build executive presence and digital acumen.

We also used the Periscope app to broadcast interactive leader sessions for the programme—all these were much appreciated.

Workshops made active use of movies and parables in order to help participants draw parallels in an effective manner. For instance, an episode from the popular television series, Flop Show, was employed to help appreciate executive behaviour- and culture-building.

Social Experiments for Employee Engagement

Nudges and experiments have been designed as part of team-building and employee-engagement initiatives.

These include:

- Designing a behavioural nudge centred on 'gratitude' to foster kinship and reciprocal altruism that leads to engagement.
- Conducting a week-long series of behavioural experiments in a specific location to stimulate curiosity.
- Designing and delivering an online game-based approach as part of a values-clarification initiative.

Online Learning for Remote Locations

A unique online learning module called 'Wipro Wide Approach' (WWA) was created to help onsite (non-India) employees to learn principles and best practices around execution excellence and nurturing people.

Since onsite employees are working in client offices, WWA had to be modular, convenient and effective.

Therefore, a 75-minute online session called 'Webshow' was designed. The Webshow was a facilitator-guided discussion on the Webex platform, but entailed visuals and short interactive quizzes.

The visual content and quizzes enabled an interactive discussion and efficient processing of core ideas.

Liberal Arts in Executive Education

Wipro has used liberal arts in various forms and for myriad applications. The flagship leadership programmes have included sessions on theatre-production (participants learn to write and enact scripts, as per guidance from a dramatics maestro). Other examples include a session on appreciating leadership and innovation from the music of S. D. Burman.

These modules help individuals appreciate nuances, see connections and reflect deeply. Furthermore, these stimuli unleash emotional energy and excitement.

Building Cutting-edge Functional Capability @ ABG

Gyanodaya, ABG's global centre for leadership learning, was established in the year 2000 with the twin purpose of developing the group's talent and to help drive the business goals. Over years we have focused on continuously evolving and improving in this endeavour.

Traditionally, the world over, the learning centres such as ours, focus on the dual purpose of developing the senior leaders and developing leadership pipeline by focusing on high potentials. We decided a few years back to broaden our business impact by launching functional academies within the ambit of Gyanodaya. These academies focus on significantly enhancing cutting-edge functional capabilities of our employees across varied businesses.

Owned and Driven by the Senior Functional Leaders of the Group

One of the foundational principles we adopted for creation of these academies was that these academies would work under guidance of the respective group functional talent councils.

So far we have launched four such academies; HR, sales and marketing, finance and IT, and so far over 2,000 participants have gone through various functional programmes. While we use the best faculty in the market for running the programmes in these academies, the design of the programme is guided by ABG's functional leaders. These leaders also spend time in the class by being the leader-in-residence, bringing in the ABG-specific, real-world, knowledge to the participants.

Large-scale Impact by Large-scale Coverage

Each of the academy starts with clear articulation of the capabilities required across the width of the function. The impact of this is that language of functional development is starting to become uniform across the group.

In order to create big impact in short time, each academy starts by focusing on development of employees occupying select crucible roles, those unique roles that create big impact on the performance of the organisation, such as store manager in a retail business, head of HR in a plant and head technical in a manufacturing location.

While the leadership programmes focus on select few people, the academies are designed to enhance the functional capabilities of the entire function. Thus academies have master classes meant for senior leaders, programmes for emerging professionals and learning labs for mid-level professionals as well. The academies cover a whole range of capabilities: from world-class partnerships to prevalent skill-development interventions. These academies, being more knowledge-driven as well as meant for large groups of employees, lay a large emphasis on technology-based learning.

Functional academies at ABG, over the next few years, will go a long way in creating cutting-edge functional capability and excellence.

10

Beyond Managing Performance

For most employees, the performance rating that they receive is in many ways the only fateful outcome from the performance management process—the emotionally impacting decision through which they make meaning out of the process.

Many years ago, we worked with Elgi Equipments Limited, a global leader in the manufacture of compressors, to design and launch a new performance management process.

Recognising the potential concerns that his employees were likely to have especially about the rating, Mr Jairam Varadaraj, the managing director (MD) of the company, wrote a mail to all his employees to offer them a new perspective through which he wanted them to view their ratings. Given his heightened empathy and concern for his people, he was able to convert his email into what we would consider an extremely eloquent communication about the meaning of a performance rating.

Here is what he wrote:

Dear Friends

Re: Ratings and their meaning
…the understanding of what a rating means has a big impact in terms of the value attached to it by the recipient.

We (at ELGI) have followed interchangeably the nomenclature of numerical and alphabetical rating points namely 1-rater, 2-rater, 3-rater and 4-rater or simply A, B, C and D. It looks like we have formed some mental connotations associated with each rating point. It was coming across that any rating below a 2-rater in the numerical system and below a B in the alphabetical system is considered as bad performance. While in a conventional rating system this may be true, in the context of our performance management system and the way it is designed, this is a dangerous misunderstanding. I have attempted to explain the interpretation of our rating points below.

A 1-rater or an A is a truly exceptional individual who has exhibited superior performance. And this performance is judged not only by his manager but also his 'customer's managers'. They would be the equivalent of the Tiger Woods or the Roger Federers or the Ricky Pontings of the world.

A 2-rater or a B would be a good performer. They would the equivalent of the Vijay Singhs or the Lleyton Hewitts or the Rahul Dravids of the world. They are solid players who are in the fringe of becoming exceptional.

A 3-rater or a C would be an average player. They would be the equivalent of the Digvijay Singhs or the Nalbandians or the Agarkars of the world. These people are a strong backbone of the company and who have all the potential to track up.

Any of the people in any of these ratings have tremendous potential to significantly contribute to the future of the company. The rating in any given year is not a reflection of their capability but a result of a combination of skills and the environment and circumstances. There could have been technology issues, or customer issues or supplier issues that may have impacted ratings across these levels in a given year.

But the fact remains that people in these three rating levels are considered to have the promise for the future.

If the past year has been a mediocre one, the company restricts the performance payout to the 1 and 2 raters. But this does not detract from the belief that a much more comprehensive envelope of people exist in the company to take the organisation forward.

When people receive their ratings it would help if they were to review them in the light of the above. As they say...

A year does not a human it can make

As does a rain not make a monsoon

Many rains and the monsoons create

The glory of nature and not so soon.

Regards...Jay

Mr Varadaraj genuinely felt that there was a place for everyone in the organisation and did not want a rating to destroy that value fabric.

His email also represents the dilemma that many progressive leaders go through every year—to let people know where they stand but also show that they matter.

From the days when every supervisor wrote a confidential report about his team members' performance and sent it to the personnel department to be filed in the confidential dossier of the employee, it appears that the function has come a long way in the area of performance management.

However, when one pays attention to the emotions that it evokes in employees before, during and after their experience of the process, things seem just the same. Whether this is a reflection of the basic human nature or the ineffectiveness of the new systems that have been designed or just a sign of the times we live in might be a moot point.

But several questions beg to be answered as we take a contemporary look at performance management.

These questions relate to purpose, philosophy, process and role boundaries.

To make the chapter more engaging and practical, our views on the subject are being presented in the form of responses to what are some of the most frequently asked questions.

What is the contemporary purpose that performance management serves and how is it relevant?

From a time when the performance management process was merely a post-mortem exercise and a seemingly rational and objective means of distributing pay increase budgets, performance management has come to be recognised as a proactive process to review, plan and manage performance of employees. With more and more organisations adopting business driven practices, managing the organisation's and the individual's performance has emerged as a vital business process rather than just an HR process. The most important job of the CEO today is to secure organisational results. Given this criticality, the CEO and his executive team is constantly looking to align everyone in the organisation towards the accomplishment of organisational goals and priorities. The use of policy deployment processes, TQM methodologies and balance score cards have aided this process. The performance management process is not the only tool that leaders rely on to drive organisational results, in the strict sense.

In large organisations with thousands of employees, leaders and line managers are embracing role-based performance standards rather than person-based key result areas (KRAs). Such role-based performance standards tightly link the performance expectation from a role to the goals of the organisation and bring about a high level of standardisation and simplicity in establishing performance expectations. These role-based performance standards do not necessarily change every year and are designed to reflect customer or stakeholder expectations. Role-based performance standards and real-time feedback also help managers assess job skills and support employees with training and hand-holding where required. This again has become a core business process.

From a feedback perspective, the performance management process was the only means by which employees received qualitative feedback about their skills, competencies, their effectiveness in the current role and preparedness for future responsibilities.

With assessment and feedback evolving into a specialised science through the emergence of assessment centres and development centres, the increasing popularity of 360-degree feedback programmes and the use of psychometric tools to provide insights into personality traits and preferences as relevant to the organisational context, the performance management process is no longer considered the best source of feedback for the purpose of development.

Amendments to the Companies Act and the growing emphasis on good governance practices have resulted in boards getting increasingly involved in reviewing policies and decisions relating to the remuneration of directors and key managerial personnel through the nominations and remuneration committees.

Given the current people portfolio management practices, a good percentage of the people who do work for the organisation are not its own employees but are those engaged through a variety of arrangements hence are more closely linked to outcome measures. The performance management process does not drive their performance, but their contract of engagement does.

Finally, with the emergence of market-oriented pay practices and the declining popularity of merit-pay increases, many organisations do not necessarily adjust pay at the end of every performance cycle.

Given all these developments, the reliance on a single system to meet diverse needs and expectations has diminished and rightfully so. In our view, the contemporary purpose of the performance management is to essentially serve as a platform for managers to engage with their team members in continuous deliberations around performance. The focus of these deliberations is to clarify expectations, calibrate priorities, discuss impediments, plan supportive efforts, provide ongoing feedback and offer encouragement and support. This, in our view, is the only thing that truly matters to the employee. While there will continue to be the reliance on using this platform to make certain judgements and decisions, those would be incidental and not primary. The more organisations steer away from this central purpose, the more unhappy and dissatisfied employees become about their experience of the process.

Performance Management in Turbulent and Uncertain Times

One of the big charges levelled against formal performance management systems is that it stifles the entrepreneurial and risk-taking abilities of employees. Every so often, we find that highly competent executives end up setting safe goals because of what is at stake in terms of rewards. Executives end up doing what makes them get good ratings for their KRAs when in fact they need to do other things keeping the changing context in mind. We also find that KRAs set in the beginning of the year quite often become irrelevant during the year given fast-changing circumstances, but organisations saddled by an inflexible system find it hard to manage this inconsistency.

Similarly, high-growth organisations seldom find their historical data backing their goals and ambitions. For these reasons, many business leaders tend to be wary of introducing a system that might end up making people play safe, and thereby dampening the spirit of risk-taking and initiative.

When the environment is dynamic, organisations expect employees to go out there and do whatever it takes to win. However, the need for form and fairness dampens the real function.

It is our view that, especially for senior executives, tightly defined individual KRAs hard wired to rewards may not serve organisations well in uncertain times. KRAs may need to be used to bring focus but sometimes ends up limiting efforts.

What is the current level of success as far as differentiation is concerned? What is the future of the bell curve as a means of differentiation?

Differentiation as a practice forms the basis for decisions regarding pay increases, a wide range of rewards—short-term and long-term—career progression, eligibility for leadership or other key positions and for the conferment of other special privileges/benefits. As much as differentiation leads to the identification of winners, it also leads to the identification of losers and their relegation within the organisation or eventual separation.

What is central to the philosophy of differentiation is the approach of assessing performance on a relative basis, in comparison with others/peers rather than on an absolute basis against pre-determined goals.

Current Level of Success

While it seems quite obvious that organisations need to follow some form of differentiation, their ability to make it work and the effort required to make it work seems quite varied. Therefore, the current situation in India is by no means uniform. This is reflected by the varied voices of the practitioners of differentiation. We are able to pick up at least four distinct voices today:

1. *Differentiation is alive and kicking and is the core of our people strategy*
2. *Differentiation is a struggle but is on our agenda and is evolving steadily*
3. *There is just too much organisation energy spent on differentiation. Is it worth all the efforts at all?*
4. *Differentiation is not in sync with our culture and ethos*

We have personally experienced all the four scenarios among the organisations we have worked in or worked with. The question is really about where the vast majority is. In our opinion, only a small minority of organisations has managed to accept and adopt differentiation as a way of corporate life and is in the first category.

The good news is that a growing number of organisations are entering the second category. From one year to the other, these organisations are constantly building their capabilities and processes to embrace differentiation in a way that fits with their approach and strategy, but not without their share of difficulties.

A good number are still in the third situation. While they are struggling to figure out whether it is the 'right' thing to do, for them, differentiation is still a far cry away. They are either far from its conceptual understanding or are driving it in a manner that is inappropriate leading to unintended consequences. They may also be encountering a lot of push back from leaders and managers.

Quite a few of the new horizon companies are of the firm belief that differentiation is inappropriate for their context and hence do not want to embrace it. However, they are encouraging individual dialogue and conversations which is all about customisation. Customisation is an extreme level of differentiation. Instead of differentiating people into four and five levels they seek to address each according to their specific need, which could even mean 100 per cent differentiation.

Clearly, differentiation is here to stay. It is on top of the agenda of business leaders in both traditional and modern businesses. The more organisations are pushed to be business-driven, the more they will be forced to embrace differentiation as a practice to remain competitive. The more they enter a phase of stability, the more they will have the ability to evaluate their value stance and take a somewhat more long-term view.

What About the Bell Curve?

In this context, it is useful to understand the reality behind the recent announcements by many 'progressive' organisations that they have done away with the 'draconian' practice of forced distribution through the concept of the so-called 'bell curve'.

The trigger for this was the large-scale discomfort in trying to force-fit people into pre-determined segments (exceptional, good, satisfactory, below par and poor performance) in a mandated ratio. In many of the new horizon business organisations—which account for the large-scale employment of the younger generations, where most people worked in small teams, each one responsible for part of the work sequence where the performance measures were invariably collective and the individual distinctions were difficult and artificial—the overwhelming need was to ensure that the whole team owned up the performance standards and delivered it. These in many ways resembled the factory shop floors of the traditional manufacturing companies. In these settings, the practice of differentiation has never been appropriate and was never practised, except for identifying the extremely poor and exceptionally talented.

These white-collar shop-floor workers were subjected to the bell curve treatment that was never perfected for people who worked in contexts that they found themselves in. The need for such sharp differentiation was never a big one. So the turn of events leading to the proclamation of the demise of the bell curve by organisations that found it largely inappropriate for most of its employees was understandable.

We must, however, be careful not to throw out the baby with the bathwater. The bell curve was and has been largely used for the managerial population where there is scope for individual distinctive contribution even in collective endeavours.

The forced fitment of people into the bell curve without adapting it to their specific context allowing for the required flexibility to ensure the sensibility of the exercise has led to the bitter rejection of the approach.

Well, the bell curve served four purposes—it helped organisations identify its best people; it helped manage pay-increase budgets; it helped identify its poor performers who needed to be separated. Of course, it was also used to ensure uniformity across the organisation in the way all this was done.

Truth is that these purposes will still need to be served, albeit, in different ways. While it is still early days for most organisations in terms of implementing these new approaches, it is not hard to come up with some plausible predictions about what the world will look like post the bell curve era.

Managerial ownership: Many organisations will give their managers at certain levels pay-increase budgets and make them responsible for managing within those budgets. The manager is then forced to distribute the pie based on performance data. This will be one possibility. In fact, many global corporations have for long been adopting this mature and empowered practice. This, therefore, puts the onus of objectivity and fairness in assessments on the manager who is closest to the action and has responsibility for managing resources and delivery of results post the pay increase as well.

Dealing with poor performers: Organisations' latitude for poor performance is often a function of the health of the business. When the going is good, dealing with the bottom is seldom a high priority. However, when the going is tough, organisations do not need the bell curve to identify and separate poor performers. I am sure you have been seeing media reports in recent times about several organisations quietly firing employees in large numbers for reasons of poor performance. Thus, going forward, separating poor performers will be an ongoing activity for which the bell curve may not be needed.

Other methods: Organisations might use other methods and models that combine data about performance and potential to categorise employees into various buckets—from the most valuable to the least valuable.

Bell curve loyalists: There are still a very large number of organisations which are struggling to convince their managers to be objective and tough-minded in their assessment process and not let their heart rule over their head. Given the inability of their managers to differentiate, these organisations will continue to rely on their HR teams and the bell curve to create a culture of differentiation.

A coaching style: Arising out of the realisation that we need to think beyond the use of a forced distribution system to manage people, organisations are beginning to encourage their managers to coach their team members for performance through the year using great conversations, rather than merely rating them on how they have performed at the end of the year.

This to us is a great step, provided managers are equipped to coach for performance. If they are indeed equipped with those skills and do it well, it can change the culture and climate of organisations and make not just ratings but also year-end performance management exercise almost redundant.

To this end, HR functions are helping managers step outside their position and start relating to their team members as persons by building trust-based relationships. They are also beginning to offer managers the skills to have good conversations.

Doing away with a system calls for courage and at least some organisations have shown the courage to do that. Replacing that with a new way, a new cultural orientation is the next big thing. The next decade will tell us how well this goal has been accomplished.

Who should actually own the performance management process? Who should assess performance and what is the role of stakeholders in the assessment?

Given the pre-occupation with using the performance management processes as a rewards tool, HR has traditionally been the process owner. This has created problems for the function, the organisation and the employee. HR has to chase managers to set goals, rate performance and fill forms. The organisation has its own mechanism of cascading the organisational planning process down to various functions and this is seldom integrated with the way the performance management process is designed. As process owners, HR has attempted to use automation to streamline the workflow. While it certainly has many benefits, even the little motivation that existed for managers to meet face to face and have a conversation no longer exists. In the eyes of HR, line managers do not show commitment to the process and in the eyes of line managers this is not a value-adding process but an onerous form-filling exercise.

In our view, the CEO and his executive team are responsible for securing organisational performance and the immediate managers are responsible for securing individual performance of their team members. The role of HR is restricted to securing the motivational dimensions of performance in the form of climate, rewards and development. However, securing an individual's performance is clearly the manager's role and every manager is the process owner. Organisations which have managed to establish this principle have been very successful in cementing the relationships and building a high-performance culture. Organisations which continue to believe that HR is the process owner suffer from diffused ownership and the absence of a strong performance culture.

While the manager is the process owner of the performance management process, the current realities of the world of work are such that the people for whom individuals do work are not necessarily their employers or managers. The IT industry is the biggest example of this phenomenon. Most employees work on clients' projects and are mostly reviewed by their client managers and very rarely by their own managers. The situation is similar in most other project-based organisations too Most business-enabling functions work for their stakeholders rather than for their managers. All front-line employees perform tasks moment to moment to meet their customers' needs rather than their manager's needs. Employees in globally distributed organisations work in remote locations with little or no oversight from their managers. Given these realities, the manager may not often be the best person or in the best position to assess his team member's performance. Given these complexities, organisations are investing significantly in capturing real-time measures about their employees' performance and productivity to support an objective assessment and aid real-time feedback rather than relying on filling a form once a year which can be completely subjective.

With the increasing use of matrix structures, employees may have more than one manager who places expectations on him and evaluates his performance.

Why the focus on experience of the performance management process?

More and more organisations are beginning to recognise that the performance management process offers several critical moments of truth for the employee and the manager. Organisations are therefore beginning to measure the employee's satisfaction with the experience of the process beyond the outcomes. In other words, organisations want to know if the process was clear, if the manager did indeed give him or her feedback, if the employee had access to a reviewer in the case of a disagreement, if the feedback process was value adding and so on.

By paying attention to the experience, organisations want to ensure that some of the principles of fairness, transparency, respect and sensitivity are upheld by managers and leaders. It also helps the organisation communicate to the employee that its focus is towards offering a fair, transparent and respectful process but not guarantee great outcomes because that is in his or her hands. This in our mind is a welcome development.

What is the most appropriate frequency to review performance in the current context?

Given the developments that we have spoken about, more and more organisations recognise the futility of reviewing performance once a year. Organisations are beginning to encourage their managers to have frequent discussions about performance to calibrate expectations, understand impediments, offer support and provide feedback.

While these conversations are expected to be informal and ongoing, organisations are also expecting that managers have at least one and up to three ongoing reviews a year outside of the annual review. These reviews are expected to be documented so that employees have tangible feedback and managers are held accountable to have these reviews. With automation, it is now possible to support managers in this process while maintaining its simplicity. In our view, at least two formal interactions a year between managers and team members would be highly desirable. This of course is in addition to numerous ongoing dialogues that managers are likely to have on an ongoing basis. However, this is easier said than done.

In the world that seems to live and die by results, do means matter? In other words, what is the place of competencies and values in assessing performance?

Organisations have been quite ambivalent about the place of competencies in the performance management process, especially when it comes to assessment.

Given the subjectivity involved in assessing competencies, organisations have been apprehensive about the merit of allowing competency assessments to influence overall ratings. In other words, it is feared that managers might score employees liberally on competencies as a means of compensating for lower scores on KRAs or performance standards. Organisations have also been concerned about the lack of skills among managers to accurately assess competencies. On the other hand, there are organisations which firmly believe that competencies are as important as results and must be assigned an equal weightage. Some organisations rate performance results and competencies separately and use the former to take decisions on bonuses and variable pay and the combined score to take decisions on guaranteed pay increases as well as career progression decisions. We also find organisations assigning varying levels of weightage to competencies, with higher weightages at senior levels and lower weightages at junior levels.

It is our view that all long-term decisions including long-term rewards and career progression should take into consideration performance, competencies and adherence to organisational values. On the other hand, decisions relating to year-on-year rewards should be based on performance ratings.

At a time when leaders of nations and organisations are recognising the need for collaboration and the breaking of silos, have HR professionals cracked the code on measuring team performance and results?

While organisational reality is that it is collaboration and team effort that helps businesses succeed, the reward systems and therefore measurement systems are essentially focused on individual performance. We also find that the goals of individuals within teams are not aligned well enough for team success.

Can this seemingly contradictory situation be resolved without compromising on performance orientation and meritocracy? We certainly think so and have seen efforts in this direction. In organisational settings where intra-team and inter-team collaboration is critical, the superordinate goals may need to be given prominence.

There are many service businesses and even sales teams that are building team results into their incentive schemes such that the entire team is rewarded. Where the 'branch' is the primary work unit, many organisations link rewards to the success of the entire branch. Often, the peer pressure is enough to deal with potential free riders in the team.

In such settings, differentiation must be used only to identify people with potential rather than to make pay decisions. Even at executive leadership levels, enterprise results need to be given as much or more weightage compared to individual accomplishments.

What appears to be the emerging role of HR in performance management?

Good HR professionals do understand what motivates employees and drives them towards peak performance. Many HR professionals have at their disposal tools to measure employee motivation and use these results to call attention to factors that are inhibiting performance. Quite a few HR professionals also have at their disposal solutions to build capabilities that can contribute to enhanced performance and design rewards programmes that will drive extrinsic motivation. A lot of HR professionals are slowly but surely beginning to shed their traditional role of being process owners and progress chasers. Select HR professionals are focusing on building the managerial capability to manage performance, provide training and coaching solutions to enhance performance, pay attention to the levers of employee engagement to create the right motivational climate and implement the right total rewards solution that rewards good performance. While there will continue to be a large number of HR professionals preoccupied with chasing progress on form filling and enforcing the bell curve, it is a role that is bound to decline rapidly.

The Role of HR in Creating a Performance-oriented Culture

A lot has been written about creating high-performance cultures. We do not see the need to restate this. There is, however, one aspect of performance orientation that seldom gets mentioned. This is to do with ensuring that the day-to-day actions of HR and business leaders are consistent with their stated philosophy of performance orientation.

The actions of the leaders throughout the year speak a lot more than their year-end mails and memos on performance and differentiation. We find good HR leaders asking themselves and their colleagues the following questions on a day-to-day basis to ensure that the culture is right. Do we:

- hire right?
- put the right person on the right job?
- steer clear of political considerations when taking people decisions?
- have the courage to unseat erstwhile 'stars' when they have failed to perform like stars?

- display latitude for poor performances in a very visible way that leads employees to perceive double speak?
- allow some of the managers to get away with violations while pushing others harder?

Once organisations embark on the path of performance orientation and differentiation, they are on watch and constant scrutiny. Any action that is inconsistent with stated policy tends to erode credibility and compromises the organisation's ability to implement it well.

Is there a place for respecting diversity in the way we manage performance?

One of the greatest dangers of any performance management process is the temptation to adopt a 'one-size-fits-all' approach. We may sometimes forget the fact that organisations are organic and human entities with significant differences within. What works for one section or group of employees may not work for another. What is easy for one group to accept may be difficult for another. Organisations are seldom made up of one homogenous group of employees. Their educational profile, socio-economic profile, tenure in the organisation and position within the organisational hierarchy have significant implications on the applicability and ease of implementation of the differentiation concept.

HR practitioners will need to ensure that they uphold the spirit of diversity as they decide in the manner in which performance management policies are applied to different groups within the organisation.

For example, when organisations hire young employees, they emphasise the fact that these employees must focus on learning and skill acquisition. If this is indeed true, it would be important to give these young employees time before they are brought under the rigors of evaluation, ratings and differentiation.

If this is not done, young employees tend to get unfavourably compared to older employees who get better ratings and rankings.

More importantly, we would end up giving the message that the real expectation is short-term performance at all costs and not really development which is essential for sustained long-term performance.

Similarly, when organisations hire employees laterally from other organisations, it might be necessary to give them the time to settle down (despite their relatively higher costs) and plan for a sustainable long-term contribution. If new entrants do not get the time they need to adjust, they are likely to focus on short-term wins, which may even compromise long-term interests.

Many organisations have programmes by which they promote employees from one cadre to another over a period of time. This could include workmen becoming supervisors or clerical staff becoming officers or managers and so on. These typically tend to be employees with sound functional skills and long tenure but without the intellectual and managerial abilities comparable with some of their younger counterparts.

This group of promotees will need time and support to build their skills and the confidence to integrate with other groups of employees and find their place. If the organisation has such a policy and is committed to its effectiveness, being mindful of the special needs of this group would be critical.

Similarly, as organisations employ an increasing percentage of women, they will need to support the needs of those who return to work as young mothers. It is quite likely that for some time their performance is likely to be under pressure given the new demands on them both physically and emotionally.

The true spirit of diversity and inclusion comes into play when organisations begin to take a more holistic view about how different groups are performing and how flexible they are in terms of performance expectations, at least in the short term.

Closing Reflections

Performance management as a process holds the potential to be a means to cement a great relationship between the manager and team member. It also holds the promise of helping employees succeed in the long term. However, the complexities of the world of business demand that business leaders have real-time means to secure organisational results beyond what a system can provide.

Organisational Experiences

Structured Performance Development and Learning Philosophy at Asian Paints

Asian Paints has been identified as a leadership factory with its philosophy for grooming young campus talent through rich job exposure including on-the-job training and stretch assignments and its development investments.

We have structured leadership and functional competency framework by level which integrates with our people processes including talent management, recruitment, development and functional capability building. Our core values—trust, fairness and caring—are the bedrock of our organisation behaviour and processes.

We believe in development conversations and these are woven in the design of our performance management and talent management processes. Annually, each employee has multiple conversations with the line management (immediate reporting manager and manager's manager): goal setting includes development objectives, mid-year focuses on development and review of business KPIs, people review process (PRP) wherein the reporting functional management reviews potential and development needs of all employees within that workgroup, job rotations (both inter- and intra-function) are heavily encouraged, MDA (My Development Aim) focused bottom-up career conversations and final appraisal is two-way conversation with focus on KPIs and learnings along the year. Organisational culture encourages line managers and employees to take joint responsibility of development with resources/processes/interventions institutionalised through HR.

Asian Paints believes in rewarding individual excellence as well as team achievements. The performance management system focuses on business goals as well as people goals. All managers have to fulfil their commitments in both these areas. The strength of the system is in the two formal reviews per year, which are led by the appraisee and not the appraiser. The appraisal system is further bolstered by a PRP feedback to the employee which solely focusses on addressing career aspirations, development required to fulfil these aspirations and in turn helping the organisation in building a healthy talent pipeline.

Our rewards system creates a healthy differentiation and motivates employees to excel as individuals. This individual reward system is balanced by team rewards where part of the compensation is tied to overall team and organisation achievements. We have been able to strike the right balance between collaboration and differentiation through this.

Ratings and bell curve have existed for long but have remained as tools for signalling the relative performance and then allocating budgeted reward distribution. The bell curve is not used as a tool to force out employees. All performance management system-related annual polls post the appraisal cycles ensure that we are alive to the feedback from employees on the spirit and rigour of the process and make amends wherever needed. Dealing with non-performance is not a result of bell curve or assigning lowest ratings but there is a continuous process of feedback and improvement where employees are fully supported in this journey. But when employees fail to respond to these feedbacks and when all efforts for performance improvement fail over a long period of time, then we do let employees go but only after we are fairly convinced.

Promotions are strictly vacancy based and adhere to the highest standards of meritocracy. We do not promote a culture of time-bound promotions.

Comprehensive Learning Philosophy in Action

Building 'leaders for life' under three powerful anchors listed as follows:

1. Invested for life: We invest in our employees to build them as leaders for life, partnering with them across various stages of their career and life. Help find a role fit based on abilities, aspirations and organisational requirements. Enabling long-term career journeys is the mantra that we believe in.
2. Learner for life: We believe in creating long-term learning journeys that let individuals customise their own learning paths based on their preferences, needs and life stage. Create multiple learning spaces and occasions for learners and teachers, enabling better ownership to learn, contribute and grow.
3. Work–life balance: Enjoying what you do through your roles, relationships and learning opportunities. We enable our employees to excel, by providing learning spaces for them. Enjoy work—be a learner for life is what we encourage. Based on this philosophy, there are three kinds of programmes we offer:

    a. Base programme: Transition/career stage-specific programmes for different levels

    b. Add-on: Functional modules, management develop-
        ment programmes, leadership skills around facilit-
        ation, coaching, org level needs (leading digital,
        building EI, and so on)
    c. Electives: As per the competency framework, lea-
        dership for life series, addressing individual learning
        needs emerging out of development conversations

Transition programmes are available for each level, as we believe in diversity of experiences and encourage job rotations heavily within the organisation. Competency-based curriculum are available for each level with electives of interest through the leadership development blueprint defined.

Feedback from participants on application of learnings, reporting manager on application on job and review of the programme objectives (to impact business agenda) are natural measures to evaluate success of capability building interventions.

We have very strong peer-network-based informal learning culture almost like campus. We wanted to cultivate this formally as well and hence have a group of internal coaches and subject matter experts are available for employees. We offer the coaches to get ACC certified and encourage cross-functional coaching. Coachee feedback and performance journeys are other impact zones. Coaching is a culture inspiring 'leader builds leader' principle. MDA is career conversation between reporting manager and employee. Along with MDA and wide choices through learning platforms, employees can plan their development journeys.

11
Money and Beyond

When Ramu walks around his village wearing his TVS uniform, he receives respect and experiences a sense of pride and recognition. Ramu's parents will find it easy to find a bride given where he works.

Sonia is working for a company which is offering her lesser than what she last earned. But the company is offering her a benefit that is hard to measure in money terms—the company allows her to work half a day and also work from home when needed and the icing on the cake is that the work itself is so interesting.

Sudha runs a centre for dyslexic children. Most of her teachers are working in the centre almost for free. Why, one might wonder. Well, most of them are parents of special children and they find the experience of working in a special school adding immense value to them as parents in helping their children with special needs.

Look at any of the best employers lists and you will find that what got companies into these lists are thoughtfully crafted benefits, facilities and rewards beyond money.

Again, look at campus placements and how students choose their employers. While everyone will talk about brand, quality of work and the learning opportunities as being key factors, the clincher is always money. In fact, news about average salaries on campus is all that the media talks about.

As we explore the subject of money, it might be useful to go back and look at some old wisdom on the subject. Yes, it seems appropriate to recollect what Frederick Herzberg,[1] a behavioural scientist, had to say back in 1959 on what motivates people.

Herzberg proposed a two-factor theory or the motivator–hygiene theory. According to Herzberg, there are some job factors that result in satisfaction (which he called motivators) while there are other job factors that prevent dissatisfaction (which he called hygiene factors). According to Herzberg, the opposite of 'satisfaction' is 'no satisfaction' and the opposite of 'dissatisfaction' is 'no dissatisfaction'.

From all the examples shared with you, it will be apparent that pay and benefits would fall under what Herzberg calls a hygiene factor. Not having enough of it leads to dissatisfaction. Having a lot of it only leads to no dissatisfaction.

It is only to ensure that all aspects of rewards beyond money are explored has this chapter been titled 'Money and Beyond'!

The Mechanics of Managing Pay

Before we look beyond money, let us see how organisations have mastered money matters.

A modern and scientific approach to compensation took birth in India after economic liberalisation in 1991. The compensation and benefits (C&B) profession also took birth around that time.

It is creditable that during this period C&B as a specialisation has earned its place of respect and deference within the HR function and its practitioners are looked up to for data-based recommendations and guidelines to manage pay.

---

[1] Frederick Irving Herzberg (18 April 1923–19 January 2000) was an American psychologist who became one of the most influential names in business management. He proposed the Two-factor Theory or the Motivation–Hygiene Theory in 1959. His 1968 publication 'One More Time, How Do You Motivate Employees?' was the most requested article from the *Harvard Business Review*.

C&B professionals have access to external and internal information, the tools to aid decision-making and the attention of senior management to shape the policy and decision-making process.

Given that employee costs are one of the most significant elements of operating costs, C&B professionals are being called upon to play a strong controllership role in managing, monitoring and controlling employee costs towards pay and benefits.

It might therefore be fair to conclude that managing the mechanics of C&B is no longer an insurmountable challenge—be it surveying the market, setting up pay ranges, designing benefit programmes or crafting incentive schemes, enough expertise is available around us.

C&B professionals in partnership with line managers and a wide range of service providers are able to design and implement a wide range of short-term and long-term programmes to attract reward and retain employees.

Organisations are also doing a good job of communicating the approach with reasonable transparency.

What then poses challenge to C&B professionals? While the expertise role seems manageable, it is the partnership dimension of C&B that poses challenges.

Whenever organisations are confronted with a need to change their approach, there can be dilemmas and conflicts.

For example, many organisations have had to embrace external equity fully or partially despite their philosophical preference for internal equity.

Many have had to practise differentiation, move towards more cash and include the manager more in the decision-making process.

Similarly, many organisations in recent times have been vacillating between paying for the person and for the position. Especially in the current context, more and more organisations are focussing on paying for the position and adopting role-based career progression policies.

Many progressive organisations are seeing the need to put in place an EVP even for their contingent workforce that reflects this philosophy. Such organisations are ensuring that their contingent workforce has access to the same facilities and infrastructure, welfare and medical assistance, opportunities for learning and advancement.

Similarly, C&B professionals will be under pressure to tinker with their programmes in the face of threats and challenges including attrition, inability to hire, inability to retain employees and so on.

For example, the last employee-engagement survey may throw up results which suggest that employees don't believe that their efforts are rewarded or recognised. A member of the board might argue that long-term rewards are critical.

Similarly, the head of a function might argue that incentives are urgently needed to drive certain behaviours. Given these pulls and pressures, it becomes all the more important for C&B practitioners to clearly establish the principles first and then shape decisions.

This starts with HR professionals asking the right kind of questions to senior management.

This brings us to all the important subject of C&B philosophy.

A Philosophical Foundation to Compensation and Benefits

In the introductory chapter of this section titled 'The Spectrum of Relationships', we spoke about a spectrum of relationships across a continuum with one end being business-driven and the other end being values-driven.

It has been our experience that the orientation of the organisation towards pay and rewards is strongly influenced by their context, their business and, therefore, their location on this spectrum. It is of course also influenced by the values of the founders, the promoters and the executive leaders in the organisation. These values translate into guiding principles which shape the organisation's philosophical orientation to pay. Simply put, a philosophical orientation helps organisations choose between two potentially viable ways of approaching pay.

While young organisations might start off with adopting an ad-hoc approach to pay and benefits, sooner or later they see the need to articulate their stance, position or philosophical orientation towards pay and rewards. Of course, one does see several examples of founders and promoters starting off with a clear philosophical orientation towards pay from day one.

So what are some of the philosophical choices that HR professionals and business leaders need to often grapple with in a deliberate way?

External Parity vs Internal Equity

Organisations which support external parity maintain that people must be paid according to what the market dictates and therefore find it acceptable to pay different people at the same level differently, if the market so dictates.

Organisations which choose internal equity maintain that loyalty and internal comparisons are important. They might find greater value in maintaining parity than differentiating. They also discourage too much of hiring from outside for fear that such hiring will create imbalances.

Differentiation vs Egalitarianism

Organisations which support differentiation maintain that good performers must be treated differently from average and poor performers. They propagate forced distribution. They may insist that poor performers are separated and that there are clear policies to take care of top talents.

Organisations which support an egalitarian approach maintain that team work and collaboration and group results are more important than individual brilliance. They believe that it is the solid performers who take the company forward. They may promote absolute rather than relative ratings and might have a greater latitude for performance failures.

Exigency vs Fairness

Organisations which support an exigency-based approach maintain that compensation and related policies must be changed as and when business circumstances change and that the employee must bear some part of the risks of doing business. These organisations will restructure pay when business circumstances are difficult.

Organisations which support a fairness-based approach maintain that any change in compensation policy must be viewed in terms of its human implications and people's ability to cope with it. They believe that employees must be insulated from the risks of business especially if they are vulnerable and not equipped to deal with it. In difficult times, they will explore other avenues of cost-saving to tide over the situation and look at C&B policy changes as the last resort.

Pay for the Position vs Pay for the Person

Organisations which support a pay-for-the-position-based approach maintain that pay and benefits must be strictly in line with job size, and flexibility in pay decisions must be minimised if it is not position-based. They adopt job evaluation and follow role-based career progression policies.

Organisations which support a pay-for-the-person-based approach maintain that one must recognise that individuals with unique competencies can make contributions disproportionate to the position they occupy. They will seek to have the flexibility to attract and retain talented individuals. They would follow broad banding and competency-based pay systems.

Confidentiality vs Transparency

Organisations which support confidentiality maintain that compensation decisions are the prerogative of management and need not be explained or discussed. They believe that compensation decisions often involve subjective judgements which are hard to justify to everyone, therefore all C&B policies are maintained in strict confidence and discussions about the subject are discouraged.

Organisations which support transparency maintain that compensation decisions touch the lives of all employees and being transparent about it is a true test of our integrity. In these organisations, while individual compensation decisions are confidential the principles are always open and transparent. All C&B policies and market-related information are shared with relevant employees.

Manager-led Administration vs Centrally Controlled Administration

Organisations which support a manager-led administration approach might maintain that it is the manager who is responsible for delivering results should also manage pay decisions and actions. They may expect their managers to manage the communication and the decision-making process on pay. Managers are allocated increase budgets, provided clear guidelines and are fully informed about pay policies, market information and so on.

Organisations which support a centrally controlled administration approach maintain that it is best to administer pay centrally and not involve managers in the process They believe that the manager's job should end with performance assessments and making recommendations. Managers are expected to provide ratings and communicate pay increases while HR along with the CEO determines the actual payouts.

All Cash vs Benefits-oriented

Organisations which support an all-cash approach maintain that employees should be given cash compensation and allowed the discretion to determine their lifestyle. In such organisations, compensation is all cash with minimal benefits.

Organisations which support a benefit-oriented approach maintain that the organisation must ensure a certain lifestyle for employees at each level given that employees are the face of the organisation. In such organisations, benefits and perquisites are linked to grades.

Making the Choices and Communicating It

Quite a few organisations adopt practices that are inherently rooted in certain deeply held values and philosophical orientations. These are businesses with a long tradition of sound people practices or promoters who come with well-founded and deeply held views about how things should be done. Many of them do not see the need to talk about it or publicise it and would rather let their actions speak for themselves. We believe that there is huge merit in organisations sending a clear and consistent message about their approach to pay. This will ensure that there is an air of openness and clarity and lack of defensiveness when it comes to making pay decisions.

Beyond Pay

After over 25 years of embracing expertise-based, market-oriented C&B practices, if there is one big shift that more and more organisations are beginning to realise, it is this: to create real engagement and satisfaction, organisations will need to look beyond pay. Organisations are realising that if they want a compelling EVP that helps them attract, motivate and retain employees in a way that sets them apart in the labour market, they need to look beyond money.

In our view, this evolution of looking at rewards as different from C&B and making the process more involved and collaborative between C&B professionals and business leaders is still work in progress.

In other words, if C&B has to go beyond pay, it will call for a very high level of empathy among decision-makers—the ability to put ourselves in the shoes of different segments of employees and understand what will truly motivate them at different times and then incorporate those into the overall programmes.

While the concept and philosophy of total rewards was formally enunciated in 2000 by WorldatWork through its *WorldatWork Total Rewards Model*,[2] the concept has been practised in spirit in India for a very long time. Before 1991, pay was a very small part of total rewards and given our socialistic and collective origins, organisations assumed a certain paternalistic approach to taking care of people. So that core spirit is very much there. All that needs to be done is to reinterpret it for today's times.

Why is a total rewards approach so invaluable for any organisation?

Very clearly, if two businesses are competing in the same industry for revenue and market share, it is fair to assume that they need to manage their cost structures somewhat similarly. In other words, the leeway available for an organisation to play around with cash compensation or benefits is somewhat limited. Take

---

[2] WorldatWork is a non-profit human resources association and compensation authority for professionals and organisations focused on compensation, benefits and total rewards. The WorldatWork Total Rewards Model recognises that the relationship between employers and employees is dynamic and not static. Given the social, cultural, local and global business environmental influences on both the employers and employees, the drivers influencing a symbiotic relationship are many. The WorldatWork model has identified six elements that can help the organisation achieve performance and results while ensuring that its employees are engaged and have a great experience working. The six elements are compensation, benefits, work–life effectiveness, recognition, performance management and talent development.

the Indian IT industry or the telecom industry or the insurance industry or the banking industry—the story is the same. What will make one organisation more attractive compared to the other are elements of their value proposition which go beyond pay.

So what aspects of total rewards will matter the most in the coming years? Presented here are our views of what will contribute significantly to attracting, motivating and retaining employees in the coming years. This is done keeping in mind the fact that a lot of this will depend on the segment of employees and the industry they belong to.

Stability and Security

It might sound somewhat strange that stability and security is seen as one important element of rewards that employees value. It is indeed so. Years of fluctuating business fortunes have had a rather deep impact on employee confidence in organisations and their ability to offer them stability. While most young employees will see the long-term prospects with optimism, they do see the short term as somewhat uncertain. Under these circumstances, any organisation with a track record of stability and sustained growth will be more attractive than its peers.

Flexibility

Given the challenges of everyday living, the deteriorating civic conditions in many of our cities, the entry of a larger percentage of women employees and the general disregard for anything rigid and fixed, organisations that offer flexibility in their employment polices and practices, be it in terms of employment structure, working hours, place of work and the freedom to pursue other interests, will score significantly in the labour market. Employees attach a significant premium to organisations which offer flexibility and measure their employees in terms of results rather than mere conformance.

The Job Itself

Employees recognise that the greatest insurance against an uncertain future is the quality of work that they get to do and the value that it will add to their CV.

While organisations might design jobs in a manner that facilitates deskilling and higher levels of standardisation and greater division of labour, employees prefer to work in organisations where the job is a lot more well-rounded and holistic with higher levels of exposure and responsibility.

Where they have a choice, more and more employees are choosing to be a big fish in a small pond—do a more complete role, albeit, in a smaller organisation.

Exposure and Experiences

Employees expect to experience some form of change every 18–24 months. Organisations which are able to offer employees a range of experiences and a variety of opportunities for exposure to different functions, problems and assignments manage to retain employees far better.

The Agenda Ahead

As is evident from the survey results that were shared with you in the chapter 'Evolving Expectations' in the first section, business leaders seem to believe that HR has managed to meet their expectations in the area of C&B. The availability of specialist service providers, the willingness to trust specialist support in this area and of course the competitive market forces have resulted in organisations making significant progress in this area.

With increased efforts to communicate pay policies and programmes, the perception of transparency has gone up. So also has the ability of organisations to make changes to reflect changing employee preferences.

Looking ahead, there appear to be at least four agendas that will need organisational attention as far as pay and rewards are concerned.

Making Variable Pay Programmes Deliver Value

A very large number of organisations have today managed to move between 10 per cent and 25 per cent of their pay into what is referred to as variable pay. While some organisations link payout to individual performance, some link it to organisational results and many others link it to both.

What most organisations have achieved to do is to establish the fact that at least some part of an employee's pay is contingent upon some outcomes at the end of the year. What it also means is that should there be a really bad year, at least all or a part of this budget is technically not payable and will serve to reduce the payroll cost to that extent. This is good news.

The not-so-good news is this: A large number of employees may not be clear about what they should do or what behaviours they should display to contribute to business results and earn their variable pay. Even worse, employees often set for themselves 'safe KRAs' just to be able to achieve their variable pay.

Beyond all this, employees who have consistently received good payouts begin to see variable pay as guaranteed pay and to that extent the ability of the programme to motivate the right behaviour might wear out.

In summary, while variable pay programmes have managed to serve as a small budgetary pool that can serve to preserve cash flow on a rainy day, its ability to drive the right behaviours for an organisation on a consistent basis is often debatable.

If new demands are being placed on leaders and managers to help their businesses grow and succeed, the variable pay programme needs to drive new behaviours to meet these demands rather than merely support status quo.

No one explains this phenomenon better than Ram Charan. In the first chapter of his book *Leadership in the Era of Economic*

Uncertainty,[3] Ram Charan says that after spending their careers in a single-minded pursuit of growth, business leaders had to now adjust their mentality.

He explains that before the 2008 crisis started for most companies, the indicators of success were *increasing earnings per share* and *growing revenues by gaining market share*. He however believes that from then on CEOs could pursue growth only if it was profitable and cash-efficient and did not consume disproportionate amounts of cash in the form of more inventory, extended duration of accounts receivable or increased complexity. Pursuit of revenue growth must give way to understanding the cash implications of everything that the company does, he argued.

In an environment of falling demand and liquidity risk, most companies have no choice but to shrink, he predicted. In this environment, he saw the need to shift focus from the income statement to the balance sheet. He considered cash to be the most critical metric at that time and believed that achieving it might call for cutting costs and raising cash, a sharper focus and concentration on the core of the business, choosing the market segments and even the particular customers they should continue to serve, the products they should continue to make, the suppliers they should continue to buy from and eliminate the rest.

Interestingly, what Ram Charan spoke about in 2009 seems even truer today. If this is the new language of business and what is described forms the new competencies for success, then it is important that our variable pay programmes are aligned to defining, clarifying, educating, measuring and rewarding these behaviours. More importantly, they must stop rewarding the expansionist behaviour of the past.

Variable pay programmes are beginning to be viewed as a dynamic performance-enhancement tool that must be constantly

---

[3] Ram Charan, *Leadership in the Era of Economic Uncertainty: Managing in a Downturn* (New Delhi: McGraw-Hill, 2009).

tweaked, keeping in mind changing circumstances. Organisations are now alive to the real danger of variable pay programmes beginning to be treated like the statutory bonus under law which workmen expect will be paid, save dire business circumstances.

To align a variable pay programme to deliver value under changing circumstances is clearly a compelling agenda for the coming years.

Managing Pay in Difficult Times

Global corporations have a fairly well-established routine to deal with an economic downturn or a recessionary phase. They tend to set a target for cost savings and translate it into the number of jobs that must be shed.

While some of the Indian corporations which have the tradition of adopting market-oriented practices are also beginning to shed jobs that is still not the norm and is not yet a widely seen phenomenon.

Organisations do struggle to find less harsh ways of managing their cost and certainly turn to HR for counsel and ideas. The manner in which these organisations go about achieving their cost-saving goals have long-term implications on their relationship with employees.

Basic Principles

The following are some of the basic principles being adopted by value-based organisations in the throes of employee cost-cutting measures.

1. Taking employees into confidence by showing them the big picture. (This takes the form of not one but a series of communications and interactions with employees to explain why this is necessary.)
2. Reporting progress. (They not only report to employees the progress made by the organisation in this particular aspect

but also progress made in other initiatives to improve the overall situation.)

3. Leading by example and starting at the top. (Firm belief that changes in employee conditions are better accepted when seniors show the way. They start the changes from the senior-most people in the organisation.)

4. Removing all visible ostentatious spends by seniors to avoid misperceptions and confused signals.

5. Doing it in stages and not implementing all changes at the same time. (Staggering the changes thus making it easier for employees to take the impact.)

6. Maintaining a sense of fairness and being careful in not impacting the lives of junior employees whose pay is low and those who are at absolute low-pay levels which hardly offer any scope for savings.

7. Signalling hope about the future. (They let employees know that the changes will be reviewed very frequently and the benefits would be reinstated as soon as things improve.)

8. Remembering legal considerations. (Section 9(A) of the Industrial Disputes Act deals with the subject of notice of change which states that no employer can effect changes in the conditions of service applicable to the workmen without giving them 21 days' notice—so they follow the required processes to be compliant with the law.)

History is full of examples of organisations that have adopted innovative solutions to conserve cash without shedding jobs. These are the organisations that tend to be respected and valued in the labour market in the long run.

Managing Growth Aspirations in Difficult Times

Organisations in India have traditionally adopted a system of pay grades to manage their pay and promotions. Typically, organisations seem to have between 12 and 14 pay grades.

Given the entry of global corporations into the country and the accompanying entry of global reward practices, organisations attempted the introduction of broad banding or work levels or levels of impact. Most ended up having four to five broad bands. Some attempted to replace their 12–14 pay grades with 4–5 work levels but soon realised that the system of broad banding did not address the social need of employees to be seen as growing every two or three years. They also had difficulties in aligning benefits and perquisites which were traditionally linked to pay grades to the new system of work levels.

Today, organisations have settled down to a hybrid system of work levels and pay grades.

While pay and benefits continue to be linked to the pay grades, the work levels serve the purpose of growth and development. In other words, organisations link their competency frameworks to work levels. They also link many of their management and leadership development interventions to the bands. As a result, there is beginning to be a distinction being made between progression within a level and promotion across bands.

Having come this far, organisations realise that they are dealing with the weight of history and tradition where a typical employee was promoted once in every three years or so. Also, given the strong push towards growth from within being adopted by many organisations, a sizable number of employees have been promoted based primarily on their performance track record, competency gaps notwithstanding. What has made matters worse is the practice of promoting people into a new work level or higher band while they continue to do the same or similar job that does not match with the jobs in the higher level or band.

While these practices were ignored during the good times they are certainly coming back to hurt organisations quite significantly in period of downturn. Organisations are beginning to realise that there has been significant grade creep, that the top is heavy and that they have more people in senior positions than they need and, worse, some of these senior people do not have the competencies to perform at those levels. Of course, all of this has costs attached to it.

While progressive organisations have been using job evaluation systems and tight controls to ensure that promotions happen only when there are open positions and such open positions fit into a higher work level, for many this is a compelling agenda that needs addressing.

We find many organisations struggling to ensure that their organisation design and structural forms and spans of control are not compromised because of faulty implementation of reward programmes. They are working hard to ensure that the aspirations of employees are aligned to their business realities. They recognise that doing this as a corrective measure in hard times is much harder than doing it as a proactive measure.

Disparities

This is perhaps the most contentious issue but one that is hardest to resolve. For a long time, progressive organisations prided themselves with the fact that they were proud of their egalitarian approach to pay and spoke about their CEO pay ratios—the number of times more that a CEO earns compares to the average employee in the company. While it was considered that a 20 times differential was considered reasonable, the differential today is as high as 300 times.

While everyone likes to talk about and even admire the problem, very little is being done to address this widening gap. Would it be fair to conclude that organisations with market-oriented practices are guiltier of bad ratios compared to those that are more values-driven? That may not be the case. The problem may perhaps need to be defined somewhat differently.

There are various reasons why CEO and CXOs are paid what they are paid. They may be promoters and shareholders and may choose to draw a salary based on what law permits. They might be professional hires who are called upon to handle what are considered 'extreme roles' with significant risks and efforts being called for. They could be people with invaluable skills of global value.

So the real issue is not about paying the senior what they deserve, although excess is not what we would be advocating. What concern us are practices that are in conflict with the manner in which top executives are paid and rewarded.

One such area of conflict is around implementing deep differentiation policies or removing poor performers at junior levels.

Michael Young[4] coined the term 'meritocracy', to which he gave negative connotations, and he became disappointed with how the concept came to be seen as an achievable concept worth pursuing.

He had meant the term 'meritocracy' to point towards an undesirable elitism. He explained: 'It is good sense to appoint individual people to jobs on their merit. It is the opposite when those who are judged to have merit of a particular kind harden into a new social class without room in it for others'.

The bottom line of Michael Young's philosophy is that what is considered as meritocracy at a certain point in time becomes a right, privilege and social class over time and fails to be merit any longer. He also advocated a much more inclusive society where everyone was respected for who and what he or she was.

HR professionals who swear by the principle of meritocracy might live to pay heed to what Young said several years ago. Sadly, it appears to be all the more true and relevant 60 years later.

It is our experience that those who reach the very top are almost always rated well, and as a result receive the best rewards. The proponents of this argument will maintain that it is only the best who reach the very top but we all know that is far from the truth. There are several reasons and circumstances for people to reach the very top and as Michael Young points out, those considered meritorious at one point in time do harden into a permanent social

---

[4] Michael Young, Baron Young of Dartington (9 August 1915–14 January 2002) was a British sociologist, social activist and politician. In 1958, Young wrote the influential satire *The Rise of the Meritocracy*, originally for the Fabian Society, which refused to publish it.

class. More importantly, there is no guarantee that those who reach the top will continue to perform at their best and deserve continued rewards at that high level. Therefore, when this class talks about deep differentiation and applies it ruthlessly on young employees who are so junior down the hierarchy, it does hurt.

It is a pity that certain principles that were designed for the senior levels are being applied in an unmindful manner to levels far below. This is what causes the problem. For example, the concept of variable pay was introduced at levels where direct correlation between personal action and impact on overall performance was more palpable. The reality also was that even if the variable pay was not fully earned the incumbent at senior levels is not impacted with respect to his ability to spend on hygiene aspects.

However, over time this concept has not only been extended to middle and lower levels, it has been attempted to increase the share of variable pay to total earnings, even when their personal action does not impact overall performance in a significant way. Moreover, at these levels, the loss of variable pay impinges on their ability to spend even on hygiene aspects. It is when this happens that the disparity in earnings between levels gets undue attention and leads to challenge and debate.

It might be the role of HR leaders to ensure that when the ratio of senior executive pay appears beyond what is acceptable, they pay far closer attention to extent of introducing variability and differentiation. Also to ensure that the process and impact of differentiation is a lot more humane.

It might also be the role of HR to ensure that the organisation is able to ensure certain minimum guarantees for the large number of front-line employees or workmen even as they make policies to take care of the executives at the very top. Global benchmark should not be selectively applied only to the top, we must remember that our social security systems and standard of living are not yet at the same levels of the developed economies and hence the organisation needs to reflect and assess its role in ensuring it for its employees, especially when we are seeking to compare them with global standards of productivity and capability.

Closing Reflections

The science of C&B has evolved and become quite strong. The force of economics has been pushing more and more organisations towards market-driven practices. In the interest of simplicity, organisations are embracing pay programmes that focus on cash rather than benefits.

Against this context, it is now becoming clear that there are limits to the power of money to attract, motivate and retain people. It will however require much harder work to identify those factors and build it into the rewards programmes of the organis-ation than it is to offer more money. The future however belongs to the ones that can do that and embrace the concept for total rewards.

Organisational Experiences

Total Reward Ideas: What Some of the Best Employers Seem to Offer

When we take a look at the list of some of the best employers in the country and examine what they did to get there, some common ideas and practices seem to emerge.

There are many things common among organisations that are often voted as the best employers. Their approach to total rewards is certainly one strong common theme. Beyond money, they do many thoughtful things which in small and large ways add quality and value to the lives of their employees.

Here is a list of 10 things, big and small, that seem to be popular with employees and are therefore offered by these organisations. The list is by no means comprehensive but certainly helps illustrate the idea of total rewards.

Flexibility and Work–Life Balance

One important element of total rewards that score high with employees is flexibility and balance. Here is what organisations are doing in this area:

- Work from home or work from anywhere policies touch a chord with employees.
- The flexibility of allowing employees to choose how much they want to work in a given week or month depending on the load and the personal lifestyle needs appeals hugely.
- Trusting employees to make their own decisions on when they want to take leave or go on vacation while remaining responsible for work output is popular with many organisation.
- This extends equally to letting employees decide when they will come to work and when they leave, as long they are available for a certain period in the day for team interaction.
- Some have of course gone all the way to make the work week much shorter—how does 4 days sound?

Women-friendly Initiatives

Women value polices that are empathetic to their needs as much or more than the money they earn. Here is what organisations are doing to get women friendly:

- One year of maternity leave is much better than what the law has now provided for and wins hearts.

- Helping returning mothers manage their re-entry effectively is an area that offers huge value to women employees and therefore pursued by many organisations, formally or informally.
- Helping women build sustainable career through mentoring support which including not just gaining skills and competencies but also overcoming some of their beliefs and apprehensions is becoming popular. This extends to networking platforms, peer-sharing forums and other forms of support groups.
- Of course, programmes and workshops to create awareness and offer skills in women safety and self-defence are also very popular.
- Sustained programmes to help mothers and fathers learn the fine art of parenting are also gaining popularity.

Health Care

Spiralling health care costs on one side and the Indian ethos of wanting to care for one's parents makes health care-oriented benefits invaluable. Here is what organisations are doing in this space:

- Awareness about health and fitness, attention to ergonomics and encouraging participation in marathons and other sporting events are all motivating employees to take ownership for health.
- Health check-up camps and exposure to alternate healing and wellness approaches and guidance in managing stress are also popular.
- Of course, a variety of insurance policies with the option to cover one's parents is becoming common.

Family Involvement/Support

Indian organisations have always been good at including, involving and recognising the family. Family days, family visit to the workplace and family inclusion in celebrations are a huge hit with the families.

Workplace Facilities

Offering employees a great physical setting that motivates, inspires and of course helps them give their best is almost foundational. The global benchmarks on this front are getting better by the day. This includes food, recreation, rest and learning.

Financial Perks

Helping employees plan their finances or make savings and investments is never easy but when done well is valued. Here is what organisations are doing to help employees in this area:

- Giving employees access to financial counsel is one such programme.
- Educating employees about planning for their retirement is another one.
- Helping employees plan and save for their children is also a valuable support system offered by some.

Growth Opportunities

Going beyond traditional growth opportunities and giving employees freedom and flexibility is what seems to score high. Here is what organisations are doing in this area:

- A very popular programme is to give employees the freedom to use a certain percentage of their time to do something that they value to gain mastery or pursue their dreams or passion.

- The other is to give employees a budget to spend on learning. This could be a new technology or just a hobby.
- Many organisations have been very generous in encouraging the entrepreneurial spirit among their employees by supporting them in a variety of ways. This could include giving them access to resources, support or in some cases even the possibility of funding if the idea is worthy.
- Beyond this, organisations also encourage and support the social consciousness of employees to do something for the community by allowing them to be part of social causes or volunteering their time for activities that enrich the communities around them.

Work Environment/Culture

The small things that organisation do or do away with also add to the rewarding experience of everyday work. Here is what organisations are practising in this area:

- At the least, organisations practise a culture of open communication, collegial team relationships and an informal workplace culture.
- Formal approval and permissions are kept to the minimum.
- An egalitarian culture where status is not given a premium either in parking space, dining facilities or travel policies also helps.
- An open office environment is becoming quite popular.

Leadership and Talent Development

The opportunity to be considered for leadership position is the greatest acknowledgement of one's potential and in fact an honour that many would give their everything for.

These organisations have elaborate programmes to identify employees with potential for leadership, give them the experiences and exposure to develop that potential and finally reward them with those life-altering opportunities.

Recognition Programmes

Recognising employees for their good work or for exceeding performance expectations or going above and beyond the call of duty has always been extremely popular and even motivating.

Be it off-sites, incentive trips, expensive gifts, vacations with families or invitations to global meets for visibility, organisations have a whole array of great ideas to make recognition really count.

12

Managing the Moments of Truth

In the chapter titled 'Evolving Expectations', our survey findings had pointed out that HR professionals had rated themselves and their contribution higher than what their stakeholders felt on many of the parameters.

Such a perception gap is not only normal but also understandable when it is approached as a service quality challenge. It becomes easy to comprehend the difference in perception when it is recognised that the HR function is in many ways the provider of a very wide range of services, albeit, to internal customers and the whole concept of satisfaction is in the eyes of the beholder.

Meet HR professionals and you find them excited about the many innovations and improvements that they are bringing about in their functional processes and products. They are ever busy rolling out one new initiative after the other, all of which according to them holds great promise for the business and its people. Listen to them and you are convinced that the function is constantly striving towards higher levels of excellence.

On the other hand, meet employees across levels in large numbers and you often get a completely contrary view. To them all our internal efforts to conceptualise, design and implement great products are of little value. Their view about HR is completely influenced by their experience of some of the everyday moments of truth. Many of their complaints, grievances, problems and wishes are very basic and devoid of all the technicalities. They find something unfair, they find something not working, they see lack of transparency, lack of care and sensitivity, lack of efficiency, lack of responsiveness and of course lack of understanding of their needs. While many do have lots of positive moments of truth, there are many who don't. That leads us to wonder why functional excellence doesn't get translated into a great service experience all the time for everyone.

This section on managing people will not be complete without examining how HR scores when it comes to service quality and what are the reasons for service quality gaps.

The term 'moments of truth'[1] was coined by Jan Carlzon, who managed the Scandinavian Airlines System (SAS).

In 1981, Jan Carlzon became CEO of the problem-ridden Scandinavian Airlines. Well before he left the company in 1994, Carlzon turned the airline around by focusing on what he later called 'moments of truth'—the various points at which people with the airline came in contact with airline customers. He used the term to mean those moments in which important brand impressions are formed and where there is significant opportunity for good or bad impressions to be made.

The HR function manages thousands of moments of truth every single day. Several moments of truth form a 'cycle of service'—what in HR is often referred to as a process. For example, the selection process, the onboarding process, the performance management process, the confirmation appraisal process or even the full and final settlement process have several moments of truth in them. The manner in which each of those moments of truth and each of these cycles of service are managed end up creating positive or negative impressions about the function and the organisation.

---

[1] Jan Carlzon, *Moments of Truth* (New York, NY: Harper Business, 1989).

When organisations manage these moments of truth well, it contributes to greater engagement and when not handled well leads to cynicism.

Using the Service Gaps Model articulated by Zeithaml, Parasuraman and Berry in their book *Delivering Quality Service*[2] (adapted for this HR context), we would like to present here one possible framework by which HR professionals can understand the potential gaps and bridge them.

The authors had identified four gaps which can contribute to poor service quality along with some insightful reasons for the same from a consumer perspective. You will notice that these four gaps and the reasons are equally true for us in HR.

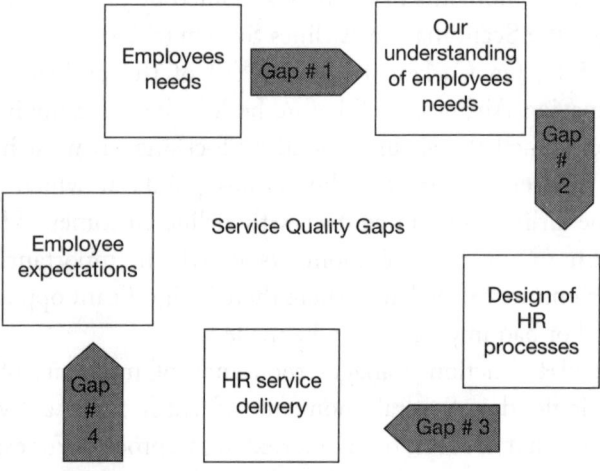

The *first gap* is between the real needs of employees and our understanding of these employees' needs. This gap can exist on account of poor action research, employee sensing, the voice of the junior HR professionals not being heard by senior HR leaders and CHROs and having too many layers or silos within the HR

---

[2] Valarie A. Zeithaml, Leonard L. Berry, and A. Parasuraman, *Delivering Quality Service: Balancing Customer Perceptions and Expectations* (New York, NY: Free Press, 1990).

function. The worst cause for this is the tendency to embrace so-called best practices or global trends and fashionable ideas without any deep research about what it means to your organisation. For example, there is a lot of buzz around 'managing the millennials', 'dumping the bell curve' or adopting the '70:20:10 rule' in learning. In doing all this, HR professionals may not be mindful of what employees really want or what is relevant to the specific context.

HR often runs the risk of making assumptions about what employees need without gathering real facts about their needs or researching it well enough.

For example, HR team members might decide that they should connect with employees and have informal chats every quarter. In reality, employees may not want to engage in such a chat and merely want the HR person to be available when needed.

The *second gap* is between HR's understanding of its employees' needs and the manner in which HR designs its processes, policies and intiatives to address these needs. This gap can arise when HR does understand their needs but does not really show commitment to meet those needs or may even dismiss them as unreasonable or just have an exploitative relationship with employees. This can also happen because of inadequate resources being assigned or people not being available.

For example, there is an enormous body of research to suggest that for every 250 to 300 employees there must be one HR generalist or partner available so that he or she is able to support those employees in all their moments of truth. While organisations recognise this, they may shy away from making those headcount commitments because of the costs involved or may not spend the time to design their jobs well enough to make impact.

Organisations might recognise that employees expect a role change every 18 to 24 months and would also expect that the internal job posting system actually works. However, management might not have the will to strictly implement a release policy to make this need a reality.

In many of the smaller organisations, this can extend to even basic infrastructure such as availability of enough number of clean restrooms, a good cafeteria, transport facilities especially for women employees and so on.

The *third gap* can occur on account of the difference between what has been designed and how it translates into delivery on the ground. This is perhaps one of the most potent gaps and there are many reasons for this.

It can happen because of role ambiguities and conflicts between CoEs, business partners, employee partners, the shared services staff and line managers. For example, employees in the various centres of excellence often see their role as specialists who must design and deploy a new programme, policy or HR product. They might see it as the role of the generalists or partners to implement them. The generalists or partners on the other hand may not even be convinced about the need for the product or programme, or may not have been involved in its creation or may not see it fitting into their priorities. This also happens where the services are rendered by third-party vendors, who do not even have the context of the problem that they are addressing in the first place. They tend to treat these services as transactions that need to be completed as per a defined process.

It may also be that the manner in which the KRAs are set within the function might lead to a fragmented approach to rolling out anything. One person pushes something out and the other might not embrace it.

The specialists and HRBPs might expect that the line managers will do their bit in making a programme successful but they may not. For example, a lot many of the moments of truth in the performance management process is in the hands of the line manager, whereas its failure is always attributed to HR.

Training is yet another area where there are huge gaps between what is designed and what is delivered. What took months to create can be dismissed in minutes as a wasteful training programme by employees because of some faults in execution.

Yet another example would be employee recognition programmes that are well-designed but poorly executed.

There is a much more serious reason for poor execution and that has to do with the lack of motivation of the HR team.

All the gurus of service quality and excellence have maintained that only happy and engaged employees can deliver great service. If that is indeed true, then it follows that only if the HR folks are happy and engaged, can they deliver great service.

The *final gap* is caused by the difference between what HR promises to employees and what HR actually delivers. Quite often despite its best efforts to deliver, HR might leave employees unhappy because of the inadvertent propensity to make tall claims and promises in the public domain or in all employee communications. In a world with an overactive social media, this can become a liability. Organisations which tend to have very strong brands in the marketplace have an even greater onus to ensure that the brand promise rubs off on the moments of truth too.

Closing Reflections

As organisations become larger and more complex and the business environment becomes more uncertain and competitive, it is our belief that employer brands and employee engagement will depend to a large extent on our ability to close these four gaps so that what we consider functional excellence does get translated into service quality in the eyes of our employees.

This might require that HR does not wait for annual survey to tell us how employees feel but leverage periodic and short dipsticks to constantly measure the employee experience across various moments of truth and quickly take remedial action.

It will also require that the various silos within the function do not widen the gaps. Most importantly, it may require us to first check how our own employees feel.

Finally, we must start with the mindset that internal service is not inferior to external service to customers and also that service quality is a science worth learning more about.

Organisational Experiences

Rivigo: The Bold Vision of Making Logistics Human

Does it ever occur to us that a truck driver is central to our nation's economy and progress? How fast and efficiently the economic produce of a nation reaches its end consumer is what determines its growth. Truck drivers drive tirelessly for long hours and traverse tough terrains day and night. They do not just drive the truck. They drive the country and its growth. While truck driving is among the highest contributors to jobs in developed countries, *there is an increasing dearth of truck drivers globally and more so in emerging economies.*

The reason is that a truck driver's standard of life lacks in many aspects. On an average, a long haul truck driver spends 25 days in a month on the highways, away from his family. He leads a lonely life, eats his irregular meals at roadside places and often sleeps in the truck. Many are affected by HIV or start substance abuse as a result of such a way of life. A large percentage of them don't get married. Those who do, fail to have a balanced and meaningful family life. For those even willing to overlook this, the profession presents some unimaginable safety hazards. A truck driver drives for 14 to 16 hours a day and sleeps in the truck. Driving in stressful, fatigued conditions puts his life at risk. In India, lack of sleep has been a prime reason for accidents and fatalities among truck drivers. An estimated 24,000 people died in road accidents because of drowsiness in 2013.

Given the stigma and risks associated with truck driving, long-haul truck drivers are subject to unimaginable social disrespect. In the Indian village, they are called the '37th caste'—the outcast. Nobody wants to be called that. Nobody wants their son, husband or father to be treated like an outcast.

Set against this context, Rivigo, which was founded in 2014, had the pioneering and audacious vision of making logistics human, faster and safer.

Rivigo's simple yet breakthrough solution was the truck-driver relay system. Through the relay model, Rivigo has fundamentally changed the driver's job from an 'away from home' job to a 'day' job. Drivers change over after every few hundred kilometres and get rostered on a trip in the opposite direction back to their point of origin. Ninety-two per cent of their 4,000 truck drivers go back home every day, while the others are able to return every other day. This means they spend less time away from their families and lead meaningful and balanced lives. This itself has fundamentally changed the way they live and the way they are perceived in society.

The relay model also cuts down any downtime on the road since the driver change happens within a few minutes and helps connect India faster by guaranteeing reduction in turnaround time by 50–70 per cent when compared to other road transport means. The endeavour of Rivigo has been to provide a sustainable life to the truck drivers. They have also built infrastructure for driver training and resting across 70+ locations in the country. They have a dedicated driver engagement team that works relentlessly with the drivers and their families towards their upliftment. From launching financial inclusion schemes to connecting them with technology and from providing family health cover to children education scholarships, they are making a huge impact—one driver and one family at a time. Once considered the 37th caste, Rivigo pilots (they are called pilots) are respected in their communities and are leading meaningful lives with their families. They are able to be around their old parents without having to uproot themselves from their village homes. Their wives are no longer worried about their safety and health. Their children do not miss seeing their father and having a normal childhood.

Their new lifestyle allows them to save more and invest in their children's education and security. Their families proudly call them 'relay pilots'. Most importantly, they feel empowered and believe they are the real heroes who are steadily and quietly ushering India into its promising future. The company has thus brought the truck driver back into the social mainstream of the economy.

The Rivigo story is not complete without taking a look at the lives of a couple of its pilots.

Rajpal Chauhan

Rajpal lost his father at a very early age. Raised alone by his mother, he looked up to her as his pillar of strength. He was doing fine as a truck driver with a local transporter. But his life shook forever when he lost his mother and could not even make it to her last rites. He was away on one of his trips and could reach only days after the funeral. He quit his job and was unemployed for some time. He joined Rivigo in September 2015 and since then goes home back to his wife and family every day.

Kaleemullah

When the mining business in the Chitradurga district of Karnataka shutdown in 2014, thousands like Kaleem lost their livelihood. The land in the area is arid and there were limited employment opportunities. Kaleem decided to take up a driving job in Dubai, but was concerned about the care of his mother and three daughters while he was away. He took the decision to move to Dubai to take up a driving job there. But just days before he was to leave, he started to feel a strange sense of apprehension and disquiet and questioned his decision. It did not seem wise to leave behind his family. He decided against going since his mother was ailing and required intensive care and routine trips to the hospital. Kaleem heard about Rivigo through a friend in April 2016 and joined in the same month. Since then Pilot Kaleem returns home to take care of his mother every day. He takes her for her routine check-ups. Determined to build a good life for his children, Kaleem also moved his daughters from Kannada-medium to English-medium schools in the 2017 academic session. All his three girls are merit holders in the school.

HR HERE AND NOW

THE MAKING OF THE QUINTESSENTIAL
PEOPLE CHAMPION

PART 4

Management and
Leadership Development

13
Aspirations and Needs

Do the aspirations of employees run contrary to the needs and interests of organisations? Do the aspirations of employees also come in the way of organisations pursuing their goals? Is that why organisations and their leaders often talk about managing expectations and tempering aspirations?

It is true that employees who contribute and make a difference are also the ones who are not always easy to manage in many ways. They know that they are important to the success of the organisation, thanks to their being well informed about their contribution and their own context. This is reinforced by the formal and informal messages that are communicated to them by their managers and others in the organisation. It is therefore natural for them to try and make the most out of the importance accorded to them for their capabilities and contribution. Their aspirations are not limited to just monetary rewards. They expect great work, access to the best positions and of course a lot of recognition and, in many ways, special treatment. If and when they feel that they are not being adequately valued and recognised they start to seek better opportunities, especially if the labour market is buoyant. Their aspirations can often seem insatiable.

The marketplace, which has a scarcity of quality resources (especially at the senior levels and in certain critical technical and functional domains) and is constantly luring these 'talented' employees, only makes matters worse.

Having said all this, we believe that the aspirations that employees nurture are a product of what organisations have offered to them. Their aspirations have been conditioned by organisational actions. They are products of our making. Even more importantly, it is this aspiration that has served as the wellspring of motivation that organisations have been beneficiaries of. If employees did not aspire, organisations would be the greatest sufferers. If employees were simply contended with where they are and want to merely coast along, organisations would make little progress.

As customers, have we all not encountered employees with little or no aspirations? Have we not been at the receiving end of their indifference? Do not leaders and managers get frustrated with employees who have nothing to aspire for?

There was a time when employees were entirely dependent on organisations to plan their careers in return for giving them their tenure and organisations certainly felt burdened by the enormity of such expectations and would often plead that employees needed to take charge of their careers and there are limits to what organisations can do.

Once the labour market opened up and organisations also embraced market-oriented practices, employees quickly learnt how to take charge of their careers and organisations found that hard to digest too. High levels of attrition hurt organisations significantly. Organisations are now settling down to a more balanced and interdependent relationship when it comes to careers and aspirations.

In this context, our efforts should be to channelise our employees' aspirations towards outcomes that are good both for the employees and the organisation. The operating word is *channelise*.

So our exploration on the subject of management and leadership development would be governed by this intrinsic value and approach. It would be prudent to see organisations and employees as equal partners in the journey and not see organisations as manipulative or agentic, as if it were a game of chess. Nor would it be prudent to see employees as overdependent and helpless.

The true objective of management and leadership development would be achieved when the aspirations of employees are channelised meaningfully and they meet the needs and aspirations of their organisations.

The section on management and leadership development therefore begins by exploring the subject of channelising aspirations. The next chapter looks at how organisations work towards institutionalising the process. We end the section by looking at the actual task of developing managers and leaders.

14

Channelising Aspirations

Is it futile to take a long-term approach to development?
There is a general sense of resignation about planning for the future given the radical changes that organisations are going through on one hand and the perception that tenures are shortening and employees are constantly seeking changes on the other.

The reality is quite to the contrary.

Beyond the cohort of employees with around 5–7 years of experience, a very large number of organisations have significant levels of stability. While the overall attrition percentages might be in the double digit, the attrition among the more experienced employees is low or even non-existent.

It also appears that tenured employees in general seem to have far better chances of growing into leadership positions. While organisations do seem to hire from outside, the numbers are still in favour of insiders. Organisations which abandon a long-term approach might actually be compromising their managerial and leadership depth in addition to losing out in the competitive labour market. Taking a long-term approach while being open to making constant changes in one's approach is what seems to be working.

This in many ways answers the much-debated question of 'make versus buy'. The decision to make ones talent calls for a long-term orientation. Investments made today will yield results much later. A buy approach is certainly likely to yield short-term results but is plagued with repercussions on many fronts. More and more mature and stable organisations seem to be adopting a make approach when it comes to managerial and leadership talent.

In the short run, these organisations might be seen as training for the street, but in the long term, once they master the 'making' process they do feel empowered and less susceptible to labour market forces.

Ladders, Paths and Lattices (Managerial and Technical)

How do organisations channelise the aspirations of employees? What organisation-design decisions and actions do organisations take to prepare the basis for channelising aspirations?

It certainly seems to take a lot of thinking and planning to create the right design elements that can support career growth which is aligned to business needs.

For channelising the aspirations of employees to meet business needs, organisations and therefore employees use ladders, paths and even lattices.

Organisations with such ladders and paths, either formally announced or informally practised, stand a greater chance of retaining and growing their employees.

Traditional Ladders

The traditional career ladder based on vertical growth typically helped employees move from individual contributor positions into positions of management and then leadership. The premium was on rewarding individuals who took on roles with higher and higher levels of accountability in terms of revenues, budgets, people and so on.

As organisations developed well-established functions, these ladders were created for growth within the function.

Sales functions had ladders which showed how an individual contributor in sales could grow to assume higher and higher levels of responsibility.

Similarly, a production supervisor had visibility in terms of how he could grow to head production for a large facility.

Quite often these ladders were clearly linked to pay grades and individuals had the motivation to climb the ladder based on visible financial incentives.

It is fair to say that career ladders ended up being established almost by default. Employees who performed reasonably well were assured of access to and ascent up the ladder.

The problems began to arise when organisational actions of assured ascent in the good times led employees to believe that it would be so all the time. Organisations failed to get employees to recognise the importance of job size and competencies. When the size of the job and the competencies required were unmoored from the ladder, aspirations turned sour and needed management.

One big agenda for the future for HR practitioners and business leaders is to clarify what it will take to climb the ladder.

Technical Ladders

The growth of specialist professions such as research, design and engineering led to a growing tribe of employees finding it hard to measure up to the expectations of job size and competence established for ascent across traditional ladders. The growth of knowledge-based businesses further fuelled the need for creating separate ladders to cater to the needs of employees in these businesses.

However, setting up such technical ladders poses a huge challenge when it needs to compare favourably with traditional ladders within the same organisation. For example, when a pharma company needs to establish a technical stream for its research and development team in a manner that it compares favourably with the traditional ladder that it has for its manufacturing and sales stream, it can pose challenges. What works for one may not work for the other.

The technical ladder system at Texas Instruments was a pioneering effort in promoting technical excellence within a business organisation context.

Based on their experience, many organisations have realised that top talent is not just about those who have general managerial capabilities but equally those who have strong functional orientation and seek to develop themselves in the functional domain. They have therefore focused their attention on both people with leadership potential and those with functional expertise.

Selective Career Paths

Organisations typically offer building block programmes to all employees. For example, all employees who get into a managerial position for the first time are nominated to participate in a first-time manager programme. Similarly, managers who begin to manage managers or businesses participate in a seasoned manager programme.

Many organisations also have role-based programmes within functions. There could be programmes for factory managers, finance heads, business managers and so on. These programmes are intended to help employees who are climbing traditional ladders.

Beyond this, organisations realise that they need to create paths on a selective basis for certain critical destination positions. Many organisations are beginning to pick on what they call crucible roles, and then crafting career paths to reach those positions.

For example, if a large manufacturing organisation finds that its unit head role which manages a multibillion-dollar, integrated manufacturing facility as a profit centre is extremely crucial, it might craft a career path that will help produce enough number of unit heads.

Similarly, an organisation that wishes to create a cadre of category managers who can manage a category of products will need to craft a career path that will help produce world-class category managers. For example, B2B businesses may want to develop key account leaders.

Such a career path might require the chosen employees to ascend not a traditional ladder but move from one ladder to another, sometimes moving horizontally and at other times moving vertically.

HR professionals will need to develop an intimate understanding of the future needs of the business and on that basis identify and select those few roles for which customised career paths may need to be created.

Customised career paths may also be created for select individuals who are seen as extremely promising with the potential to move up to executive leadership positions.

For this, organisations will need to develop an intimate understanding of each of the individuals, their abilities, their aspirations and on that basis map them to potential positions and create career paths to get there. Of course organisations will need to know the areas in which they are likely to have requirements in the coming years.

The Career Lattice

The term 'career lattice' is used to refer to the process of an individual moving in his or her career pretty much the way Spiderman would—using a web or mesh to move around in a manner that is exigent and dynamic but with some underlying needs, assumptions and interests in mind.

With radical changes in the nature of work and job portfolios that we have discussed earlier, it is now evident that traditional ladders and even customised paths may not be able to meet the aspirations of employees or needs of organisations.

Individual employees might use the career lattice approach to move from one position to another horizontally or vertically based on their needs. They might even make such moves based on their personal exigencies. For example, we see several young mothers returning to the workforce choosing jobs that are quite different from what they did earlier.

Employees in hi-tech businesses facing obsolescence often use the lattice approach to remain employable. Employees also make deliberate choices to shift their professional stream or industry and under these circumstances use the lattice approach. Free agents use the lattice approach to do a wide variety of assignments, acquire a wide range of skills and move up in their professional practice.

Of course, for the ever-growing tribe of contingent workers, the career lattice is the only hope of employability, mobility and, hopefully, growth. Organisations are leveraging the career lattice approach when it comes to grooming leaders for extremely critical executive leadership positions in an accelerated manner. Career lattices are emerging as an extremely customised and bespoke approach to career mobility within organisations.

Separating Growth from Development and Handling Social Pressures Without Creating Illusionary Growth

The need for social recognition and social prominence is quite high in our context and that invariably translates to regular promotions and changing designations (including visible perquisites) that signal growth. This is a need for all employees and it is further heightened when it comes to the white-collared and managerial population. Many organisations have found an easy option by creating artificial levels and differentiated designations to meet this socially visible growth aspiration. In doing this, they have also created a problem of multiple levels and artificial differentiation leading to complex organisation structures and a vicious cycle of unproductive growth hallucination.

Today, a number of corporates are taking steps to correct the imbalance in their organisation design consequent to the mindless artificial growth syndrome. They are aligning to the concept of *work levels*, originally propounded as Stratified Systems Theory by Elliott Jaques.[1]

This and other similar systems categorise the nature of work into levels and ensure that the right kind of work is done at each level and through that we restore a proper shape to the organisation. This is intended to ensure that the progression of people between these distinct levels is based on real growth in responsibilities.

In addition to looking at the position, organisations are also looking at the capabilities of the person. Organisations are also beginning to make an objective assessment of their capabilities so that they can support their professional development and prepare them prior to such elevation. Employees are slowly beginning to recognise that this is not something that can happen every other year but will call for sufficient time gap to help them to acquire and develop competencies for the higher-level role. This is real development.

However, the social pressures for continuous progression and recognition have not entirely disappeared. Therefore, organisations continue to tinker with job titles or create mezzanine levels to create some illusion of progress within the same work levels.

This is certainly a significant agenda for HR practitioners.

---

[1] Dr Jaques graduated from the Johns Hopkins School of Medicine and earned a PhD in social relations from Harvard University. During his extensive work with the US Army and Corporates, he developed an objective scientific process for testing and measuring human capability through a validated methodology applied in the context of time-span of discretion as measurement of the level of complexity of work in an organisational role. His research became the Jaques' Systems Theory. He has published over 20 books.

Elliott Jaques, *Requisite Organisation: A Total System for Effective Managerial Organization and Managerial Leadership for the 21st Century* (Baltimore, MD: Cason Hall & Co., 1989). This book outlines the model of work levels.

Respecting Diversity

Can birds of different feathers really flock together? Can diverse groups within organisations receive an equal opportunity to succeed and grow? Can employees with different profiles and backgrounds or with different views about careers manage to find a place for themselves?

The delightful fable (also a video) *A Peacock in the Land of Penguins*[2] most truly describes our message. Through the engaging story of Perry the Peacock and other exotic birds who struggle to be themselves in the conformity-minded *land of penguins* the book brings home the message about the problems of respecting the diversity of talent.

As society begins to celebrate and promote a more individualistic orientation, we will find employees making their own unique choices about careers. There will also be employees with varying profiles at the workplace.

HR functions will certainly be called upon to respect and value such diversity. The problems of talent diversity will take several forms.

A Place for Those Downshifting

In vibrant and high-growth economies, executives are confronted with the need to decide what they will do in their ladder or path every two or three years, because every two years they are lured with hard-to-refuse invitations to shift to a higher gear or climb more steps even if their heart pleads with them to take a pause or their head tells them that they are not ready for this. For most executives, not doing anything or turning down an invitation does not appear to be an option.

---

[2] B. J. Gallagher Hateley and Warren H. Schmidt, *A Peacock in the Land of Penguins: A Fable About Creativity &Courage* (Oakland, CA: Berrett-Coehler, 2001). Originally a book, but now also a video echoes the dilemmas that businesses face in terms of the increasing diversity of their workforce.

Some succeed in the choices they make while many others fail because they accept jobs for which they not have the competence or join work environments that do not suit their value system or may sign up to work with managers whose style is incompatible with theirs. So what is the way out?

Many executives are beginning to recognise that it is smarter to downshift. Downshifting might mean sticking to doing what one is very good at or passionate about and not venture into unknown or unsuitable terrains. Downshifting might mean that one stops choosing jobs that call for excessive personal and family sacrifices. Downshifting might also mean taking a calculated reduction in pay and benefits so that on a sustainable basis one is still fine. However, downshifting does not mean one is resisting change. It only means one is adapting to it in a harmonious way.

By choosing the right time to downshift, executives might be able to build sustainable careers which allow them to move out of restrictive tracks, paths or ladders and take the road less travelled. Downshifting is one interesting way of using the career lattice.

The question is this: Will organisations have a place for those who choose to downshift? Is there at all a place for those who are productive but contended with where they are?

Diversity of Educational Qualifications

Organisations have MBAs and non-MBAs, engineer MBAs and pure engineers, engineers and MBAs from tier I institutions, tier II and tier III institutions, diploma holders, ITIs, graduates, class XII and so on. The list is very long!

What really causes the problem is not the fact that organisations hire from diverse sources. Obviously, they must. The problem is when they keep reminding them and others that they have come from different sources in a very dysfunctional way. As Professor Alison Wolf, author of *Does Education Matter?*, said, 'We are creating societies in which the sheep and the goat are marked for life in their teens'.

Organisations complicate the situation by creating separate pay structures and progression charts for each educational source instead of quickly integrating them into a common platform beyond a point. As a result, many individuals live their professional lives with an inferior identity and deep regret. Can organisations give employees with diverse educational backgrounds a fair chance to succeed?

Diversity of Tenure

The issues of tenure-led diversity are even more debilitating.

Organisations have old timers and new comers, those who have grown from within and those that have come from outside. Newer organisations also have the 'original founding team' and 'others'.

Employees with significant tenure view the new breed as rolling stones that gather no moss. They see them as opportunistic people who run away in the face of adversity.

The newcomers complain about the inability of the old timers to think afresh and embrace change freely, while the old timers talk about all the turbulent changes inflicted upon them by their footloose colleagues.

Founding teams lament about the lack of ownership in the next generation and the next generation talks about the original coterie and its non-inclusive ways.

The Push Towards Localisation

As organisations move to new geographies within their national boundaries or across countries, they are under pressure to ensure that their workforce in that location represents the same mixture as the overall population in that region. Given protectionist pressures as well as pressures for equal opportunity and affirmative action, organisations seek to invest in the development of management and leadership talent from the local area as a sign of respecting diversity.

Gender Diversity

This is easy to understand. Even organisations which start with a 40 per cent female representation in their workforce end up having fewer than 5 per cent in their senior management and leadership group. The lack of gender diversity has begun to occupy the attention and mind space of leaders across organisations and HR is being called upon to come up with programmes to support women managers and leaders to build sustainable careers.

Getting Managers to Engage in Career Conversations

While organisations keep asserting that the individual needs to own his or her career, such assertions do not in any way take away the responsibility of the immediate manager in guiding and championing the career development process for his or her team members.

At the least, the manager is expected to engage in periodic conversations with his or her team members to listen to them about their dreams and aspirations and share his or her perspectives on how such aspirations might be realised. Unfortunately, this seems easier said than done.

Coaching Foundation India[3] had undertaken a research project among HR and business leaders to understand the current talent management practices within organisations in terms of its state of evolution, its role and effectiveness. The idea was also to understand the human dimension of talent management in terms of what leaders and managers are supposed to do and actually do for talent management.

The research pointed out that the biggest talent management challenge seemed to be around the ability and willingness of

---

[3] Coaching Foundation India Limited (CFI), 'The Human Side of Talent Management: A CFI Research Project'. (Chennai: CFI, July 2013).

managers and leaders to engage in a developmental relationship with their talented employees. Specifically, the gaps seem to be around their ability to:

1. Establish a genuine, positive and empathetic relationship with their employees
2. Make the time to engage in active listening
3. Provide consistent feedback
4. Take out quality time to have engaging career and developmental conversations with the ones who are making important transitions or preparing for future roles

The research showed that while top management support was very high and the processes to support talent management were robust, the weakest link was around the quality of conversations.

The research also pointed out that in highly competitive work cultures, where belonging to a fast-track programme carries a huge premium, the managers who make these fateful recommendations are under huge pressure.

Given their own emotional attachments, notions and biases on who is highly talented and who is not, it seems to be very difficult for managers to dispassionately engage in a range of conversations that can truly help nurture talent. Very often the talent identification process is polluted by present-day exigencies of listing as top talent employees who perform today even if they fail to show promise and potential for tomorrow. As a consequence of this, the tendency for a TM intervention (like any other organisational process) to be *reduced from a scientific to a socio-political process* is high.

For the employees who are identified as top talent, they experience their organisation as being somewhat impatient in terms of expecting them to produce sustainable results and deliver excellence early on. This creates stress and performance anxiety and does not make it easy for them to engage in candid conversations with their managers or show their vulnerability.

It could also be possible that the manager is himself or herself not on the list but has to support a team member who is on the list. There are several reasons why this might happen.

The manager might be new to the organisation and may not have met the qualifying criteria that might have been set up. It is likely that the manager is a good sound functional specialist but does not fit the organisation's definition of top talent. The manager may be at a life stage where he is confronted with other priorities. The manager may still be a very valued performer but may have fallen short of the bar which becomes steeper as one goes up.

Whatever might be the reasons or circumstances, this is where the rubber hits the road.

Managers cannot be expected to know how to have these conversations. They need training and support to have great conversations. They need insights on how to talk the language of ladders, paths and lattices. They need to know how to give feedback. Most importantly, they need to know how to make development plans and support their implementation. They need to know how to be great mentors and coaches.

This is the moment of truth and needs to be managed well.

Closing Reflections

The aspiration of employees can be aligned to the needs of the organisation if they are channelised at the right time with the involvement of the right people. This will call for designing solutions in terms of career ladders, paths and lattices. It will also call for resisting the social pressure of creating illusionary growth. It will also call for our ability to respect the diversity in aspirations among different groups in the organisation. Most importantly, it will call for the time and attention of the immediate manager for engaging in meaningful career conversations.

Organisational Experiences

Placing Bets on People: The Murugappa Way

The Murugappa Group has always been a votary of growth from within. For years, a good majority of its senior management positions have been filled from within, save some exceptions. This enviable state has not been achieved by accident.

The Corporate Advisory Board (CAB), the apex forum in the group, consisting of the chairman and the lead directors representing the four key sectors of the group, spend a week to ten days every year discussing the senior management of the various group companies.

The managing directors of the respective companies represent the achievements of their people to the CAB in order to facilitate deep discussions around performance, course corrections and potential growth opportunities for each individual.

Thanks to this process, the CAB has complete visibility on the performance, potential and development needs of the top 250 leaders across the group. As a collective, the CAB is in a position to understand the needs of individual executives for growth and development and match them with the opportunities available in group companies for such resources. This process of dialogues aids in the movement/rotation of senior leaders with the buy-in of all the stakeholders.

This has enabled the group to offer all-round developmental experiences to senior leaders who have the ability and demonstrate the willingness to move from functional roles to business roles, or from one business role to another.

For the individuals, the fact that the group has reposed faith in them and the fact that they have seen several of their predecessors benefit from these movements motivate them to take the leap of faith.

For the MDs of the businesses, when they see their people being considered for significant growth opportunities, they readily release them. They know that this is good for them and for the group.

Clearly, a robust talent-review process conducted with discipline at the highest levels, the track record of supporting people who have taken the leap of faith to move and the underlying principle that talent belongs to the group have helped the Murugappa Group promote job rotation as a sound developmental experience.

Texas Instruments Technical Ladder

The Texas Instruments (TI) Technical Ladder is their technical career path with increasing levels of responsibility and influence on the company's technical direction. The Tech Ladder at TI fuels innovation, supports business goals, and recognises, attracts, develops and retains top technical talent.

The TI Tech Ladder titles are:

- Member of the group technical staff
- Senior member of the technical staff
- Distinguished member of the technical staff
- TI fellow (fellow)
- TI senior fellow (Sr fellow)
- TI principal fellow (Pr fellow)

Given the history of this process, these titles are well known and recognised even externally.

How Does One Get into the TI Tech Ladder?

Based on individual contributions, achievements and initiatives, technical contributors in TI can stand for election via an annual peer-election process. Election criteria includes history of technical contributions made to technological advancement while working outside of TI, evidence of current contributions, potential for future technical contributions and high level of performance relative to peers. The election process is worldwide and is fully owned and managed by the technical community at TI. Once the technical community has voted/ranked the nominations, the management draws the cut-off line. The ranking order obtained from the election cannot be changed by any external input.

An employee joining TI can also be nominated as part of the joining process. Such nominations go through a special election process. There is no minimum job grade associated to a title level. This process is not about which job grade the person is currently in, it is focussed on whether the contributions are high enough to deserve a tech title.

The Re-election Process

Title holders will be up for re-election every five years from their last election or re-election to a title. The tenure limit ensures that the Tech Ladder is a reflection of TI's top technical talent continuously contributing at the highest level, providing sufficient opportunities for aspiring talent to get on to the ladder and for top contributors to move up the ladder.

If a title holder does not get re-elected he moves to 'Emeritus' status. A technical talent can also voluntarily move to an 'Emeritus' status.

15

Institutionalising the Process

Should management and leadership development efforts be directed towards a chosen segment of the population or should it be broad-based? The responses of organisations to this question will depend on their philosophical orientation.

We find more and more organisations veering towards the view that they should do a bit of both. They direct some of their efforts towards ensuring that all employees receive a base level of developmental inputs to make them effective in what they are doing. They then direct some of their efforts to address the needs of employees who are perceived to have a lot of potential for future growth.

Providing a base level of inputs is simple. It calls for the ability to design the right learning interventions for the right group of employees.

Making investments for a select few employees is often not just time-consuming but also fraught with a lot of conflicts, emotions, expectations and disappointments.

The former hold out the promise of making people effective while the latter holds the promise of creating a leadership pipeline. It holds the promise of grooming future leaders.

Given that the latter involves judgement and the painful process of including some and excluding many others, there is the need to be seen as fair and objective.

Finally, we have the task of championing development or doing something with the people who have been identified as having potential—the task of living up to the promise that leaders have made to themselves, those identified and to the organisation.

And this needs to be done consistently over time.

This entails institutionalising the process of development: defining the competency expectations, assessing employees against these expectations to make the decisions on whom they would like to make what kind of investments and then identifying the right governance forums. So what does this mean?

To develop managers and leaders, organisations first determine what skills and competencies are required of managers and leaders across various levels. This calls for the collective abilities of HR and business leaders.

Once organisations establish what the needs are, they help decision-makers judge which of their employees have the potential for growth and can be chosen for differentiated investments for development. This requires HR professionals to put in place the right tools and methods to make those judgements.

Finally, organisations champion the actual development process by understanding where the employees are in their journey of development, determining what actions need to be taken and then ensuring that those actions are being taken. This may involve setting up supportive, helping relationships, the right forums to monitor and champion these processes and of course establishing the right policies that will create a supportive environment for those with potential to actually realise their potential. In this chapter, we will explore some of the challenges in doing all of this.

Forming a View of the Management and Leadership Imperatives

How do organisations go about establishing what they expect from their managers and leaders? Are such expectations based on realistic needs and demands or do they sometimes fall prey to the temptation of over engineering such expectations? Do our expectations help us appreciate what we already have and build on it or do such expectations seem out of reach? With functional expertise, technology and innovation becoming so important for businesses, we are beginning to see organisations asking themselves some important questions about what they really expect from their managers and leaders and whether such expectations are grounded in reality while respecting diversity.

This brings us to the subject of competency frameworks.

In the July–August 2007 edition of the *Harvard Business Review* (HBR), Norm Smallwood and Dave Ulrich[1] talk about something interesting they did in a workshop for nine companies that were all household names.

They asked the representatives from each organisation to send them their leadership competency models, which listed the 'unique' characteristics that they sought in their leaders. They then deleted the names of the corporations from each model. During the workshop, they asked the representatives to pick out their own. Few were able to do so. They found that there was little difference between the models of a telecommunications company, a consumer products company, a financial services company, and an aerospace company. Their conclusion was that by focusing on the desirable traits of individual leaders, the firms ended up creating generic models. They go on to assert that vanilla competency models generate vanilla leadership.

Yes, for large and global organisations that have spent years living and working with competency frameworks, vanilla competency frameworks are of little value. On the other hand, for organisations which are uninitiated to the practice of using competency frameworks, a good vanilla framework is still a great place to start.

---

[1] Norm Smallwood and Dave Ulrich, 'Building Leadership Brand', *HBR* (July–August 2007): 82–90.

In essence, there is a wide variety of ways in which we can determine and establish the management and leadership ask. There are several ways in which competency frameworks can be crafted. None of them is right or wrong.

Several possibilities exist when organisations decide to develop competencies and it may not even be possible to describe all of them though we will attempt to do so.

Role Specific

Some organisations with very diverse job families and professional streams find it necessary to define competencies for each unique job family or role. For example, banks may find it necessary to define the competencies for their relationship managers in the private wealth management role.

Sales function within a technology company may find it necessary to define competencies for their sales team specifically for hunters and for farmers.

In both cases, they might combine functional and behavioural competencies into what they define as key to the roles.

Functional and Leadership Competencies

Many organisations have a universal leadership competency framework and a separate functional competency framework for each function or job family. They define the functional competencies for all or some of their priority functions.

Work-level Specific

Many organisations choose to map their competencies to each work level or band. When they do this, they either have separately defined competencies for each level or use the same competencies across levels but with different behavioural descriptors with ascending levels of proficiency.

Universal—Simple

Some organisations choose to have a very simple set of competencies or leadership behaviour which they believe need to be demonstrated by all their leaders across levels. These behaviours include leadership competencies as well as values.

Elaborate and Granular—Managerial and Leadership and Values

Some organisations choose to separate managerial skills from leadership competencies. These organisations also have values called out separately. In addition, they have functional competencies as well as some workplace principles.

All of these approaches are valid in a certain context provided HR practitioners make the right choice keeping the context in mind. Therein lies the challenge.

There is a need for HR practitioners to ask themselves and their businesses some very fundamental questions before they set off on the task of defining their needs. Here are some questions that often get asked:

- Should the organisation look at competencies as standard job requirements for full standard performance or look at competencies as explaining the difference between the average and exceptional performers?
- Would the organisation like the competencies to be thorough and comprehensive or would they wish to keep it simple and sharply focused?

The answer to these two sets of questions often forms the basis for defining the competencies and it will depend on the specific context of the organisation.

For organisations that are embarking on the journey of moving away from subjective judgements about people to defining skills and competencies, the journey of making it thorough and comprehensive might well be necessary. Such a journey helps its leaders and managers become comfortable with the language of competencies and guide them in their actions.

Unilever had developed a comprehensive competency and skills framework for its managerial employees with a common leadership competency set (11 in number) cutting across functions with work-level-wise descriptors of how this may be demonstrated and a professional skills framework—function wise (10 functions). This was a seminal work that was undertaken at the turn of the century to introduce a common integrated approach to management development across 80 countries that Unilever was operating in at that point in time.

As organisations spend years working with competencies, their maturity increases and the whole literacy becomes tacit and ingrained within the organisation. These organisations can afford to take as read many of the foundational competencies and focus only on the vital few.

The same Unilever a decade later, by which time the rigour of detailed assessment and development feedback using the competencies and skills framework had been institutionalised in an uniform fashion across the different geographies, introduced the usage of a simplified framework referred to as 'Standards of Leadership' with just 5 elements.

Ultimately, it always seems useful to keep the expected competencies as few as possible. It brings focus and clarity. At the same time, oversimplification may have its perils. It is beneficial to articulate competencies or behaviours as distinct for each work level rather than use a universal framework across work levels. It will be hard to explain why young individual contributors should think strategically, when in fact they need to learn to think logically. Similarly, for some roles it might make greater sense to have role-based competencies rather than even level-based competencies, especially at mid to junior levels where across levels there could be a huge variety of roles needing specific knowledge and behaviours.

Where organisations are building functional competencies as a priority using a role-based approach, it seems beneficial to integrate

functional and managerial competencies into the role requirements and define what is expected of the role holder to deliver full
standard performance.

Of course, some of the foundational managerial competencies
such as planning, problem-solving, decision-making and dele-
gating are rather universal. These may be necessary for every
manager—in every function, at every level—to be effective.

On the other hand, leadership competencies may need to be
built around what gives life and identity to that organisation and,
more importantly, what is contextually appropriate for that
organisation at that time.

What really matters is that HR practitioners and leaders are
constantly engaged in the quest of figuring out what matters to
them most. It is best that this process of defining what matters is
seen as 'work in progress' all the time rather than be seen as done
and dusted for good and preserved in expensive leather-bound
books.

Judging

Organisations which embrace the philosophy of getting selective in
their management and leadership development investments are
keen to adopt a scientific approach to identifying those with potential for future leadership. Such a group is referred to by various
names—HIPO (high potential), top talent, listers and so on.

This has given birth to an entire industry and professional
practice—leadership assessment.

Organisations rely on the performance track record of the individual as the primary criteria to select individuals for investments.
The performance score over a typical three-year period ends up
being plotted on a scale.

To assess potential, organisations set up assessment centres
to assess a larger pool of employees at certain levels and pick
the most promising candidates. Some organisations also rely on
psychometric tools to support their decisions about potential of
employees.

While many organisations plot performance and potential on the two axis and through that place individual on a nine-box grid, others look at more than these two dimensions. Organisations might look at values or culture fit as the third dimension. They might also look at the employee's willingness to be mobile across roles and geographies as additional inputs to make a decision.

HR practitioners are charged with the responsibility of facilitating the entire process and boiling up a list of employees who deserve selective investments for development.

While there are several obvious benefits for organisations to know who their most talented employees are, the process itself poses several challenges which HR professionals need to be mindful of and deal with. Here are a few that we consider important to call out.

Universal Benchmarks

Third-party consulting firms that offer assessment services to organisations find it convenient to use their universal model of leadership competencies to drive the potential assessment process. They also rely on a battery of psychometric tools including personality-profiling tools to support their selection process.

What concerns us is the fact that the more scientific the yardsticks of measurement, the more universal they are likely to be and often removed from the realities of the organisation. We were once talking to the talent manager of a very large and successful organisation which was part of a global conglomerate. The global organisation required the leaders in the local company to be assessed on certain global competencies and most leaders fared poorly. What irked most employees as well as the talent manager was the fact that the local company was actually delivering far superior results on a consistent basis compared to the parent company and that was a contradiction that many could not digest.

While the need to adopt a system that is objective and free of bias is understandable, over engineering the specifications can end up creating unintended consequences.

The Acceptance of Such Assessment Data

The more elaborate and minute the definitions of what is needed from leaders, the steeper the expectations become.

Assessed against this daunting list, the leaders of even a consistently high performing organisation may come out looking quite bad and give the CEO and his team some sleepless nights if not read in context. This is no different from all the elaborate lists that exist today of what good looks are, what good health is, what physical fitness is, what a happy life is and so on. The more these standards are defined in almost idealistic terms, the more people look bad, feel terrible and think catastrophically. Read those lists every day and you can wake up feeling hopeless.

For one, most leaders who have been through these assessments see it as 'a test to pass and clear' rather than as an opportunity for self-discovery and self-awareness. Employees seldom identify with the results if they are debriefed to them. They also struggle to attach developmental value to what they see as a selection tool. Many of us who work as executive coaches therefore encounter a lot of cynicism when we talk to our coachees and we ask them about their assessment centre results and what it means to them.

Finally, what concerns us the most is that some of the firms that run the assessments often spend a single session to debrief the executive about the results and as a result leaving the executive with more questions and shock than answers and acceptance.

Technical and Ethical Concerns

There are also technical and ethical issues with the use of psycho-metrics for making judgements. First, the correlation between psychological preferences and traits and workplace behaviours is not well established in all cases. While individuals may have certain preferences and orientations, they might have adaptive abilities as demonstrated at the workplace that may not be reflected in the results. Also, many of the tools clearly specify that they are not intended for selection but are still used by many for this purpose.

Undervaluing Managerial Judgement

The average manager in an organisation if asked to name his very best team members—the ones who are performing well, who are learning well and quickly, who can take on a lot more in their existing roles and can grow at least two levels in the perceivable future—he or she might be able to respond quite effortlessly.

Similarly, if the manager was asked to name the ones who are consistently failing—don't try hard enough, do not show initiative, are in the wrong job, do not learn and are a burden on the team— he or she would not have to think too hard.

Good managerial judgement should not be blindly replaced with tools just because there is fear of bias among a few. On the other hand managers must be trained in the art and science of assessment and invited to sit on skip level panels for such assessment and selection purposes.

Integrating Assessment and Development Needs

When organisations start planning developmental interventions for the ones they have chosen through a rather elaborate assessment process, they are often confronted with the peculiar problem. The assessment data may not lend itself easily to developmental actions. The debrief done at the time of assessment is often not adequate for use in development and finally, those tasked with designing developmental interventions also find the need for additional or different assessment data.

In fact, we often encounter a certain level of assessment fatigue among senior executives who experience too much assessment and too little support. Also, when assessment data is not handled with sensitivity it can lead to snap judgements and labelling of the executive.

Many organisations struggle to balance between the need for competence and the need for acceptance. The ability to see each executive as a complete and unique person with a combination of abilities and limitations is sometimes missing.

There are also times when assessment may not even be necessary. Assessment of leaders against competencies which are alien to them or are new and represent a new ask are best avoided when a certain assessment outcome is obvious; it may be prudent not to pursue it. Organisations can instead spend that time and money to develop their leaders. Of course, assessment after imparting the inputs to see if they have started demonstrating actions at the workplace is certainly welcome.

HR practitioners can often be so caught up in the activity end of these complex projects that they may fail to pay attention to these nuances and challenges.

Matching Supply with Demand

Organisations often encounter other challenges with the process of identifying their so-called HIPOs and top talent.

Organisations are not sure if they need to make the list public or keep it private. Whether public or private, the actions of the organisations eventually indicate that they are special and that ends up creating all the associated concerns of 'managing aspirations' for this group.

In times of muted business growth, organisations do find themselves with a larger list of employees with potential than they really need or can manage.

To make matters worse, when organisations invest in the development of this group by exposing them to a range of developmental experiences, the expectations of a big break thereafter can only grow larger.

The nature of messaging that organisations adopt, the meaning they convey to those on the list and the actions that they take are all crucial in the process of matching supply with demand.

Championing Development

Marrying what the organisation needs with what they have and then making plans for the chosen individuals and the organisation is a rather complex and dynamic task.

The task becomes even more complex given that organisations wish to build consensus around the choices that they have made about individuals and want to ensure wider acceptance and mobility.

This need has given birth to the creation of talent councils within organisations. In fact, organisations have such councils at multiple levels depending on how far deep into the organisation they choose to implement the process.

HR leaders are responsible for creating these forums, convening them, collating the information necessary for these forums to discuss, crafting the agenda for the forum and of course following up on the actions agreed to in such forums.

By design, talent councils are expected to review the recommendations about those nominated as talent, review the needs for talent across the organisation and against that discuss development plans to help the person realise his potential and fulfil organisational needs.

The talent council members themselves end up releasing or receiving executives and that has consequences.

Making all of this work is an onerous but important task for the HR practitioner.

Given that the talent council members are also the sponsors of talent, there are a few critical expectations from them in their role as leaders and council members. These are also often the roadblocks to the process of championing development.

Managing Release

At the heart of an organisation's ability to grow leaders from within is its deeply held conviction and value that talent belongs to the organisation and not to the manager, that managers cannot hoard talented people. This has to be translated into affirmative policy and programmes by the council and cannot be a mere wish statement.

Whether leaders and managers will release or not release their team members depends on how well this belief is translated into action and how much the council members walk their talk. It is well recognised that release always leads to disruption for the releasing manager and most managers do not like disruption and will therefore resist release.

Should release be managed through use of force or should it be managed through social processes of alignment to purpose, dialogue and recognition is often a dilemma. Under compelling circumstances, mandates and force might be necessary but the dialogue process needs to keep happening within the councils to foster sustainable ownership.

Nobody Is Ready

One of the stark realities of growing leaders from within in today's environment is that nobody internally is ever completely ready for a job. Even the best employees will never be plug and play. There is always an element of risk and developmental headroom. The paradoxical situation seems to be that the very same leaders who were beneficiaries of others placing bets on them, hesitate to perpetuate the virtuous cycle of placing bets on the people that are identified. The talent council has a special role in encouraging their teams to take bets and often lead by example on this.

Overvaluing External Hires

The odds are typically stacked against internal talent as compared to external hires for the simple reason that organisations know a lot more about our internal talent and don't think too well about what they know. On the other hand, organisations know so little about external hires from the brief interviews they do but out of anxiety and hope ascribe a lot more to them than they deserve.

Talent councils do engage in deep discussions about external hires and ask themselves if they are taking risks with internal candidates. Obviously, organisations will need to strike a balance between upholding growth from within and finding the right person. It is only recommended that other things being equal, internal candidates must be given a better score.

Making Talent Fungible

Meeting our needs from within requires that our talent must be somewhat fungible across functional and other boundaries. In other words, unless a talented person can be utilised in multiple areas he or she will never be an organisational resource. This will call for people to be trained to work across functions. Organisations may need to avoid the tendency of making jobs so super specialised that no one can fit into them easily unless found from outside. This is where career paths and lattices will become critical.

Another factor that promotes growth from within is the ability of individuals to broaden their perspectives and worldviews. This includes the ability to respect other functions and other points of view, adjust to other styles, be able to work with diverse people and so on. This happens only when the individual gets to work with different people and is not stuck with one person for too long a time.

Ensuring that chosen executives use the career lattice to navigate the organisational network rapidly does make a difference.

Talent councils often review policies of job rotation and see if they are rotating employees well enough to produce well-rounded leaders.

Making Time for Conversations and Interactions

Talent council members like members of the board are effective, only when they go beyond the dossiers submitted to them and develop a first-hand understanding of the people considered valuable. They may be required to find the time and the motivation to meet, engage and understand them well.

Beyond all this is the delicate task of ensuing that there are candid and constructive conversations in these forums. Organisations that are designed to function in silos and have fostered a culture of competition among divisions and functions find it an onerous task to get their leaders to wear the organisational hat and discuss people dispassionately and even selflessly. However, the more organisations discuss their people, the more intimately they understand them and the less they need to rely on assessments for this purpose.

Closing Reflections

What view organisations take about management and leadership will in many ways influence what they look for and value. If they look for the predictable, they will get predictable results. When they look for stretch they will create stretch, look for the essential few and there will be focus.

That organisations must form judgements is well understood. However, such judgements must result in clarity and empowerment and not leave everyone overwhelmed. Organisations must trust managers to judge and not undervalue their ability to judge.

The senior-most leaders may need to champion the developmental process by playing the role of selfless senior citizens. The intent of these seniors must be to understand employees better so they know what they can do to develop them. Such understanding will always call for assessment data but here again assessment needs to promote self-awareness and be empowering and affirming.

It must be conceded that the process is anything but mechanistic. When the aspirations of employees begin to be channelised, organisations stand to gain. Such channelising includes the effort of holding the mirror of reality in front of employees—the reality of the business as well as the reality of who they are. All of this calls for courage, conviction and of course a lot of influencing.

Organisational Experiences

Airtel's Experience with Talent Councils

In a tight talent market, succession planning becomes a core part of any organisation's workforce management and development plan. Building a pipeline of talent ready to take on progressively greater responsibility and leadership in an organisation is key to driving success, especially in the constantly evolving telecommunications market.

Airtel believes in building a strong 'bench of talent'. Talent councils as a talent management process provide business leaders a platform to discuss talent profiles and information, agree who the high-potential employees are, facilitate a collective understanding of the employee strengths and create essential development plans.

Talent councils are helping Airtel leaders to create a visibility of talent across functions and levels, identify talent across lines of business and ensure that the high potential talent gets an equal chance to grow.

Talent councils ensure that a standard 'one view' of talent is created among all leaders. On an average, each of the senior leaders (numbering about 400) are spending at least 5–7 man-days in a year on talent development through the talent council framework, besides their one-on-one time with their teams. Talent councils are used as a way of reviewing against organisational talent requirements of today and future and creating a high potential workforce ready for the future.

Key points of discussion in a talent council include:

- Performance and potential
- Next roles for HIPO talent

- Development plan for the future
- Succession for critical roles
- Way forward for people who have hit the ceiling and are weak performers

Talent Councils Levels and Framework

Airtel's telecom operations in India are conducted by 22 circles. Talent councils operate even at the circle level. The bands in Airtel are (in the ascending order of seniority): F, 1, 2, 3 and SVP+.

The hierarchy of the council framework is:

Circle Council ———▶ Functional ———▶ Cross Functional ———▶ AMB Council
and below   Council B3 +   Council B3 +   B2 All SVP +
employees   Circle EC   Circle EC ready   top 100
                               ready for next   for next role   leaders
                               role talent   talent

(Note: Circle EC is Circle Executive Committee; AMB is Airtel Management Board; SVP is senior vice-president.)

Role of HR

HR is the process owner and facilitator of the process of talent councils (for nearly 7,000 people). HR ensures that holistic dialogues are captured on the system and all talent actions arising out of talent council discussions are implemented as per the action plan. These talent actions can be related to talent development, succession planning, career progression, employee engagement and retention and ensuring that an internal talent pipeline is created within Airtel.

The Talent Forum Framework and How It Works in HUL

People and brands are at the heart of what we do in HUL. Both of these are assets that will leave a lasting impact on organisations and consumers respectively and yet with the fast moving, VUCA (volatility, uncertainty, complexity and ambiguity) world we live in, we need to constantly reinvent how HR helps managers manage their people and their careers to enable them to be their best and in turn, give their best to the organisation.

Our talent philosophy is not new, but it has definitely taken on a whole new meaning, in today's world. Our focus has always been on building robust talent pipelines and early identification of potential towards that pursuit. Even though we exist in a matrixed and multistructural global organisation, we have always taken an enterprise view of talent over time to ensure right people, right roles and right opportunities are made available. This ownership of individuals and talent, their growth and development is in built within the organisation and has been one of the success story for the HR function.

The intent is to create an environment where everyone can be at their best thereby unleashing the capacity of all our employees. The talent forum is the forum which identifies the 'Big Bets' and 'promotable talent' while also focusing on every individual's development support.

Every function/business category has its own talent forum which comprises of the functional head/category head and the team of directors reporting into that role. This talent forum hence has direct oversight of all managers in its structure.

The talent forum meets formally once a year to review the performance, potential and development plans for every manager in its purview. The following are the highlights of the talent forums:

1. A qualitative discussion on the people takes place.
2. Based on the information compiled about their performance track record, assessment of potential and the multi-source feedback results are formulated.

3. The forum would have each individual's line manager/ skip line manager, so they have directly seen the work of the individuals.

4. Due to matrix structure in the organisation, it is normal to have more than a couple of managers in the forum who are familiar about an individual's contribution and style of operation. For every individual discussed at least three people in the forum can add value, including the HR partner, who also is expected to have a point of view on every person.

5. Hence, when individuals are discussed, there is a healthy challenge/discussion in which all those who are knowledgeable about the individual participate in a meaningful fashion.

The output of each talent forum is consolidated by the HR partner and the promotion recommendations or the development programme nominations are taken up for next level review/action.

The management committee (MC) of the company acts as the apex talent forum for the enterprise level and discusses the senior-level managers, who are the members of the individual functional/business category talent forums. They also review and approve the recommendations of each of the talent forums.

Apart from the decisions about the promotions and placement of big bets on a few individuals, the talent forum focuses a lot of its attention on the status of capability in the function/business and the action steps required to be taken to keep it in sync with the emerging needs and expectations. More important is the pre- and post-forum engagement with the people.

The enabling culture is key in making the process of talent review and development effective. Lot of emphasis and time is spent on capability building of line leaders and HR organisation for having development conversations, giving authentic feedback, assuring confidentiality, managing perceptions/prejudices and so on. HR plays a key role in this regard. Also, leaders and line managers understand the importance of this and do this quite well in the organisation.

16

Developing Managers and Leaders

Three critical ingredients make the subject of leader development eternally captivating and intriguing.

This is one subject about which the most has been written and said, and yet it appears each day that the last word has not been written and said. The field lends itself to multiple interpretations, possibilities, ideas and of course research. Thought leadership is at its best in this field.

This is one subject that seems to be keeping business leaders, boards and promoters of businesses awake at night more than any other. There is overwhelming agreement that the lack of availability of competent leaders can singularly impact the ability of any organisation to grow and perform.

This is one field where the demands from the environment seem to be ever increasing, making the task onerous even for the most accomplished. The rules of success, the styles and slants needed to make a difference seem to be dynamic and ever changing. The change is enormous here.

Given this context, HR leaders and professionals have always felt privileged to be looked up to for support and contribution in the area of leader development. They have attempted to develop an accurate understanding of how leaders are best developed and then used that understanding to design and implement programmes and solutions that can in the most predictable manner contribute to developing leaders. However, the task has been anything but easy.

HR professionals are required to find answers to several difficult questions and grapple with several dilemmas and decision points when it comes to conceptualising, designing and implementing leader development solutions. Most importantly, they are expected to ensure the best possible returns for the fairly generous investments that organisations are today willing to make towards leader development. Learning and leadership development professionals who can find the right answers and navigate these dilemmas and make the right choices end up doing what is right for their organisations.

In this chapter, we would like to step into the shoes of these learning and leadership development professionals and articulate some of their questions and dilemmas and present our views and perspectives.

Who Should Own the Process?

One of us was invited by a very reputed conglomerate to evaluate their current approach to leader development and suggest changes to the same.

Instead of looking at what was wrong, the consultant looked at what was working. He had detailed conversations with all the MDs in the conglomerate to understand their journey of growing as leaders within the group to see if there was any insight, a pattern, maybe.

What emerged from these conversations was extremely interesting. There seemed to be several commonalities in the manner in which all these leaders were groomed for leadership.

First, someone senior spotted this person as one with potential. This person responded by showing the initiative and the willingness to take on more.

The second step was that this person was offered the opportunity to move to another function for a specific opportunity and the person took on the invitation.

This is when the person got that big career break—a higher position in the same business or a new business or an important and mission-critical project. This came with the comfort and assurance of being supported to make it a success.

On the back of this big break came one or more job changes which brought with it high visibility within the group at the top management level. The person was now clearly seen as a group resource of significant value, winning the trust and confidence of the promoters and other seniors.

At this stage, the group was willing to make significant investments in the person's executive education and development to add skills, perspectives and stature.

From here on the person had clearly established himself as a trusted leader in the group.

Clearly, the ingredients appeared to be the presence of one or more sponsors who spotted and took bets, the willingness of the individual to take on the challenges, the exposure to some real job challenges, the visibility among key decision-makers and then of course the exposure to formal developmental inputs.

To convert what appears to be a very natural, organic, long-drawn grooming process into an institutionalised process that can be championed by the HR function is certainly a huge challenge.

The biggest challenge for leadership development professionals is this: They would like leaders to own the process of grooming future leaders and champion it. At the same time, they would like fairness, transparency and a certain process that drives it. In leaning towards a process, they recognise that they might rob the leaders of the ownership but by not having one they fear that it might be subjective.

Successful leadership development practitioners manage to find the right balance between keeping it naturally occurring with a high dose of business ownership and supporting it with the right deliberate processes.

They work to ensure that the organisation and its top management have the culture of being concerned about the quality of its managerial and leadership talent. They implement the right processes and establish the right forums but let the businesses drive it.

What Should Be the Scope of Leader Development?

As long as the development of leaders is viewed as event-based, leader development too logically belongs to the learning function.

With the subject of leader development, including the process of identification of leadership talent and the grooming process, being seen as distinct, calling for specific focus, attention and effort, we are beginning to see more and more organisations separating these two.

If there are talent managers, they are assigned the responsibility of managing leader development. In other organisations, senior HRBPs are called upon to champion the process.

While separating leader development from learning makes sense, its scope needs to be expanded to include all aspects of developing managerial and leadership capabilities across levels including functional and behavioural abilities to enhance role effectiveness as well as prepare for future needs. This includes putting in place a range of developmental programmes, experiences and the establishment of career ladders and paths.

The scope of leader development needs to include the development of managerial abilities. The subject of developing good managers has seldom received the attention it deserves. Yet, most of us attribute all problems in the organisation to poor managerial abilities. Be it task management or people management or business management or relationship management, we continue to see that some of the most common coaching needs of senior leaders continues to revolve around managerial skills and abilities. This may be called the problem of missed developmental milestones. A person misses to learn what he should have learnt as an assistant manager and waits until he becomes a vice-president to learn the same on an urgent basis.

It is for this reason that many organisations have well designed programmes for each level of management so that those entering the level are duly prepared to succeed in that level. As leader development professionals pay attention to all aspects of leader development, they will partner with the learning team to design and deliver specific class room learning events and interventions to address such needs.

There is one other question around the scope that needs addressing: Should leader development always focus on preparing individuals for the future or should it also focus on current role effectiveness? Well, all developmental investments are for two purposes: to solve problems of today and to leverage potential for tomorrow.

One of the biggest follies of current leader development pro-grammes is that it positions these programmes as intended to develop leaders for tomorrow. This has two unintended conse-quences. First, executives begin to believe that they have nothing to learn for their present positions. Second, they believe that as soon as the learning process is complete there must be an open position waiting for them. Neither of these two assumptions are true.

Given the new demands being placed on businesses every single day, it is hard for any leader to believe that he or she is completely sorted out for the current position. Even the best of leaders have a lot of headroom left to learn, to be effective in what they are doing today. Learning practitioners and sponsors who fail to make this clear will end up compromising the leaders' motivation to learn.

Similarly, it is hard to promise that every individual who learns will be rewarded with an open and challenging position immediately. For this reason, it is always risky to promise something as a guaranteed future because that future itself may be fuzzy.

On the other hand, it would be necessary to ensure that leaders are certainly challenged on the job with the right kind of experiences and assignments so that they are able to develop themselves adequately. This is a fair thing to expect.

How Do Leaders Develop?

Do leader development professionals clearly understand how leaders develop?

The Center for Creative Leadership (CCL)[1] gives us outstanding insights into this subject.

According to CCL, all experiences that a leader goes through are not developmental in nature. For example, the first year in a new job is more developmental than the fifth or sixth year. CCL has concluded that for any experience to be developmental it must contain three essential ingredients. They are:

1. Assessment: Data about oneself that promotes self-awareness and helps one know where one stands against certain benchmarks and standards and forwards actions.
2. Challenge: Experiences that throw a person out of one's comfort zone and forces one to learn new skills, develop new perspectives and abandon old ways and approaches.
3. Support: That serves to make the challenge enabling by providing a sense of assurance and safety.

CCL has outlined six developmental experiences as being most powerful in developing leaders. Three of these are formal and three are naturally occurring:

---

[1] Ellen Van Velsor, Cynthia D. McCauley, and Marian N. Ruderman, *The Center for Creative Leadership Handbook of Leadership Development* (Chichester: Jossey Bass Wiley, 2010).

Formal developmental experiences include 360-degree feedback, feedback-intensive programmes and coaching relationships.

Naturally occurring developmental experiences include job assignments, developmental relationships and hardships.

This in many ways also aligns with 70:20:10 principle to learning that learning professionals swear by.

Essentially, leader development is a slow and life-long process, something which takes time. It is also evident that most of the effective developmental experiences are integrated with not just work but also life.

Unless leader development professionals understand the science of developmental experiences, they may end up engaging their learners in a variety of activities hoping that they will lead to development.

A little later in this chapter some of these developmental experiences and what it takes to make them effective will be explored.

How to Create Development Plans That Work?

Most leader development practitioners will insist that every single leader has an individual development plan (IDP) in place. This is intended to serve as the basis for all learning investments and is meant to convert the assessment data into tangible outcomes.

While the practice of creating a development plan is excellent, the process is quite often ineffective. First, there needs to be clarity on who will have the developmental conversation and craft the development plan. Second is the clarity on how it should be done. Third is about who owns the implementation.

Here, it must be clarified that the process of creating a sound development plan is a fairly specialised skill and does not come so easily to any manager. The support of external coaches or internally trained coaches or HR practitioners who understand the art and science of creating sound development plans through great developmental conversations may be required.

Second, we sometimes observe a huge gap between the people who implement the assessment processes and the ones who support the leader in development. The ones who conduct these assessments, the debrief, the development planning and the subsequent hand-holding in implementing the development plan need to be well integrated to avoid gaps and doubts in the minds of the leader.

Like many HR processes, the IDP process often degenerates into a form-filling exercise. Unfortunately, leader development is anything but form filling. It is about conversations, reflections and actions. Leader development professionals may need to recognise that the process is dynamic, iterative and evolving and must aid development rather than result in a form being filled.

One of the fundamental assumptions of a sound development-planning process is that it is done in partnership between the leader who is developing and a person skilled in the process who is helping the leader. It is also assumed that the partnership lasts until the goals of development are accomplished. In that sense, the process and steps are conversation enablers and not columns to be filled.

What Developmental Experiences Matter?

Let's now pay attention to some of the most powerful developmental experiences and see how leader development professionals make the best use of them.

Leveraging Assessment Data

Often employees may have difficulties in understanding or even accepting the outcomes of the assessments that have been done. When the manager, the coach or HR partner uses a range of coaching skills to help the employee come to terms with the assessments and uses those as a basis for development planning, it really helps.

Executives also need help in challenging themselves, their current ways of thinking, current behaviours, current perspectives so that they are able to discover why they are where they are. For example, if somebody's ability to influence the system is poor the report will merely say that it is a development need. However, leaders need to discover why it is so. They need to discover which aspect of their behaviour, thinking and personality and what lack of information is inhibiting their ability to influence the system. Without understanding the root cause, it would not be prudent to make a development plan. Once people are able to identify what is holding them back they are likely to be in a better position to determine what needs change.

The assessment reports throw up several areas for development. It is not possible for the individual to work on all those areas. It is also not necessary to work on all of them at once. Ideally, having identified the root causes the employee can carefully select one or two specific areas that if managed will give maximum benefit and result in the greatest pay off. Development plans which promise to serve several development needs are quite often ineffective. An IDP put through a careful filter and which has a laser sharp focus is far more effective. One well-chosen area for development is often wise choice.

Executive Coaching as a Developmental Intervention

The field of leader development has made rapid advances in its understanding of how leaders develop and its approaches to make such development happen. The role of one's personality, strengths, preferences, beliefs and the very personal nature of effort involved in becoming an effective leader is now being increasingly recognised.

Given this recognition, executive coaching which is a very personal, humanistic, result-oriented and one-to-one developmental experience has become a very central and integral part of all leader development interventions.

Presented here in the form of a fictitious (but very common) case is the approach that Ajit, a management and leadership development professional, adopts to get the best out of coaching and embed coaching as an integral part of his leader development interventions.

Validates the Coaching Need

Ajit recognises that coaching is not a silver bullet and cannot cure all organisational problems. When there is request for coaching, Ajit puts the request through a few simple filters:

1. Is the focus on empowering that executive to realise his potential?
2. Is it to help the executive develop an important skill, perspective, a style or a certain way of thinking?
3. Does it pertain to the person and is not systemic or organisational in nature?
4. Is it a precursor to deciding whether the employee should stay or leave?
5. Are we looking for solutions and quick answers through coaching?

Ensures Sponsorship

Ajit understands the importance of an active executive sponsor for the engagement. He also knows that his role is a lot more than finding a coach and approving the payment or providing some cursory support. He ensures that the immediate manager supports the engagement as a sponsor and holds the boundary of the business need and constantly validates and confirms that the business need is being met. He gets him to articulate his expectations from the coaching engagement and more importantly support the coachee as he attempts to apply learning and practise new behaviours. In effect, while the coach is engaging in an external developmental relationship, the sponsor engages in an internal developmental relationship too.

Ensures Coachee Readiness and Motivation

Ajit knows that the coachee's motivation is the single biggest contributor to the success of the helping relationship. To this end, he has positioned coaching as completely voluntary. He requests the coachee to clearly articulate a compelling need that he would like to fulfil through coaching. He informs the coachee that he must be willing to be challenged through feedback and gain insights. He also ensures that the coachee's current job context should give him the mind space to make such a time investment.

Empanels Coaches

Ajit has empanelled a coach provider as his partner for the process. He also uses an independent panel of senior coaches for certain needs.

Ajit applies a clear set of criteria in making the choice. He checks to see if the values of the coach or the institution are aligned to the principles of a sound helping relationship which is about being non-directive, non-judgemental and about creating a safe space for the coachee to engage with the coach. He attempts to understand the approach that the coach will take to run the engagement, the mechanism that the coach has in place to assure quality and the ethical boundary that the coach will uphold.

Matches the Coachee with the Right Coach

Ajit takes the time to ensure compatibility in a coaching relationship. He looks for perspectives and points of view that the coachee needs and to that extent values diversity while ensuring that the coach understands the coachee's context.

He leaves the final choice to the coachee and in fact gives him the opportunity to meet at least two coaches and then take a final decision on who he would like to work with.

He also personally gives the coaches a good briefing about the business, the context and the needs of the executive as understood by him.

Monitors Key Milestones Without Intruding

Ajit understands the place of confidentiality in a coaching context. He recognises that the purpose of confidentiality is to create a safe space where the coachee can freely discuss his situation, issues and concerns without being judged or having fear of consequences. To that extent, he never seeks any details that are discussed within the coaching setting.

However, he ensures that the coachee's manager and others, including himself, have visibility into certain key milestones of the engagement to ensure progress is happening. Some of the key checkpoints he looks for are:

1. Has the coach obtained adequate assessment data about the coachee to zero in on areas needing attention?
2. Has the coachee arrived at concrete coaching goals and the same been shared with the sponsor?
3. Have the goals been translated into specific action plans?
4. Have the action plans been converted into tangible results on the ground?

On occasions, he does intervene when there is reluctance, lack of sponsor support or the coach is struggling for lack of some additional insights. Ajit has learnt to play a very nuanced role in leveraging coaching to help his leaders realise their potential without intruding but also not taking a hands-off stance.

Mentoring as a Developmental Intervention

Mentoring is usually described as 'the relationship between a senior and more junior member of an organisation directed towards the advancement and support of the junior member'. It is a long-term relationship (either formal or informal) associated with the provision of support, guidance and 'passing on of wisdom'.

Mentoring can be a very impactful leadership development enabler when seniors choose to give their time for promising leaders across levels.

The challenge with mentoring is its very nature. Mentoring by definition is a naturally occurring process. It works best when a protégé voluntarily chooses his or her mentor and engages with that person on an open ended basis.

Given this reality, attempts to formalise it are fraught with challenges.

When HR practitioners launch formal mentoring programmes, pair up mentors with mentees and mandate that they log in meeting dates and report progress, the programmes just does not take off. Mentees would like to see mentoring as a support when required rather than as a procedure they need to follow. Similarly, many leaders may have professional credentials but not the skills or the inclination for mentoring.

The best programmes are the ones that create a market place for protégés to be able to meet mentors and then choose the ones they wish to work with and then work with them as long as they see a need and for needs that they find important.

Having said so, there are specific contexts in which offering a helping relationship is beneficial.

These contexts include socialising new entrants in a system that finds it hard to accept outsiders, helping promotees get to understand the demands of the new role, helping individuals gain technical expertise from a skilled senior and so on.

Even here, making available the opportunities and then leaving it to the individuals to leverage them as needed is far more effective. The focus is on making the support available rather than on insisting that the same is utilised.

Making Available Job Experiences and Assignments

As is evident from the 70:20:10 principle, it is the job itself that offers the best developmental experiences when carefully set up.

Such experiences and assignments tend to take many forms.

While job rotations is one of the most traditional methods of offering select individuals a range of diverse experiences, there are several other ways in which those with potential are exposed to rich developmental experiences on the job.

There are several things that organisations do in a spontaneous or planned manner to give their talented employees exposure. Here are a few popular ones:

1. Handling a mission critical project
2. Being a part of a cross functional task force
3. Leading a consulting project, working with a global consulting company
4. Setting up a new project, facility or business division
5. Working in a new geography or business division
6. Solving a difficult problem or a difficult situation to clean things up
7. Working as an executive assistant to a very senior executive leader
8. Working in an entirely different function, as a full-time resource
9. Working on a transformational agenda for the organisation
10. Deputed to a key business partner/vendor organisation

Closing Reflections

Despite all the research and insights, the task of developing leaders and managers continues to be challenging. However, when the process is owned by sponsoring managers and the needs are well defined and the developmental experiences are well thought through, effectiveness is experienced.

Organisational Experiences

The Seven-step Leadership Pipeline @ L&T

L&T has a well-established seven-step process for creating a leadership pipeline. The thrust is on facilitating the transformation of engineer-managers into leaders and leaders into 'corporate entrepreneurs'. The strategy is to create a pool of leaders who can envision, inspire and successfully deploy global growth strategies, thus creating a result-oriented culture of multiplying value. This is to cater to the talent needs of the company. L&T is amongst the fastest growing infrastructure companies in the world. Talent management is its no. 1 strategic priority to be in step with the ambitious growth plans articulated in its five-year strategic plan.

Each step of the Seven-Step Leadership Development Process is bespoke to equip managers at various levels, with the required knowledge, skill and mindsets to transition seamlessly to the next level of leadership and global entrepreneurship.

Step 1 begins with a Management Education Programme conducted by IIM Ahmedabad. Young managers in their late twenties and early thirties are identified, and they go through a two-year executive education programme at the institute to instil in them a holistic management perspective. The participants are HIPO managers, excellent in execution skills or domain expertise, but may require basic management education. The programme has been designed on the lines of a post-graduate executive management education programme to provide these future leaders with a broad spectrum, strong foundation in strategic management and leadership.

Step 2 is a programme in which potential leaders are groomed in 'leadership', through a Leadership Development

Programme. Leadership is all about demonstrated leadership behaviours. The focus of this programme is to enable leaders to discover their own leadership style and concentrate on behaviours that reward them with respect, rather than relying only on knowledge and skills. The participants are high performers handling medium-sized projects or roles, for example, in a business unit for high-rise residential projects, hydrocarbon projects in the Middle East or challenging city metro projects. They are young high achievers in their own right, but this intense programme takes them to the next level of leadership. The programme is designed for various leadership archetypes, to groom them into mega project directors, functional leaders and business leaders.

Global Leadership Development Programme, which is Step 3, covers globalisation from the perspective of finance, strategy, human resources, leadership and entrepreneurship and is conducted in collaboration with the Stephan M. Ross School of Business, University of Michigan. Identified leaders, who already head projects in India or the Middle East in functional or domain roles and have an experience profile of around 20 years, go through Step 3.

Step 4 is the Transforming L&T into a Global Corporation programme conducted by INSEAD for top management executives covering global strategic thinking, global economy, M&A, risk management, driving change and building a leadership agenda. Business leaders, who head businesses or major mega projects in the various businesses of L&T, or functional heads, with an experience profile of about 25 years, go through this programme that challenges mindsets, builds competencies and capabilities that are required in a global corporation.

Step 5 is the Global CEOs Programme, conducted by professors from Harvard Business School and is for those in leadership positions. This powerful programme covers business model innovation, strategies for globalisation, organisational leadership and personal leadership. The participants are business heads or emerging chief executives (with large profit and loss [P&L] responsibilities) of businesses in India or overseas.

In Step 6, which is the programme of International Executive Education, senior leaders are nominated for Advanced Management Programmes offered by globally renowned business schools such as INSEAD, Wharton, Harvard, International Institute for Management Development (IMD), London Business School, Darden School of Business and the like.

As a part of leadership development at the top echelons of the organisation, a structured and systematic approach to mentoring has been initiated as Step 7, which is known as Mentoring. The Chairman and MD–CEO mentor 'hand-picked' future leaders to prepare them for senior leadership positions.

Chairman Mr A. M. Naik initially started mentoring four leaders in 2008 and has today mentored more than 50 leaders who are either on the board and/or are heading businesses. The chairman is now focusing on mentoring young emerging leaders about 35 years of age for the next level of leadership. The focus is to equip them with the skills, competencies and strengths of character to steer the company through future challenges. Personalised development discussions of about one-hour duration are organised as a part of the mentoring agenda. These discussions are video recorded and shared with the mentee, so that they can reflect on the conversation. Specific action points are identified and reviewed by him in every meeting to monitor their development journey.

From Steps 1 to 7, each step addresses select executives at various levels in the leadership pipeline. The programmes are designed with the best, internationally ranked institutions to provide inputs on innovation-based strategies, finance, integrated business models which provide relevant and holistic inputs appropriate to each step in a progressive manner.

In addition to the seven steps, bespoke functional leadership programmes for boosting up the competencies of the CoEs are conducted. One example is the Strategic Finance Leadership Programme, which was conducted in association with Wharton School of the University of Pennsylvania to develop carefully identified finance and accounts leaders into effective strategic business partners. The intensive two-modular programme along with an action learning project focused on experiential learning aimed at honing their business, strategic and behavioural competencies.

Building a Developmental Culture @ Aditya Birla Group

ABG has been a story of sustained growth and sustained success. Over the past two decades, the group has grown 20 times in its revenues and today the market capitalisation stands at USD 50 billion. This exponential growth has been possible due to the leaders developing at a fast pace and driving the businesses at the speed of change. This journey of the past two decades has seen many a transformation and none bigger than the HR transformation. Starting with establishing of Gyanodaya as a global centre for leadership learning 17 years back, to initiating the talent management process more than a decade back, the group has embarked on many contemporary HR initiatives. With dozens of such initiatives behind it, it's no wonder that the ABG is seen as a best employer and a top company for leaders.

To further build on this, the group embarked upon a journey of creating a development culture across the group as a part of its HR 2020 strategy.

The Foundation: My Development in My Hand

The foundation of creating a development culture in the group was put in 2011 by implementation of My Development Plan (MDP) that each of the management employee creates. The inputs to the MDP comes from varied sources: the manager's feedback, employees' own aspirations as well as organisation-conducted assessments and so on. Today, more than 95 per cent of ABG employees in management cadre have a documented MDP on the Human Resource Information System (HRIS). Employees do feel that development, indeed, is in her/his hands at ABG.

Culture Built Top-down

We started on this journey by introducing a transition coaching process for our senior-most leaders. So far about 25 per cent of our senior leaders have been through this transition process supported by external executive coaches. As these leaders are being coached, they are also imbibing the characteristics of being a coach. Soon we will be embarking on the next phase of this journey—creating certified ABG coaches who in turn will formally coach the future and emerging leaders of the group.

We have also created a rhythm of talent councils in each of our Indian as well as global businesses. The senior leaders of the businesses as well as of different units come together to discuss the talent within the business, their destination roles as well as the development journeys. In any given month, hundreds of such discussions are being held by senior leaders of the group with the identified talent, creating a development mindset in them.

At the group level, we have created different kinds of functional talent councils. In a functional talent council, the functional leaders of different businesses come together and discuss that function's talent in each business, their development journey as well as their future roles. In order to accelerate the development of employees, these functional leaders act as the mentors for them. These talent discussions as well as the mentoring interactions help these senior leaders create an environment for development within the group.

Leaders are actively engaged with learning programmes at Gyanodaya. As leaders-in-residence, they act as co-facilitators with the external faculty to contextualise the learning to the real workplace. As steering committee members in key learning programmes, leaders mentor and review the learning application of the participants over a longer period of time.

Conversations That Count, Employee by Employee

One of the senior-most business directors at ABG said, 'Coaching happens in every moment that a manager meets the employee, every interaction is a mentoring opportunity'. Through the six-month process that starts with a two-day workshop called CTC (conversations that count), we are teaching all the managers across the group, the foundations of coaching. So far we have covered more than 2,500 mid- to senior-level managers through these workshops and sub-sequently sustained the learnings of the workshop through a series of tech-based activities. Participants as well their managers have come back sharing that this has helped them in having good developmental conversations in their teams.

Impact: Higher Score on Learning and Development and a Higher Score on Engagement

ABG conducts Team Vibes Survey, a development tool for managers, on a regular basis. According to the recently concluded survey, over the past two years the score on L&D for the group has gone up by 7 per cent and the overall engagement score has gone up by 8 per cent. Neither was Rome built in a day and nor will we create a development culture at ABG overnight. However, the scores like the aforementioned do give us reassurance that we are on the right journey.

HR HERE AND NOW

THE MAKING OF THE QUINTESSENTIAL
PEOPLE CHAMPION

PART 5
Making the Organisation
Effective

17
Leading Change

For all of us as human beings, being *effective* in our lives is the ultimate goal. Personal effectiveness includes many dimensions such as physical, emotional, social and spiritual effectiveness. It is about achieving our fullest potential and being all that we are capable of. At a more basic level, it is about coping effectively with the environmental stress and pressures while still upholding commitment to our larger purpose.

Similarly, for organisations, effectiveness is about going beyond the mere pursuit of profit and realising its full potential and fulfilling the expectations of all its constituents by doing it in the most socially responsible, commercially ethical and environmentally friendly way. Like in our personal lives, organisational effectiveness most certainly calls for quite a bit of planned change and, in more recent times, the ability to manage a large amount of unplanned change.

Over the last hundred years, the world has been subjected to a lot of change. Initially at a slower pace and then at a faster pace and now at breakneck speed. In the realm of organisations, these changes have been across different dimensions. Initially, it was about new products that were developed and were in great demand, hence the need to plan and organise for mass production. Later, it was about how to improve productivity in the factories, and then it was about managing the costs associated with the production and distribution of the products so that they become more affordable leading to increased sales as well as improved profits. Then came quality improvement techniques which tried to leverage human capability in the pursuit of efficiencies, then the advent of computers first in our offices and then soon after in our factories and marketplaces. The globalisation and boundary-less nature of our markets have brought their own changes in the way businesses have been organised and managed. The Internet has changed the way all of us access knowledge, share information, buy products and deliver services.

The change agenda within organisations today is on an accelerated path. In fact, there are too many things being changed all at the same time and all of which are projected as key to the organisation's vision and future.

Organisations that have made a name for themselves in the management of change are the ones that have not just survived but thrived in this context of continuous change by mastering the art and science of change management. Many have perfected it to the extent their approaches to Change has been marketed as models for other to follow.

General Electric (GE) company's change acceleration process (CAP) model is a generic benchmark for change management.

According to the CAP model and other such models of change, it is quite clear that for change to be successful it has to be assiduously planned and implemented and not allowed to just happen. Hence, the need for specialist knowledge and support to the CEO, the top team and other leaders of change in the organisation across levels.

Leading change has therefore become a core leadership competence for every leader, something that leaders are measured on. It is no longer the preserve of HR or OD professionals or external consultants alone to lead change or contribute to organisational effectiveness.

Having said so, there continues to be a crucial role for HR professionals in supporting and facilitating organisational change. Across many organisations, change as a subject matter is seen to fall within the purview of OD. Some organisations are beginning to value the need for OD as a specialisation and even consider in-house staffing of the OD role. Our research suggests that the role of such internal OD specialists is evolving. Many are right now assigning all large-scale HR projects of a transformational nature to the OD team if they have one.

Others are adding OD as an additional responsibility to one of the specialists within the HR team or to their HR business partners. Almost all of them are expecting mid- to senior-level HR professionals to have the skills in facilitating change. In many cases, there is an emerging element of change facilitation in every HR specialist's role, be it employee relations, L&D or corporate HR.

Therefore, OD work will not be restricted to 'OD professionals'. Business leaders, HR leaders, HRBPs, HR specialists from various disciplines and OD specialists, where they exist, will be called upon to contribute to organisational effectiveness by facilitating change.

Whatever might be the model, it would be useful to explore the contemporary role demands that are beginning to be placed on anyone charged with the responsibility of facilitating change.

The Emerging Role of HR and OD Professionals in Facilitating Change

Even as organisations are becoming far more global and far more complex, there is a growing realisation among its leaders that they need to go back to first principles to develop a much more contemporary and accurate understanding of individual, group and organisational behaviour (OB) to shape their systems, processes, policies and actions. There are at least seven areas where HR professionals (with OD capabilities) and OD consultants are being sought out and have been expected to make a significant contribution in recent times.

A Fresh Understanding of Human Motivation

The birth of the employee-engagement movement that organisations have been witnessing in the last two decades is bringing to the foreground the important role of human motivation in shaping organisational performance. Organisations are now convinced beyond doubt that the presence of motivational factors can shape successful organisations.

However, more and more organisations are seeing the need to go beyond buying engagement models off the shelf and developing a far more psychologically intelligent appreciation about how and why certain factors impact motivation and what they can do to shape it in their specific context.

Especially in India, organisations are perplexed by the fast-changing social and emotional fabric, the emerging demographics and the new sociotechnical challenges posed by the way they have designed jobs. They want to reconnect with different segments of their employees and understand what really motivates them. They are slowly beginning to realise that therein lies their effectiveness and sustenance.

Understanding How Leaders Develop

For years, good leaders were supposed to be functionally sound, strategically minded and simply great gifted men! However, there is an increasing recognition that the leader's emotional intelligence and style has a far greater and a more direct impact on the effectiveness of the team he leads. The increasing use of tools such as 360-degree feedback in addition to psychometric assessments, the extensive use of executive coaching and, most importantly, the focus on Emotional Quotient (EQ) in executive education programmes has firmly established the critical role that psychology plays in shaping leaders and leadership.

OD consultants are being called upon to understand how leaders actually develop and what contributes to their development. Their help is being sought in designing assessment programmes and deploying them to provide feedback to enable development.

Discovering What Drives Collaboration

Collaboration at the workplace is often seen as an interpersonal thing. In other words, it is believed that if people like one another they can then work with each other more effectively. Based on this understanding, organisations invest quite significantly in improving interpersonal relationships through a variety of training interventions often with limited results. Hence, OD consultants are being invited to support businesses in understanding the psychology behind certain elements of teamwork such as trust, openness, appreciation and interdependence and design interventions to strengthen the same, hopefully leading to better interpersonal relationships.

Designing the Organisation for Effectiveness

Concerns around performance and costs are driving more and more organisations to simplify their organisation structure, reduce layers, increase accountability and prevent the organisation from becoming heavier than it needs to be.

There is also a huge pressure on organisations to increase the productivity of employees and grow without adding headcount.

Shaping Organisational Culture

Organisations are recognising that the greatest source of competitive advantage comes from their culture. They see culture as the hardest-to-imitate secret weapon in their arsenal. It is their belief that what differentiates two organisations doing similar things is not resources, technology or other tangible factors—it is the way these organisations go about doing things that might really set them apart.

They are turning to OD and HR professionals to help them in retaining certain aspects of their culture which give them the competitive advantage or embracing certain new aspects of culture currently alien to them, to give them the new edge that they are looking for.

Cultural Integration

Most M&As, global hiring, joint ventures, alliances and partnerships have either failed or succeeded not because of the quality of the deal or the intellectual property (IP) but because of the manner in which they have addressed the cultural integration in a seamless and sustainable fashion.

Hence, organisations are paying a lot more attention to the cultural integration of businesses, organisations and people to enhance the chances of what on paper looks like a great opportunity to actually come together and become a successful merged entity.

In fact, in a number of M&As as well JV instances, business leaders, HR professionals and OD consultants are undertaking due diligence studies from a cultural perspective to map the differences and similarities between the target groups and then find ways to integrate better. This of course includes cross-cultural integration too.

Promoting Wellness

Large-scale sociocultural changes are sweeping societies and placing huge demands on the life skills of individuals to cope with the impact of these societal changes. As a result, we find that the problems of living are far outweighing the problems of working. While work itself might pose problems, the range of problems arising from societal changes seem to be far more difficult for most people to handle.

Organisations are beginning to recognise this quite well. They are realising that their most valuable cohort of employees who are in the age group of 25 to 45 are also the ones in whose lives the most is happening. If not for any other reason, just out of enlightened self-interest, organisations are beginning to see the value of addressing the wellness needs of employees, covering both mental and physical health.

Be it employee assistance programmes, programmes for young mothers or ageing employees, assistance in financial planning, programmes and policies aimed at offering flexibility and better work–life balance, programmes to promote the safety of women employees, programmes on diversity and inclusion, organisations are looking at every aspect of wellness and coming up with programmes and policies.

This in many ways is an extremely important dimension of organisational effectiveness and it is heartening to see organisations recognise that its employees need support in coping with the numerous changes that take place, as a consequence of organisational and social context.

The Specialist and Generalist Role in Facilitating Change

Among all the role holders in HR, it is the HRBPs who are very well positioned to work with business leaders to facilitate change. HRBPs who are assigned to support an entire business division or geography are closest to the point of action and are often expected to play this role.

Businesses might be impacted by a wide range of problems—high attrition, low employee morale, inability of teams to collaborate, low productivity and so on. This calls for change management skills.

HRBPs are expected to understand these problems and come up with solutions.

To do this, these business partners need training in internal consulting skills. They need know-how to define the problem, frame a starting hypothesis, gather sufficient diagnostic data, present their proposal and of course effectively implement them. HRBPs are also called upon to prepare the employees in the organisation for radical and disruptive changes that are often inevitable. These could be technology changes, regulatory changes, ownership changes, business model changes and so on.

The HR professionals in specialist roles such as L&D and C&B are also required to handle change agendas in their areas of responsibility. Hence, they too need similar skills of facilitating change—internal consulting and problem-solving skills.

While they often rely on the HRBPs to roll out their programmes, they need to play a hands-on role in the assessment of the need or opportunity, then design the proposition and gain the support and sponsorship of the leaders for their ideas. HRBPs are also being increasingly called upon to participate and contribute to significant change projects that are led by cross-functional teams. These are also in areas other than the people domain such as innovation and strategy.

Similarly, employee relations professionals in manufacturing plants too need significant skills in facilitating change given the constant changes that manufacturing leaders are keen to make in their domain to remain competitive.

In the next two chapters, we explore in detail two specific dimensions of organisational effectiveness—designing for effectiveness and shaping organisational culture—and explore in detail the opportunities for HR to add value in these areas.

Closing Reflections

Leading change is the responsibility of every leader—something that every leader should be good at.

However, HR has a special role in supporting leaders in such efforts.

Their expertise in understanding individual, group and OB demands that they support these efforts.

Organisational Experiences

Digitisation @ ICICI Prudential Life: A Story of Change and Transformation

In the aftermath of the financial crisis of 2008, the Indian life insurance industry underwent regulatory changes leading to significant reorientation of the existing business model. At the same time, disruption in the form of digitisation and emerging social media, mobile, analytics and cloud technologies presented new challenges and opportunities for change and transformation. Hitherto, technology adoption in the life insurance industry had been comparatively slower than in the banking world. Banks had embraced and adapted technology in customer acquisition and servicing through ATMs, Internet banking and, subsequently, mobile banking and robotics. However, the prevalent belief in life insurance was that it was a people-to-people business driven by deep relationships between customers and distributors, and that intermediation through technology would weaken the customer–distributor relationship. Also, a commonly held view was that life insurance was a push product and not a pull product like banking, and digitisation would alienate distributors and adversely impact business growth. It was in this context that the digitisation journey at ICICI Prudential Life started in the year 2011–2012. A simple yet overarching vision was defined—'making customer acquisition as easy as buying a bank fixed deposit through a one-click process'. To counter the existing mindset against digitisation, the narrative was framed as providing convenience to distributors and sales employees for enhancing business growth and not as a technology initiative that promoted direct interaction between customers and the company.

A web platform was first launched for customers and distributors that enabled sales employees and distributors to complete the customer onboarding process from their base location. A big leap forward was taken with the launch of the mobility platform, NEO, which enabled the sales fulfilment to be completed anytime, anywhere. With the scan and upload feature, this application radically decongested the documentation process. Essentially, this meant that the hassle and time spent in filling, collecting documents and traveling to the branch for timely submission of documents, checking if forms were correctly filled in and whether all documents were in order, couriering/scanning of documents and rechecking them at the central operations unit would now become a thing of the past. Additionally, system integration with bank and distribution partners, Credit Information Bureau (India) Limited (CIBIL), Aadhaar, National Securities Depository Limited (NSDL) and insurance repositories eliminated the need to collect documents from the client as verification of customer details could be completed online. The web platform and NEO had huge impact in reducing dependency on physical branch offices thereby paving the way for front-office elimination. The median time to issue a life insurance policy came down from two weeks to 30 minutes guaranteeing immediate customer satisfaction. Currently, 96 per cent of all applications are logged via the web platform and NEO.

Developing the application was only the start of the digitisation initiative. The larger challenge was to get the teams to adopt mobile devices such as tablets as way of doing business. In fact, the initial thinking was to ration tablets and give them to new recruits only after they reached a threshold productivity level to save expenses on tablet purchase. The mindset of technology adding to cost and not a productivity enhancement lever was challenged with the analogy of soldiers going to battle with bare hands and being given equipment to fight and defend only after they had proved themselves in battle. The key point here is not that technology enablement happened and that it led to enormous productivity and efficiency gains apart from enhancing customer satisfaction. The process of change management involved cultural transformation and it was initiated with the introduction of humility—the willingness to learn and adapt as a core value. Humility was reinforced in every forum and colleagues were encouraged to exorcise phrases such as 'it does not work' and 'it only works like this'. Ceaseless engagement and communication with colleagues facilitated alignment with the demands of the changed reality over a period of time and giving up of the traditional way of doing things that were clearly not working.

At the same time, digitisation was never positioned as a panacea for business success in which case it may have remained a stillborn child. It was constantly reiterated that business teams would always be evaluated on market share growth and health, quality and efficiency parameters, and that they retained the choice of achieving business goals with or without technology adoption. This was consistent with the philosophy of trust and empowerment that was implemented by moving from a functional structure to a micro-market structure where the head of the business in every market was made accountable for business outcomes of growth, profitability, quality, health and efficiency. Accountability had to be necessarily accompanied with devolution of decision-making freedom to allocate resources based on assessment of business opportunities. There was no doubt apprehension whether the next level leadership was ready and capable. However, the proposition that the role of leadership was to grow, nurture, mentor and hand-hold talent and that in a complex world no one would be ever fully ready or fully capable helped in assuaging this apprehension.

Another key enablement for change and transformation was facilitating the ownership for digitisation with the business leader in each micro market and not just with the head of digitisation. While strategic platform capabilities would be built by the head of digitisation, each and every business unit leader was encouraged to see herself as a technology evangelist who leveraged technology to the maximum and worked with the digitisation team in making digitisation a competitive business differentiator by providing input on usage, deployment and next-level enhancement opportunities on a real time basis. As part of the organisation design, the head of digitisation reported to the chief operating officer who reported to the chief business officer thereby, facilitating full ownership by the business teams as they saw digitisation as a business initiative and not merely as a technology initiative.

Navigating Change and Transformation: The Opportunity for HR

Changing beliefs to bring about lasting transformation is a slow process and needs to be done in a calibrated manner. Moving too fast or using a sledgehammer approach to break resistance may result in causing fear and paralysis. Sensing the pulse of the organisation, surfacing the feedback in an appropriate manner, containing the fear of change and uncertainty, role modelling organisation values, embracing and advocating the vision of the new reality and lubricating resistance to change through dialogue and discussion, resolving conflicts and making forward movement possible are essential for management of change and a role that HR is naturally suited for in the organisation context.

Enabling Culture Change at HUL

Last year, Unilever embarked on the Connected4Growth (C4G) programme—a rewiring of the entire organisation to empower those who are closest to the consumers to run the business, aligning processes to allow quick decision-making and encouraging leadership behaviours of collaboration, empowerment and experimentation—to build an organisation that was designed to win in the twenty-first century. This was and still remains a big cultural change, building an owner's mindset within all our employees and HR has been central to making this change happen.

For a shift in culture to happen, the change has to be led across all elements—structure, processes and leadership.

Structure

This change has required us to bring down complexity in our ways of working and move towards a faster, simpler, more consumer- and customer-centric and future-proofed organisation. Key elements of the change are the global roll-out of country category business teams (CCBTs) which are empowered cross-functional business units. Each CCBT is now an independent business team comprising of a business head (mostly from marketing, but could be other functions too), the brand managers in the country and a team of cross-functional managers fully accountable to manage the complete business. All business decisions—be it sales and operations planning, innovation management, planning new launches or competition tracking and so on—are taken by this team. The most fundamental aspect of this change is that the CCBT is an intact organisation team cutting across functional boundaries.

Formulating the new structure, communicating it widely and landing incumbents into the new roles with minimal disruption was key. However, the more fundamental role of HR was in stepping up capability of individuals to fit into their new empowered roles. A holistic capability calendar for CCBT members was constructed around three pivots-deepen functional expertise, broaden cross-functional understanding and sharpen business and financial acumen.

Process

Next came the overhaul of all organisational processes such as annual business planning, innovation management, performance management, goal setting as well as individual and team evaluation process. Cross-functional teams were formed to review each of the core business processes and rewire them to fit the new organisational reality. As the custodians of the performance management process, HR drove the process—individual goal-setting process is no longer a boss-subordinate activity alone, but one that is informed by the CCBT team members and the CCBT leader and signed off by the line manager. At the start of the year, the HR team undertook a massive 'goal-alignment check' exercise across the organisation—all goal plans for CCBT members were aligned to the CCBT goals and each other's. Similarly, the year-end performance evaluation too has been redesigned to be a true 360-degree process where 'stakeholder feedback' is no longer an input but the pivotal element that defines one's performance rating.

Leadership

As CCBTs took charge of their businesses, our leadership teams have seen the scope of their roles enlarged—both geographically (taking charge of more markets) and strategically (leading strategic priorities for the business). A two-pronged approach has been followed on the leadership front:

1. Redefining the new roles of the category/divisional leadership teams—As CCBTs take charge of their respective businesses, what would the new role of the senior leadership teams be?

2. Stepping up leadership quotient of the newly appointed CCBT leaders especially on two relatively under-developed skills—general management and cross-functional leadership skills. Through a holistic 70 (on the job learning), 20 (learning through coaching) and 10 (formal training) framework, we have built a robust development plan for all CCBT leaders.

18
Designing Organisations

There are few who understand design as well as Steve Jobs did. About design he said, 'Design is not just what it looks like and feels like. Design is how it works'.

French writer, poet, aristocrat, journalist, and pioneering aviator Antoine de Saint-Exupery said, 'A designer knows he has achieved perfection not when there is nothing left to add, but when there is nothing left to take away'.

Organisation design is no different. The goal of organisation design is to ensure that the organisation works and does what it is supposed to do. Designing an organisation is about adding nothing extra and not leaving anything unwanted behind.

Organisation design gives the organisation a form and shape, stores organisational capabilities, regulates movements and work-flow and supports business activity.

There are two common myths about the subject of organisation design among HR professionals—first, that organisation design and organisation structure are the same thing; second, that HR's role in this area is somewhat limited.

The role of HR in the area of organisation design will become very clear and obvious when the subject itself is understood better.

Components of Organisation Design

Organisation design has three distinct but interconnected components:

1. Complexity
2. Formalisation
3. Centralisation

Complexity

Complexity is the extent of differentiation that the organisation requires in its structural form in order to be effective. Such differentiation could be across three planes—*horizontal differentiation, vertical differentiation and spatial differentiation.*

Different organisations see the need for different levels of horizontal differentiation or dispersion in terms of roles, professions or occupational specialties, diverse work units, departments, functions, divisions and so on. Given the nature of the business, the organisation might have seven or eight functional groups, five or six product divisions, dozens of unique roles. More the horizontal differentiation, more the level of organisational complexity. More the differentiation, the more challenging the integration process.

Vertical differentiation is about establishing the right levels of impact and the freedom to act and accountability at each of these levels. This has implications for speed, seamless accountability and also the incumbents' expectations in terms of role efficacy.

Vertical differentiation also has implications for real and illusionary career progression, layering and cost escalation without responsibility escalation over time. (The global movement towards broad banding is a case in point.)

Organisations which need to reach out to multiple geographies tend to ensure that they have geographical overlays in their organisation structures to address the need to be 'locally present'. Establishing the geographical overlay over the horizontal differentiation is what we refer to as spatial differentiation.

Changing complexity needs may call for continuous changes and periodic tinkering of work units, structural forms or layers and all of this needs HR support.

Formalisation

Formalisation is the extent of standardisation that the organisation attempts to achieve in the way it gets work done through its people. Service-, operations- and delivery-intensive organisations require a high level of formalisation.

While formalisation can be achieved through written job descriptions, standard operating procedures (SOPs) and so on, it is also achieved through pre-socialisation at the job skill development stage (like the hospitality industry employees and nurses) or through professional ethics and intensive training.

Understanding the extent of standardisation requirement helps HR and business leaders to determine the appropriate processes in the following areas:

- Employee selection: Should we hire from ITIs or polytechnics? Should we pre-socialise students to our job requirements? Should we have apprenticeship programmes to observe and then select? Should we have written tests or psychometric assessments for standardisation of whom we hire?
- Role-clarification processes including role documents: Should we have clear SOPs and performance standards?
- Capability frameworks: Should we establish functional, technical and behavioural competencies as a means of standardisation?
- Work procedures and policies: Should we have very clearly documented dos and don'ts, policies and work procedures including the number of breaks that people should take, how they should dress, what reports they should file and so on?
- Job-skill training and certification processes: Should we have certification processes for a high level of job-skill

standardisation? How do we use skill training for stand-ardisation of work methods and behaviours? How do we use training to build our culture?

- Rituals: What are the cultural rituals we will establish to bring about a sense of standardisation among our employees—a common tribal language so to speak?

Centralisation

Decisions about centralisation help us determine the extent to which the formal authority to make discretionary choices are concentrated in a single individual unit or level. It is also about evaluating the centralisation needs of the organisation based on the stakeholders' needs and expectations, the role holders' skills and capabilities, expectation from the role and of course the need for speedy response.

Outcomes

The study of the organisation's need for complexity, formalisation and centralisation leads to several outcomes.

The organisation is able to arrive at its structural form (func-tional, divisional, process-based, committee, task force, matrix, network and so on). The organisation is then able to design its various work units.

The organisation is able to determine the professional classific-ations, job titles, approaches to standardisation of hiring, training, job descriptions, rituals, operating procedures, rules, performance measures, job evaluation systems and so on. This also leads to determining ports of entry, pay grades and levels, policies for promotion and so on.

Prepare or Repair—HR Has a Role to Play

When we begin to look at the entire canvas of organisation design, it becomes clear that there are several opportunities for HR to add value across various levels.

At the strategic level, HR leaders are able to prepare the organisation for business by advising and guiding the CEO and other leaders on all aspects of managing complexity, standardisation and centralisation. HR leaders play a significant role in job design, especially when a new position is being conceived.

HR leaders and professionals are almost at all times involved in a fair amount of repair work around organisation design.

Organisations are constantly making changes to one or other aspect of their design (complexity, formalisation or centralisation) and each of these changes have human implications. HR supports businesses in conceiving these changes well or help in its effective implementation.

Organisations are constantly moving from centralisation to decentralisation or vice versa given certain business realities. Organisations are constantly creating new roles, merging existing roles, shifting accountability from one role to another, launching new business divisions, seeking greater formalisation or task standardisation and so on. In all of this, they turn to HR for expert counsel and also for support in managing the human implications of the change process.

We have also noticed that many organisations make decisions about people (promotions, reporting relationships, increasing numbers) prompted by some exigencies. They do not realise that such decisions have an implication on the organisation design. Over a period of time many such unconnected and seemingly reasonable decisions lead to the design of the organisation being changed considerably making it quite a confused and misaligned one. Quite often people wonder how the organisation allowed itself to lose shape and rational design! It is on account of the cumulative effect of several short-term incremental actions.

Following are the aspects of organisation design that require the attention of HR and business.

Strengthening Functional Capabilities

As more and more organisations attempt to embrace growth, the question that crops up is this—what is the best structural form for a company that is on the path of high growth?

Preserving the foundation of a sound functional structure is crucial for a high-growth organisation. While many organisations overlay other structural forms such as matrix, process, division, team, network, project and so on over their functional structures, they realise that it is not prudent to replace the functional structure.

In designing an organisation and choosing a structural form, leaders are influenced by the *input side of complexity* such as functional skills, expertise and technologies required for building the business and delivering great products and services. In the early days, leaders built organisations along these input dimensions through some form of a functional structure.

As the business becomes more complex, organisations are required to pay far greater attention to the *output side of complexity.* They then see the need for dedicated attention to each of their business lines and dedicated resources and leadership in their chosen geographies. They start to realise that different customer groups or verticals demand special attention, dedicated focus and that some of their large customers demand a dedicated structure to address their special needs including a key account management structure.

As a result of these pulls and pressures, leaders start to tinker with their original functional structures and put in place divisional structures, business verticals, dedicated units for customers, geographical territory structures and so on.

While it is necessary for leaders to respond to the environmental demands by making their structures a lot more flexible and aligned, the biggest price that they pay is in the gradual compromise and neglect of the input factors which in many ways is the foundation of the organisation design.

Let us illustrate this with an example. A manufacturing organisation started with a single product for one segment of the auto industry. At this stage, it was a simple functional structure with functional heads to manage sales, production, engineering, maintenance, materials, quality, design and so on.

As business grew, the organisation started adding new product lines. Some of its customers also became strategic partners demanding special and dedicated attention. In the interest of focus and clear accountability, the organisation set up new units for the new product lines and carved out a dedicated unit for each of their key customers.

While the business grew, problems cropped up. The business heads of these discrete units who were measured by revenue and profitability focused entirely on getting work done and delivering the quarterly results. When they needed talent, they adopted an exigency approach and hired from outside. When experienced resources left, they were often replaced by junior resources in the interest of containing costs. Soon the divisions were bereft of any depth of functional skills and expertise and as a result their ability to solve problems and achieve scale got inhibited. The functional heads within the SBUs were helpless because they were governed more by business goals and less by their functional goals. The organisation as a whole found itself out of depth in being able to solve the emerging complex functional problems because it had failed to build the necessary functional expertise and leadership over these years.

Look closely at any of the respected and successful global corporations and you will find that at their heart is a very strong functional organisation. In fact, global organisations are so obsessed with respecting functional discipline and expertise that they have functional verticals that are aligned globally, cutting across geographical and business division boundaries.

These organisations have recognised that building functional depth and deep expertise is a great source of competitive advantage as the organisation becomes large and goes global. These organisations have also learnt to respect their functional leaders as much as they respect their business leaders. There are lessons to learn from them.

HR leaders have the opportunity to partner with business leaders to come up with many innovative solutions to preserve the functional depth and expertise even as they overlay other structural forms over their original functional structure in response to growing business complexities. Here are a few examples.

Centre of Excellence

Many technology companies have successfully leveraged the *centre of excellence* concept to build functional depth. While they might have multiple businesses and geographies, they make all or some of them a centre of excellence for a specific skill, competence, technology or practice. This way, the dual focus is emphasised and expertise is preserved and enriched by communities of practice.

Functional Cadres

Many organisations have used functional cadres to build and preserve functional expertise. Take the example of our civil services or our special protection group. These special cadres have served the purpose of creating expertise that no individual state will be able to replicate. Many global organisations are building these cadres by locating them close to supply sources and offering them to solve problems across the globe. Building these cadres has meant centralisation of hiring, training, allocation, rotation, ongoing development, rewards management and so on.

The creation of the accounting back offices in India by the four big accounting firms is a case in point of a specialist functional cadre of accounting and auditing in a geography that is rich in this typical capability at a reasonable cost.

The establishment of global research centres by many of the consumer goods companies and the technology development hubs created by many of the technology majors in a focused manner in a few locations and paying special attention to both the functional and career development of people in these centres is another concrete example of the functional expertise-building agenda.

Horizontals

IT service companies have quite successfully leveraged horizontals to build and preserve specialisation even as they have had to organise themselves around industry verticals. While each vertical focuses on a certain industry group, the horizontals focus on building precious and hard-to-replicate functional/specialist capabilities that can be deployed across the verticals.

The functional organisation has long been criticised for creating silos, overspecialisation, fiefdoms, turf wars and control from the top. While some of this might be true, many successful organisations have realised that the solution is not to kill the functional core.

Job Design that Preserves Employee Engagement

Why is the average modern factory worker much happier with his work than the average technology worker? Why is the nurse who works in the night shift much happier with what she does than the average BPO employee who also works in the night shift? Why do some jobs have higher levels of attrition and some don't? Why is it that the best talent doesn't always produce great results? Is it to do with the industry, the people or the HR practices?

Beyond the more obvious things such as working conditions, pay, rewards and career advancement lies a much more serious but little understood driver of employee engagement and productivity —job design. Very few HR practitioners have understood the real power that good job design has on business results and also on people effectiveness and satisfaction.

Job design is the scientific process through which the various elements of a job are carefully identified, balanced and seamlessly integrated to ensure that the twin objectives of peak performance for the organisation and satisfaction for the job holder are secured. Job design is also the science of ensuring that technology, processes and people's humanistic needs are harmonised to produce meaning for people and results for business.

While the Taylorist era essentially focused on designing jobs to increase efficiency by breaking it down and monitoring and measuring it, the quality of work life (QWL) moment in the 1950s began to focus a lot more on the human side of job design. Today, as Indian business leaders build organisations that grow larger by the day, they also run the risk of going back in time and applying the Taylorist principles to designing narrow jobs, adopting tight division of labour with the singular intention of increasing efficiency. In the bargain, they fail to pay enough attention to the needs of the employees for more fulfilling jobs that are a lot more humanistic by design.

As the needs of business get more complex and the expectations of the customer a lot more demanding, existing jobs are being constantly redesigned and new jobs created. In doing so, seasoned HR professionals tend to pay attention to two key principles of good job design.

Balance Culture with Design

One of the realities in many of today's jobs especially executive jobs is that they are all what one would call 'extreme'. In other words, the demands placed on the executives quite often far exceed the resources at their disposal. For example, leaders are expected to get things done by influencing people around them—people over whom they have no formal authority, using shared resources or resources that do not belong to them. This is especially true for all business-enabling functions.

The good news is that such extreme expectations do manage to get the best out of people and very quickly shape their abilities as leaders. However, for executives to succeed in such jobs, they need an enabling cultural context. When the culture of the organisation does not foster collaboration or promote respect for commitments to colleagues through SLAs or otherwise it can be hard for executives to rely entirely on their personal authority or influencing skills and relationships to get things done on a daily basis.

Successful organisations pay attention to nurturing the culture appropriate to the organisation design they have enshrined. Taking a holistic and integrated view to shaping organisational effectiveness by seeing the connect between culture and design is crucial for sustained business success.

Make Work Meaningful

While organisations are constantly tempted to deskill jobs and embrace an assembly line approach to job design, they soon recognise that they are leaving several human needs unmet. Some of these human needs include the need to know how one is making a difference, the need to use all the skills that one has and the need to be able to determine to a fair extent how one can go about doing one's work.

While a lot of us tend to complain that young employees do not seem to take ownership, we fail to recognise that they are being treated as puppets in a neo-Taylorist era.

As the next generation of Indian employees begin to meet their basic needs of money and security quite early in their work lives, they soon start looking for jobs that provide meaning and self-role integration (integration between self-concept and role demands) and influence (a feeling that one's role can make an impact on the system) (Role Efficacy Model, Dr Udai Pareek).[1]

---

[1] Udai Pareek. *Making Organisational Roles Effective*, 141–152. (New Delhi: Tata McGraw Hill Publishing Company Ltd, 1993).

The high levels of attrition is actually on account of competent and motivated employees moving to more aspirational jobs (both in terms of money and meaningful job content). This hurts much more as organisations start to hire fewer people and expect each one to deliver their best.

Organisations that spend time on job design will in the long run beat the malice of alienation and low productivity. Those that choose to run twenty-first century businesses based on the nineteenth century approaches to job design will continue to suffer.

Balancing Between Adhocracy and Bureaucracy

In the ultimate analysis, there are only two kinds of structural forms—adhocracies and bureaucracies. All the other structural forms are somewhere along this continuum.

Adhocracies are characterised by adaptive, integrative and creative behaviour which helps the organisation to respond very fast to a changing environment. While the value of an adhocracy lies in its ability to be adaptive, creative and responsive with few limitations on how one will reach a final goal, they are also plagued with conflicts, ambiguities over authority and responsibilities and very little structure and standardisation.

Typically entrepreneurial organisations, start-ups, businesses in a high-growth phase, small businesses, creative businesses and professional service firms tend to be characterised by adhocracy.

Bureaucracies are characterised by standardised procedures, formal division of responsibility, hierarchy and impersonal relationships. Bureaucracies are also characterised by a well-established system for hiring and career progression, clear hierarchies and of course informal networks that connect role holders for information and cooperation.

Adhocracies are often envious about bureaucracies and the many gifts they possess just as bureaucracies are also often envious about adhocracies and the many gifts they possess. The grass is always greener on the other side!

But why do adhocracies want to become bureaucracies and vice versa?

As young organisations become large and the making of people decisions goes far beyond the realms of the founder, there is a need for standardised procedures, formal division of work and allocation of responsibility, a strong hierarchy, well-defined work levels, clear policies, hiring criteria and clear delegation of authority. There is also need to ensure fairness, transparency and meritocracy. In other words, adhocracies seek to embrace elements of good bureaucracies.

Most often, however, the problem occurs when adhocracies give up the soul of being creative, adaptive and flexible and end up embracing systems that tend to dehumanise and demotivate their members and also stifle their initiative. Most importantly, they also end up losing the flexibility that once gave them the competitive advantage.

Is it possible for highly adaptive and adhocratic organisations to retain their core while they also transition to embrace certain functional elements of a bureaucracy? Yes, there are examples of several leaders who have managed to get the best of both worlds.

Why do bureaucracies want to embrace adhocratic ways?

Even as adhocracies attempt to embrace certain elements of bureaucracies, bureaucracies themselves struggle with injecting certain elements of adhocracy in the way they work.

Fed up with the lack of speed and responsiveness, they create change agents, set up cross-functional teams and task forces, remove layers, promote autonomous teams and encourage a culture of dissent.

Some even create a separate organisation or division to seed new ideas and new ways of working.

HUL has constantly adopted the approach of building a nimble-footed, flexible-and-fit-for-purpose business units. It helped the company to navigate through the VUCA world and successfully overcome new aggressive competitors, for example, popular detergents team to counter the challenge of NIRMA. Similarly, when it decided to compete with the well-entrenched player Aquaguard water business, it designed its Pureit business organisation quite different from its other traditional businesses.

In today's business context where young organisations are able to conceive of and deliver transformational results and create unicorns and disruptive changes, large bureaucracies are looking to urgently embrace some of the adhocratic ways.

When organisations are at such crossroads, they naturally turn to HR for counsel and support in making those shifts. When such needs do come up, they may not be presented as problems of organisation design. Very competent HR professionals use their functional expertise and their partnering and consulting skills to respond effectively.

Managing Structural Conflicts

One rather obvious aspect of organisation design that continues to consume the time and attention of HR professionals is around managing conflicts arising from issues of complexity.

There are inevitable conflicts over resources and priorities between businesses and business-enabling functions. There are also conflicts amongst different business functions in terms of resource allocation.

There are conflicts that managers in matrix roles face in balancing the demands from their multiple seniors.

There are conflicts between corporate headquarters and local business units around issues of centralisation and decentralisation.

All of these conflicts come in the way of performance and results and of course organisational climate.

HR professionals are constantly challenged to come up with solutions that are aimed at fostering collaboration, greater alignment and reduced interpersonal animosities.

Organisational Experiences

Accel's Venture Development Practice

A lot has been written about the vibrant entrepreneurial energy in the country and the success of start-ups. While most of these reports focus on the funding that start-ups receive, little is known or documented about what venture capital (VC) firms do post the investment to develop these ventures.

With the VC space getting crowded and many firms chasing good ideas and entrepreneurs, how do companies genuinely differentiate themselves regarding the value they can add to their portfolio companies beyond investment? Put differently, what contributes to the success of ventures beyond the money they receive?

It is in this context that Accel's venture development practice deserves mention.

Accel is a global VC firm that partners with exceptional founders with unique insights from inception through all phases of growth.

The belief statement of Accel in many ways describes its approach to investment. The statement reads:

> The firm seeks to understand entrepreneurs as individuals, appreciate their originality and play to their strengths. Because greatness doesn't have a stereotype. From the early days through all phases of growth it is our responsibility to support unique founders with unique insights as they take the seats of promise and grow them into amazing, enduring companies.

Some of Accel's industry-defining investments in India are living testimony to this belief being converted into reality—bookmyshow, freshdesk, Portea, Flipkart, Power2SME, UrbanClap, Universal Sportsbiz Pvt Ltd (USPL), Mitra, BlackBuck, PropTiger, Swiggy and many more.

Some of the global Accel company investments include Facebook, Dropbox, Slack and Supercell. Accel's venture development practice covers four areas, namely, product and marketing, engineering, organisation and people and business operations. In each of these practice areas, Accel has very senior practice leaders who are like an operating partner, working with their team to develop the practice and make available its benefits to the portfolio companies.

For example, the product and marketing practice looks at things such as user interface and user experience and marketing strategies for its portfolio companies. The engineering team looks at the technology architecture and scalability and the ability of its platforms to work in different environments as well as data security for its portfolio companies.

The practices work on projects and tasks that are of short-term, medium-term or long-term nature. They are of course available on call to address any of their emerging needs.

The organisation and people practice looks at a range of consulting services from culture, talent acquisition, organisation design, people strategy, statutory compliance and policy interpretation. The business operations practice helps in building business-operational capabilities such as sales and logistics, allows entrepreneurs pivot their business models or works with entrepreneurs who may have more critical operational or strategic challenges. In all of this, Accel adopts the credo of respecting the entrepreneurial autonomy and allowing them to seek these inputs rather than imposing anything on them.

Accel partners with founders very early to understand founders' aspirations and works towards realising their ambitions. The People practice team begins with talent acquisition as first helps to understand the desired behaviour and capabilities and on that basis helps the founders create a talent pipeline. The team also helps run campus connect programmes, hackathons and international hiring through a unique platform called #SmartMove.

#SmartMove was initiated to enable talent acquisition globally. Under this programme, the portfolio companies of Accel visit the US and share opportunities available in their companies. Till-date the programme has covered over 1,000 professionals in areas including products, technology and marketing.

Culture is at the heart of a start-up's evolution. Accel has developed a platform to codify culture so that founders can identify their current and preferred culture. This model is gaining momentum and is evolving to support the founders.

Recognising that not all start-ups are the same and neither are the hurdles that they encounter, Accel has created best practices in Formation, Validation, and Growth stage based on factors such as funding, years in existence and number of employees.

Accel also puts together training programmes that might be critical for entrepreneurs. For example, they have an online course that entrepreneurs take to become familiar with issues of ethics, integrity and prevention of sexual harassment.

Accel also creates an ecosystem of partners and service providers whom portfolio companies can leverage for the benefit. These could be technology, products and solutions, global firms for advice on founders' compensation or local organisations for C&B for rest of the organisation.

The Accel story demonstrates that for start-ups, the people portfolio should go beyond hiring its employees and must leverage other sources for building critical organisational capabilities. It also illustrates how world-class VC companies are contributing to create corporate capability within their network in an empowering way.

19

Contributing to Leadership Effectiveness

The CCL in their *Handbook of Leadership Development*[1] define 'leader development' as an expansion of a person's capacity to be effective in leadership roles and processes. On the other hand, they define leadership development as the expansion of the organisation's capacity to enact the basic leadership tasks needed for collective work: setting direction, creating alignment and maintaining commitment.

While the former is about the person the latter is about the organisation capacity and naturally follows that such capacity must be present across multiple leaders, groups, teams and also embedded in the organisational culture and systems. We call this leadership effectiveness.

Having looked at the subject of leader development in an earlier section, we would like to explore the subject of leadership effectiveness (leadership development) in this chapter which is deliberately placed under the section of organisational effectiveness.

---

[1] Velsor, McCauley, and Ruderman, *Handbook of Leadership Development*.

The Role of HR in Leadership Effectiveness

It is typically the CHRO or the senior HRBPs who have the opportunity to play a facilitative role in contributing to leadership effectiveness, given their stature and seniority.

This happens when they are seen as trusted advisors to the CEO and other leaders in the organisation.

Presented here is an array of opportunities that exist for the HR leader to contribute to leadership effectiveness.

Setting the Vision or Direction

Direction can be in the form of a vision, statement of purpose, or can be a lot more specific such as a goal or a business plan. Direction can be for short term, medium term or long term but must pass the test of being able to show people the way.

Business leaders invite HR leaders to facilitate the process of setting the direction in a manner that secures buy-in. This means involving the right people in setting the direction to ensure that the direction once set has the support and commitment of all the people concerned. HR leaders do it themselves or seek suitable external help for facilitation.

Mobilising the Team Towards the Vision

Sometimes the direction is visible but people still need to be rallied around it. It requires communication in a manner in which people feel inspired to follow the direction set by the leader. For this to happen, leaders need to be persuasive and also deeply empathetic. Where leaders naturally have these abilities, they do not need much help. Where they don't and they recognise it, they seek help from their HR partners in making it a shared leadership process. Where the leaders have a blind spot about it, the HR professional tends to bring to their attention the fact that people are not excited about the direction or don't get it.

Direction setting is not a one-time job. With every change in the environment, with every change in the team setting and with the emergence of new challenges, there is need to reaffirm the direction and renew the communication effort. This is the greatest challenge for leaders. Leaders who are successful in rallying people around in the early days of the organisation by the sheer power of their ideas fail when the organisation becomes much larger and the visibility of the direction a lot more diffused. They may even be blind to this need. Some even shy away from this in difficult times. HR leaders, who have their ears to the ground, alert the leaders to this situation and help them reconnect, clarify and re-establish the direction.

Setting direction is relevant for leaders at every level. A programme head, a factory manager, a business head—all of them need to set direction and all of them can do with good help and support from their HR partner. By helping leaders at every level set the direction clearly, HR helps to show employees how their work integrates into the bigger picture and help create a strong performance-oriented culture.

Alignment to Goals, Strategies, Actions and Priorities

At the most basic level, leaders must ensure that the entire organisation is aligned to the short-term goals, strategies, action plans and priorities. It is common for organisations to experience misalignment. Functions may not be aligned with one another, geographies may not be aligned with head office, staff functions may not be aligned with line functions, unions may not be aligned with management, juniors may not be aligned to seniors, young employees may not be aligned to old employees, the leadership may not be aligned to the board and so on. It is the job of the leaders to be able to sense these misalignments and proactively engage in narrowing the gap.

Using the performance management process as well as the planning processes and other top team workouts, HR leaders can support this alignment process. When there is a leadership change, the new leader (typically, the CEO) looks to HR for help in aligning his direct reports to his vision and strategy and line of thinking or to even talk about these issues. For example, CEOs may constantly receive feedback about the need for decentralisation to speed up decision-making. At other times the CEO may see the need to rationalise the structure to optimise costs.

The way reward systems are designed might be in conflict with the goals of the organisation. CEOs look up to HR for help in getting to the bottom of these misalignments and then support the painful actions that may need to be taken to set things right.

The periodic off-sites that HR leaders are called upon to organise are typically exercises in alignment. Good HR leaders show enormous leadership in shaping these off-sites.

Resolving Differences and Conflicts

While many organisational conflicts start off as substantive differences on a professional point of view, they soon degenerate into interpersonal conflicts if they are not attended to in time. Leaders seek help from HR in spotting these conflicts and then finding solutions to resolve these conflicts through a range of interventions. In many cases, respected HR leaders personally get these conflicts ironed out. In many cases, HR leaders with credibility counsel the warring leaders to see eye to eye. Others reach out for professional external help to support the leader.

Designing for Alignment

The structure of the organisation, the goals and the rewards systems can greatly support or derail alignment. Leaders pay attention to these hard aspects too in their pursuit of alignment and for that they seek support from HR.

They also use values as the basis for having difficult conversations in the executive councils when they are confronted with dysfunctionalities at their levels or levels below them.

HR tends to engage in an internal consulting relationship to diagnose the root cause and then come up with solutions to redesign these variables.

Using Values, Trust and Communication as a Means of Ensuring Alignment

HR leaders and business leaders often work together to leverage the power of the organisational value fabric to secure alignment among employees. They use values to help establish that there is *one right way* of doing things in the organisation and this automatically serves to narrow down differences. When articulated and deployed effectively values serve to enhance alignment.

Understanding Motivation

Leaders seek to remain tuned in to the needs, expectations, aspirations, fears and anxieties of their people, and through that understand what drives them. Leaders rely on HR to sense and understand what different groups of employees within the organisation aspire to accomplish and use this understanding to create the climate that will ensure commitment.

Leaders like HR to come up with programmes and mechanisms by which they can first-hand assess the climate in the organisation. This is in addition to relying on more formal engagement survey mechanisms. They expect HR leaders to have that deep intuitive sense to assess climate and engagement beyond what surveys will tell them. Once this is known, they like HR to come up with programmes and solutions to ensure that the factors contributing to motivation are present in abundant measure.

Moderating Style

In most organisations, the style of the leader has a direct impact on the performance, climate and engagement levels of employees and also influences the culture of the organisation.

While more and more leaders are becoming aware of their styles, they also find it hard to make changes to their style, even when it may be necessary. Some believe that they do not need to change and their current style is what will get results. In those cases, where the style has certain dysfunctionalities, there can be collateral consequences for the teams below and even for the entire organisation.

HR leaders with courage and credibility take the risk of having conversations with leaders about their style and tentatively point out that they need to pay attention to certain dysfunctional aspects of their style.

Leaders who are often alone in their journeys even open up to the HR leader once they establish a trust based relationship.

At times, other senior leaders in the organisation also look up to the HR leader to bell the cat—let the leader know that his operating style is hurting. This is not easy but can be an invaluable contribution to the leader and the organisation.

Those HR leaders who have earned the right to contribute to leadership effectiveness need to have first established their personal credibility. They have also honed the skills to engage in crucial conversations. Let's explore this dimension further.

Conversations That Can Contribute to Leadership Effectiveness

The success of HR leaders depends in good measure on the quality of their conversations with a wide range of stakeholders. Given that the heart and soul of HR work at the senior-most level is listening, consultation, advise, expertise sharing, data gathering, collaborating and joint problem-solving, all of which rests on trust, confidentiality and credibility, effective conversations is at the very core of what makes all this impactful.

HR leaders who contribute to leadership effectiveness seem to be skilful in five different kinds of conversations with their CEO or anyone else in executive leadership.

Conversations to Build Trust

All good relationships are built on trust. For trust to develop, HR leaders learn to move out of their role boundaries and communicate with candour, openness and of course sensitivity. They learn to connect at a human level with the leader or manager in the business. It also helps build a genuine and trust-based relationship which can form the foundation for deeper work.

Conversations to Demonstrate Empathy

Leaders and managers may express issues, concerns and problems. Good HR leaders resist the temptation and anxiety to offer ready-made solutions and instead tune into their worlds, listen with empathy and respond with understanding. To be seen as someone capable of listening and understanding is by itself a huge virtue.

Conversations to Bring New Perspectives

HR leaders often share with leaders and managers organisational issues and concerns arising out of their sensing effort—issues that can impact organisational effectiveness. They also present their professional views and opinions when called for. This calls for being precise, firm, respectful, objective, sensitive and of course being open to engage in a dialogue.

Conversations Around the Leader's Agenda

Leaders and managers often look to HR as a neutral colleague to discuss some of their dilemmas and use them as a thinking partner to make certain critical decisions. In these conversations, the seasoned HR leaders not only demonstrates great listening but also asks good questions, presents his/her perspectives in a neutral and unbiased manner to facilitate clarity leading to objective decision-making.

Conversations to Bring a Teachable Point of View

There are times when leaders and managers look to HR for expert advice or guidance. These are typically in areas where HR has expertise. In these conversations, the trusted HR leader or specialist seizes the opportunity to present his or her knowledge and insights with precision and confidence.

Internal Consulting Skills and Values

World-class HR leaders possess strong internal consulting skills to support leadership effectiveness agendas. They know how to define problems, how to diagnose, how to use tools and methods to facilitate group processes, how to sell ideas and drive change.

These leaders of course have a strong value orientation in order to remain neutral, apolitical, selfless and professional.

The greatest value any HR leader can add is to contribute to the becoming effective of leadership processes within the organisation. This is the CHRO's single-most important role.

Governance of Effectiveness

There are occasions when things go wrong within organisations. Employees might blow the whistle and raise ethical concerns. Someone might file a formal complaint about an ethical violation or point out a fraud or a misdeed by someone senior. These are symptomatic of organisational decay and need to be attended to. HR leaders need to play the role of ethics officers, conscience keepers or ombudsmen to uphold organisational values.

Closing Reflections

The task of leadership which includes setting direction, creating alignment and maintaining commitment is complex and is something which even the best of the leaders can do with support.

HR leaders with credibility and competence are often invited to support in leadership effectiveness. Contributing to leadership effectiveness would rank as one of the most strategic contributions that any HR professional could make.

Organisational Experiences

The Shadow Board at TVS Logistics

The Idea of a Shadow Board

Given the global nature of its business operations, TVS Logistics was keen to launch a global talent development programme that would help it nurture rising stars across the globe.

The need was to identify and cultivate employees with high potential to grow into business-critical leadership roles.

The idea was to hand-pick HIPO employees who had the ability, sound experience, strong qualifications and were deeply engaged. The idea was to groom these individuals to be able to lead critical projects for the organisation.

The experience of other Indian and global corporations of leveraging shadow boards served as a source of inspiration for the organisation to give it a try.

The Framework

TVS Logistics which has five entities across the globe wanted regional shadow boards to be established in each of these entities. These shadow boards were expected to conduct their monthly meetings and submit their suggestions and proposals to the board, executive committee or the respective CEO. The monthly shadow-board meeting was to be chaired by the respective CEOs. The group's corporate function heads were invited to attend these board meetings at random.

The top talent from the shadow board of each country is to form a global shadow board of six or seven members under the chairmanship of the deputy MD.

The Benefits

The shadow boards are expected to work on projects that are of strategic value. These could be around fostering cross-functional working, engaging in research, coming up with breakthrough solutions to problems, looking at new business development opportunities and so on. In the process, the organisation is able to develop its talent on a global platform.

For the individuals, it offers great exposure and accelerated growth.

The Results on the Ground

The US shadow board has set up an 'innovation hub' to show-case advance technological capabilities to our current and future customers. After successful pilot, the voice-picking systems are deployed in our warehouses with significant increase in accuracy and productivity.

Our UK shadow board has introduced the MRO (maintenance, repair and operations) capabilities. We are witnessing excellent response from the market and are confident that this new vertical will emerge as a strong business unit soon.

The India-based shadow-board members have fine-tuned and strengthened our Green Logistics offering. With increasing focus on the triple bottom line (people, planet and profit) by several organisations, Green Logistics has a bright future.

20
Shaping the Way Organisations Work

About three years ago, the totus HR School created on an experimental basis a peer learning forum for CHROs—a forum that would bring them together to talk about issues of common interest concerns and to learn from one another. In all, about 18 very senior CHROs participated in the process.

In preparation for our meeting, we engaged in an iterative process to build consensus on the topics that they would consider most important to discuss and learn.

While several themes came up in the initial rounds of exchange, 'shaping organisation culture' came right on top.

You will recollect that our own survey for the book presented in the chapter titled *Evolving Expectations* also threw up shaping organisational culture as one of the new asks from HR.

Clearly, businesses seem to recognize that they either need to fiercely retain certain aspects of their culture which are giving them the competitive advantage or they need to embrace certain new aspects of culture currently alien to them, to give them the relative edge that they are looking for.

It is acknowledged that the culture of an organisation might often be shaped through serendipity or situational responses rather than through deliberate actions. However, it is felt that greater understanding of culture and its drivers might help shape it in more deliberate ways. In this chapter, we will therefore first attempt to arrive at a common understanding of what culture means before exploring why this is important and what the role of HR is.

Culture as a Source of Competitive Advantage

First things first: Why is it that business and HR leaders are increasingly paying attention to the subject of culture? Their everyday experiences, from their strategic vantage point, tell them that the greatest source of competitive advantage comes from the culture they have been able to help create in their organisation. They see culture as the hardest to imitate secret weapon in their arsenal. It is their belief that what differentiates two organisations doing similar things are not resources, technology or other factors—it is the way these organisations go about doing things that might set them apart.

Culture: A Working Definition

Culture can be defined as a way of working, as something that is seen through the visible behaviours, rituals, practices and norms of an organisation and the culmination of many values and principles that are practised actively by the people in the organisation and influenced significantly by those who lead the organisation.

The Two Dimensions of Culture

There seem to be two dimensions to culture:

Values in Action

Values in action shape the content of what organisations do. These are things that organisations consider important or value in their business—what organisations choose to pay attention to in reality rather than those that are merely espoused.

For example, organisations see being close to the customer, embracing speed, being innovative or striving towards excellence as key dimensions of their organisational success behaviour.

Workplace Principles

Workplace principles shape the context in which work is done and reflect our demonstrated preferences in terms of how employees actually engage with or relate to one another, how employees do their work, how they treat one another, how they communicate or the kind of workplace they end up creating.

In other words, the workplace principles address the internal behaviours and actions or commitments between employees, functions or across the organisation.

For example, an organisation may want to avoid silos, demonstrate respect and integrity, collaborate or foster development. Organisations have internal norms on how meetings should be conducted, how time should be valued, how colleagues should treat one another, how managers should encourage risk-taking and so on. Many of these principles are intended to set the tone of internal working.

It must be clarified that while we are attempting to bring out a subtle distinction between values and workplace principles, most organisations will present both as organisation culture.

The Power of the External Context

While values end up determining what organisations actually pay attention to because they value it and the workplace principles shape the internal context in which work gets done, the external context is seen as having a very dominant influence on all of this.

This could include the industry that one is part of and its influence on certain cultural elements, the macro-economic environment and its influence on culture in a short-term-oriented society, the national culture of the place one does business in and its influence on cultural elements and the ideologies, cultural shifts and other breakthrough developments in the times we live and its impact on culture.

The unprecedented changes in the external environment across these dimensions is well documented and well understood. Its impact on business models and strategies is also well understood.

What is not as well understood and appreciated is the fact that changes in the context are so strong that they are forcing organisations to change the way they do things—their culture. Organisations decide to consciously respond to changing external contexts with a shift in their way of doing business/working to be most successful in the marketplace. These decisions are in a way related to the evolution of a new organisation culture emanating from workplace principles.

This need to change the way they do things takes the form of new demands on the styles and behaviours of the people in the organisation as well as building new capabilities.

Traditional Indian companies have often enshrined a culture of deference to seniority and experience. These companies would always seek approval of plans and proposals from the senior-most member in the family or team before they implement the same. They would have the ritual of the key family members or senior team leaders meetings every week to review and approve pending proposals.

However, with the changing competitive scenario and their venture into the technology- or internet-driven businesses, these same business houses have adopted agility and empowerment as their new cultural characteristic. The ritual of weekly review is not sufficiently fast to be competitive in the marketplace and hence this adoption. They also know that changes in such an operational culture will keep evolving to meet newer needs and may not be long-lasting like their culture of integrity and social consciousness which have more to do with core values.

Many business houses such as TATA and TVS are known for their cultural anchors such as trust and ethics which will never be changed. They have also been known for their employee-oriented culture which was demonstrated by their practice of life-long employment. However, with the change in the market conditions they too have changed this cultural dimension in tune with the times and today follow the culture of fair treatment of their people during employment or termination.

Why Is It Becoming Important to Pay Attention to Culture?

Following seem to emerge as some strong contextual factors that are making it necessary for organisations to review and contemplate changes to their existing cultural milieu:

- The macro environment and its accompanying uncertainties/ turbulence require organisations to display greater tolerance to ambiguity while also requiring employees to demonstrate greater performance, results, cost consciousness and profitability focus under much more trying circumstances.
- The growing power and influence of external stakeholders requires organisations to display greater empathy and responsiveness. This could include the increasingly evolved consumers and their expectations.
- There is a growing need to make sustainability a value in organisations, given the increasing ecological concerns.
- There is a need for respecting and working with the values, attitudes and expectations of a young workforce who are products of a radically different sociocultural context. This could include dimensions such as work–life balance and embracing technology.

- New social consciousness is driving a greater need for upholding diversity, inclusiveness and equal opportunity, also leveraging the power of diversity.
- Given the environment of alienation, there is a need to help employees get connected to the larger purpose of the organisation.
- There is a growing need to promote a culture of collaboration and bring about a shift in focus from individual excellence to collective excellence (connected thinking), given the contextual complexities.
- There is a need for nurturing innovation as a cultural element to respond to contextual complexities.
- Reputations of organisations are up for scrutiny by anyone in the community and this has also led to organisations adopting not only a standardised way of dealing with issues and people but also making themselves more open to public scrutiny.

In fact, it is believed that organisations that remain successful are the ones that respect this changing context and evolve. Culture which disregards context, it is feared, may become irrelevant.

It is even believed that since changes in the context are continuous rather than sporadic, organisations and therefore its workforce should engage in making adaptive cultural changes that are proactive and incremental. This will avoid the more painful process of large scale reactive cultural changes.

If proactive and incremental cultural change is necessary, it follows that the ability to continuously predict the emerging contextual changes and the resultant cultural response seems critical.

The Enduring and the Adaptive Layers of Culture

As we begin to recognise the power of context and the need to embrace change, the inevitable question in all our minds is this: If culture defines us and gives us life and character, can organisations keep changing it? Does that leave organisations almost soulless or bereft of a stable and unique identity?

It emerges that when organisations talk about culture (including values in action and workplace principles), they are referring to two layers:

1. The enduring core
2. The adaptive exterior

The Enduring Core

The enduring core is the DNA of the organisation. In the language of appreciative inquiry, it is the life-giving force and this is what sets it apart—the thing without which the organisation would just not be what it was or what people would like it to be.

This is fiercely protected and does not change under most circumstances.

However, it may need to be emphasised that it takes deliberate work to retain the enduring core and not allow external or internal forces to dilute it.

The Adaptive Exterior

This adaptive exterior includes values that the organisation might need to reinterpret to meet the needs of today or workplace principles that it might incorporate or change in response to changing demands.

It may be driven by external demands or internal decisions. It may also be driven by the styles of new leaders leading organisations.

It appears that most of the deliberations around culture change revolve around this adaptive exterior.

Successful organisations are able to recognise this combination and know what to retain and what to change when needed.

There can of course be potential conflicts when the adaptive exterior clashes with the enduring core. Unfortunately, the implications of this conflict can only be noticed after a length of time, by when much damage may have got caused.

For example, many businesses might be defined by their ability to follow process and instil a sense of discipline among its workforce to conform. When these organisations suddenly see the need to embrace innovation or even induct a workforce of a different kind, there are significant conflicts. Many of the brick-and-mortar engineering industries in India are seen to be going through a cultural transformation journey. Bosch Ltd—part of the globally renowned Robert Bosch GmbH, Germany—a global technology major and a leader in auto-component industry, has been a successful company thanks to its technological superiority and organisational culture of process excellence. Its products have defined the industry standards for many decades in India.

In today's context of eco-friendly environmental norms being embraced by the governments, auto manufacturers are looking to adopt engines with significant environmental-friendly performance and even move to electric-powered vehicles. All of this needs to happen in an extremely short span of time, making a company like Bosch Ltd seek to become much more 'agile and customer-centric' (as key cultural characteristics) to be able to continue with its strong market share (and market capitalisation) in the auto-engine systems/component domain.

Role of Leadership in Shaping Culture

It is well understood that leaders and their style have a huge impact on the culture that evolves within the organisation. There is a famous saying that culture is the shadow of the leader. To that extent, the personal values and beliefs of the leader end up finding a place in the organisation's culture.

This is especially true of founders and leaders of start-ups. These leaders have a huge role in shaping the enduring core of the organisation. They lay the foundation of what the culture might look like.

Much depends on the style of the leaders in terms of nurturing this core or attempting to change it and the adaptive exterior.

It appears that enlightened and selfless leaders might end up shaping or positively impacting the enduring core of the organisation. On the other hand, less enlightened leaders might create cultures that do not endure beyond their time. These organisations might revert to their old ways once these leaders move on.

Leaders especially have a very huge role to play in predicting the need for cultural change, articulating the aspects that need change and then be able to simplify their communication around the enduring core and the adaptive exterior. Leaders who communicate effectively and consistently are likely to influence greater assimilation and change.

Leaders may also rely on honey bees or lantern bearers to help employees cope with cultural change. These are individuals who are neither new nor seeped too deeply in the past and can therefore serve as role models of adaptive behaviour and act as a bridge between different workplace generations.

The leader's style-infused culture is usually the adaptive exterior kind. We have seen in many large organisations with multiple divisions or conglomerates with different business entities, the much empowered leaders who are in-charges of the different parts of the business invariably create a distinct stamp of their own with respect to what is preferred and how things are done in their parts of the organisation. It even makes us wonder if these are parts of the same large company/conglomerate.

HR's Role in Shaping Organisation Culture

Commenting about HR's role in shaping culture seems rather tricky.

At one level, HR based on its expertise in understanding organisations and OB is considered to be best equipped to bring the body of knowledge around the subject to the organisation.

However, it is also clear that it is not HR's sole responsibility to shape culture. In many cases, HR does not even have the mandate to define what the culture needs to feel and look like.

In fact, it is clear that it is the job of the CEO and his team of direct reports to define the enduring core, the adaptive exterior, to recognise the need for change and lead from the front, the efforts to communicate the inculcation and change process.

The board plays a role in providing the governance to ensure that the enduring core is preserved and the adaptive exterior is changing as needed.

HR, however, is called upon to play a supportive and facilitative role in shaping culture through several significant actions.

HR professionals often help the CEO to articulate the enduring core values and work principles. They also help the CEO stay alive to the need for changing certain aspects of the culture.

Determining what kind of a culture the organisation needs is often not an easy task. What is even more difficult is to use the range of levers at the disposal of the function to bring those elements alive.

HR of course has a huge role to play when it comes to championing the culture-change processes. They are required to assess the efforts needed to bring about the changes. They also need to support the CEO in the communication efforts.

Senior HR leaders of course need to spend a fair amount of time educating business leaders including the CEO about how their actions and deeds end up having such a huge impact on the culture of the organisation. Many of them also demonstrate the courage to call out behaviours of leaders that run contrary to what is preached.

Levers at HR's Disposal

HR has many levers at its disposal which it uses to reinforce the chosen core values and workplace principles.

These include determining who will be hired into the organisation, how people will be trained and inducted to some of the values and workplace principles, how performance will be defined, reviewed and measured, how outcomes will be rewarded and good behaviours recognised. HR also ensures that its policies and communication mechanisms contribute to shaping culture.

HR of course plays a huge role in helping implement changes to the adaptive exterior through its expertise in change management.

By aligning all the functional processes to the values in action and guiding principles, HR certainly shapes the organisational culture proactively.

Closing Reflections

Culture change is not just an area of interest for HR professionals but also an area where business leaders are increasingly seeking HR support. While a lot of the onus for culture change rests with the leadership, HR must contribute in a very significant way by understanding what aspects of culture need change and then leveraging the appropriate change-facilitation skills to make it happen.

Organisational Experiences

Sundaram Finance: 'Enduring Values. New Age Thinking'

The tag line says it all—'Enduring Values. New Age Thinking'.

If one were to search for a shining example of an organisation that has been able to retain and cherish its enduring core and yet demonstrated the ability to adapt and make changes in response to external demands, opportunities or internally felt needs, Sundaram Finance (SF) would stand out.

SF, part of the TVS Group came into existence on 11 August 1954. Its founder Mr T. S. Santhanam's vision was quite simple—'It is the customer who pays us our salary and therefore we must do everything that is right for the customer'. For over 60 years, this simple vision and the accompanying values have shaped the decisions, actions and destiny of the institution. The values of service, discipline, prudence, fair play, honesty, integrity, humility, openness and relationships have shaped the Sundaram way. These values have always been non-negotiable.

In the first 50 years of the organisation's existence, the values or the Sundaram way were not documented in any manner. It was passed on from one generation to another through what is often described as the Sundaram Finance Gurukulam. In other words, it was the leaders who chose to lead by example and through their tacit ways and hundreds of everyday actions; the values were practiced and passed on and the DNA got ingrained.

Their single-minded focus on customers from their founding days soon helped them transform the transport industry in South India. Thanks to their service orientation, cleaners and drivers could realise their dream of becoming vehicle owners. Single-vehicle operators began to aim at maintaining a fleet. In all this, these customers would always call upon the SF executive for counsel and guidance. On many occasions, Mr Santhanam would himself spend time with those who walked in.

Many years later, when the non-banking financial companies (NBFCs) were being regulated by law and had restrictions on the amount of deposits that they could collect, SF faced a different problem—they had to turn away investors because they had reached their limits much to their disappointment. For many in the south, a fixed deposit in SF was considered the safest and most secure form of savings. Safer than a nationalised bank too!

As much as there was clarity about what employees must do, there was also clarity about what employees should not do. Two phrases that were a complete *no-no* at SF were 'at any cost' and 'by hook or crook'. While growth was valued, means were valued even more. In fact, one often emphasised element of the employee value proposition at SF is that its employees can sleep well at night knowing that their organisation would never ever pressurise them into doing anything that might compromise their personal integrity or the credibility of the organisation.

Unlike many financial services companies which have separate verticals for sales, collections and credit, SF is organised around its branches. Each branch is established as a full-fledged and self-sufficient entity and each branch head is expected to be the CEO of the branch and is empowered to take all the decisions.

As a culture, all plans and commitments are made bottom-up, and performance and results are achieved not through pressure but by people routinely going beyond their call of duty because of their sense of pride and responsibility. Stories of legendary acts of customer service are almost routine at SF.

The organisation does not fire people on grounds of poor performance. Thanks to the sense of safety and commitment, this has not resulted in the organisation compromising on growth.

SF does not believe in, leave alone promote, a culture of superstars. Teamwork is considered far more important than individual brilliance. Many of their awards and incentives are designed to reward the entire branch rather than individuals. Of course, the organisation does recognise individuals with talent and rewards them.

Despite being in the competitive financial services space, the organisation enjoys a very low level of attrition.

The organisation has had to grapple with the need to revisit some of its beliefs, assumptions and mindsets and embrace change, and it has been able to do so every single time.

In the 1980s, the organisation took the big step of moving out of the south and establishing businesses across the country. A little later, the organisation ventured out of truck- and bus-finance business to learn more about the leasing business and set one up. In the 1990s, the organisation undertook a nationwide survey to listen to its customers and non-customers to understand what they needed to do differently. The resounding feedback was that their needs were changing and they wanted the organisation to do a lot more.

Based on this feedback and the emerging opportunities around them, the organisation entered the mutual fund business, the home finance business, car finance business and general insurance business over a period of time. Today, SF has gone well beyond truck and bus finance to become a full-fledged retail finance company.

SF was also among the first to embrace technology and develop its own homegrown technology platform.

As the organisation looks into the future, it is confident that the coming generations of employees will continue to embrace these values even better, given that they have strong social consciousness and a strong desire to live a congruent life. They only need the right leaders who will lead by example, the organisation believes.

Clearly there is a lot to learn from SF, when it comes to combining enduring values with new age thinking.

HR HERE AND NOW

THE MAKING OF THE QUINTESSENTIAL
PEOPLE CHAMPION

PART 6
Managing the Relationship
with Employees

21

Boundaries Redefined

The foundation of any healthy relationship is the ability to appreciate and respect the boundaries that delineate the relationship. Every boundary establishes what is acceptable, what is not; what one can expect, what one cannot; what one needs to respect and value; what one needs to stay out of; where one will be included, where one will not be included; what can be said and what cannot be said and so on.

What is true for boundaries in parent–child relationships and marital relationships is equally true for employer–employee relationships.

When both sides in the relationship respect, value and honour the boundaries, there is peaceful and productive coexistence. When boundaries are consciously or unconsciously violated, there can be conflicts or even breakdowns.

It is fair to say that the relationship boundaries between employers and employees have been altered significantly. Has the alteration been a conscious process with both sides signing up for the new arrangement or has it been that the new boundaries have just emerged out of rapidly changing values and preferences on both sides? Are both sides happy with what they see as the new emerging boundaries or are there regrets on both sides?

Given that employee relations is all about relationships it would be crucial for us to examine how the boundaries of this relationship have been redefined across several dimensions and what its consequences are.

There are at least five such boundary dimensions that are worthy of exploration.

The Contractual Boundary

The contractual boundary which defines the very nature of how employment will be structured has been altered significantly. We have spoken a lot about the changing approach to people portfolio management but it is worth re-emphasising this point.

The new employment structures are determined based on the high need for flexibility and cost reduction. Companies are looking at being able to predict and control employee-related costs over a long period of time. Therefore, the emphasis is on third-party manufacturing and services, outsourcing, minimal permanent headcount and a fairly large contingent workforce. Some companies run with almost 100 per cent contract workmen, over 25 per cent of staff from manpower service providers such as Addeco and TeamLease, many specialists on fixed-term contracts, almost all non-core operations outsourced to service providers (canteen, housekeeping, security, gardening and so on) on a contract basis and with only a few permanent employees. Practices such as factory within factory are quite prevalent. These kinds of arrangements have resulted in HR and administration managers having to manage vendors of such services to ensure compliance and effectiveness.

Clearly, the contractual boundary in terms of who employs someone and for whom one offers one's services has been altered significantly. While this brings many benefits, it also causes a lot of friction and conflict when the new arrangements violate the basic tenets of fair treatment, equal pay for equal work and so on.

While the boundaries of employment have changed, so have the boundaries around separation.

The movie *Up in the Air*[1] explains it all.

Ryan Bingham works for an HR consulting firm that specialises in termination assistance—basically, firing employees. Natalie Keener is his new apprentice. Ryan is called back to office to be familiarised with a new web-based programme to do the termination, to save costs. Ryan opposes it because he considers the process impersonal. He is also advised to get Natalie ready to eventually replace him on the virtual termination platform. Eventually, Ryan helps Natalie appreciate the need for humanness even in termination.

The audio clip uploaded on WhatsApp by a dismissed employee in an IT major that recently went viral (where the employee counselled to resign over a phone call recorded the conversation and posted it on WhatsApp) seemingly made the HR lady to be the apparent cause of all the trouble. The issue is understandably much deeper. And the movie explains it quite elegantly.

If one thinks more deeply, several realities and questions come up:

1. In the IT industry, employees are not considered 'employees'. They are often and unfortunately viewed as 'resources' hired for deployment to client projects and sites. That is why, in the great days of growth, organisations started to adopt SCM techniques for managing the hiring process. Now organisations are wondering how to deal with the excess.

2. Employees in the IT and other modern businesses liked the 'market-oriented philosophy' of global mobility and competitive pay for skills when the going was good. Now,

---

[1] *Up in the Air* is a 2009 American comedy-drama film directed by Jason Reitwan based on the 2001 novel of the same name. The movie has George Clooney in the lead role.

a bit of protectionism with a socialistic and benevolent approach seems favoured by them but organisations are not listening.

3. Given the employees' lack of attachment to any ideology or collectivism, trade unions never took off in IT/ITeS industry. What we see now is the formation of 'interest groups' in and around specific issues using social media.

4. Asking an employee to resign or face termination is one of the oldest methods adopted by HR professionals for decades. It was not invented by the IT industry. The only difference is that in the past the HR profession had more Ryans doing it, with experience and maturity. Today, there are very few Ryans left. Young Natalies with scripts are expected to do this. The audiotape clearly reflects the lack of experience and conviction, poor HR leadership and capability-building processes. The individual was not solely at fault.

5. The issue is certainly not about whether organisations will go into restructuring and resorting to lay-offs. Of course, they will. That is the new order. The question is, how will it be done.

6. This brings us to the last point. In the coming years, will organisations develop this skill and value or will they outsource the task to firms like the one Ryan worked for, or will the wave of technology that is sweeping all of us offer an automated solution to make this devoid of human contact? Will organisations end up changing the boundary of our relationships with employees so drastically that it will become so cold and impersonal?

Legal Boundary

A labour court in Chennai recently held that a senior service programmer of HCL Technologies was a 'workman' under the Industrial Disputes Act.

While the company argued that the software engineer was in a supervisory position and on that count did not fall under the purview of labour laws, the court did not agree.

'It cannot be denied that the job of an engineer in a software company involves skills and technical knowledge. Therefore, it can be easily concluded that the job of a software engineer can be termed as skilled or technical one', said first additional labour court presiding officer S. Nambirajan.

Rejecting the company's objections, the judge said that the software engineer was indeed a workman. According to the Industrial Disputes Act, 'workman' means any person employed in any industry doing any manual unskilled, skilled, technical, operational, clerical or supervisory work, for hire or reward, whether the terms of employment be express or implied.

His order read:

> The Company has not produced any evidence to show that failure to improve the performance or failure to measure up to the expectations of standing orders of the company would amount to an act of misconduct. It is not known whether the company has any service rules and regulations, and it has not produced any materials to show what acts constitute misconduct.[2]

This is not the first instance in which a court has held that IT engineers are workmen. In January 2015, the Madras High Court restrained software major TCS from retrenching an employee who had been issued termination orders by the company. The employee moved the High Court saying the retrenchment move

---

[2] Times of India, Indiatimes.com, Chennai, A. Sunramani, 11 May, 2016, 'Reinstate Sacked Techie, Court Tells HCL'. Available at https://timesofindia.indiatimes.com/city/chennai/Reinstate-sacked-techie-court-tells-HCL/articleshow/52215401.cms, accessed 1 February 2018.

was illegal and in gross violation of the Industrial Disputes Act 1947.

Admitting her petition, Justice M. Duraiswamy granted a four-week interim injunction restraining the company from retrenching her.

In her petition, the employee said she was a 'workman' within the meaning of Section 2(s) of the Industrial Disputes Act 1947, as her main duties and responsibilities are technical and clerical in nature.

Well, the hard reality is that the IT industry in India, which recorded revenues of over USD 150 billion in FY 2017 with exports crossing USD 100 billion and a workforce of 3.9 million, is not governed by any national labour legislation except the local Shops and Commercial Establishments Act!

A few attempts by the Government of Karnataka around the year 2012 to bring the industry under the purview of the Industrial Employment Standing Orders Act was given up with the government finally granting it exemption for another five years effective 1 January 2014. However, this exemption has been under threat now and then. Recently, a new trade union representing 250-odd IT employees has been granted registration in Bengaluru, Karnataka. This has confused people in the industry even more.

So with no sensible legal framework in place to guide employers and protect employees, we are beginning to see a series of such individual cases springing up to set precedence for more and more in the coming days.

All major and significant industries in India are covered under an industry-specific legislation. Thus, factories are covered under the Factories Act, plantations under the Plantations Labour Act, mines under the Mines Act, port workers under the Dock Workers (Regulation of Employment) Act, construction workers under the Building and Other Construction Workers (Regulation of Employment and Conditions of Service) Act and so on.

The Shops and Commercial Establishments Act which was really intended to address the needs of small units of establishments such as a retail shop or trading establishment, a bank, an office, a hotel or a restaurant, a cinema or any other place of public entertainment is hardly the right legislation to cover the IT industry.

For an industry with such great talent and such a huge equity with the government and all other stakeholders, one would wonder why there isn't a suitable legislation to protect its employees or regulate the working conditions.

One might wonder how businesses within the industry would define working conditions or deal with contentious issues relating to grievance redressal, termination and disciplinary procedures.

One argument which is often proposed in favour of not having any legislation is that the big firms are supposedly doing better than the law. Well, that might be true for manufacturing companies too, isn't it?

Take the case of Contract Labour (Regulation and Abolition) Act. The act is supposed to regulate and abolish the employment of contract labour in industry. By that logic, almost all manufacturing companies would be in complete violation of the act. Organisations and the regulators seem to believe that if law is seen to come in the way of economic activity, economics should win. Many also argue that laws are antiquated and tend to stifle businesses, and also lead to exploitation and corruption.

On the other hand, activism and strong public opinion seem to play a role in shaping some of the decisions by the government to amend existing laws or introduce new ones. For example, the recent decision to introduce a new law for the prevention of sexual harassment [The Sexual Harassment of Women at Workplace (Prevention, Prohibition and Redressal) Act 2013] is a case in point. It also appears that instead of a framework of labour legislation, more and more individuals and interest groups will raise civil disputes to find redress for their grievances. In other words, as employees become increasingly aware of their rights and privileges, it is litigation that will form the basis for resolving issues rather than an appropriate and contemporary legislative framework.

Power Boundary

Where unions exist, business uncertainty and competitiveness have forced managements and such unions to look at areas of common benefit and have resulted in proactive engagement between unions and companies led by progressive union leaders. There is a realisation amongst union leaders that the business scenario is no longer steady and stable, and that workmen and employees need to engage seriously with issues of productivity, costs, automation and so on. Unions have become more progressive. For example, the union in an ailing company took a decision not to ask for a raise after the settlement expired until the company became profitable and volunteered to do additional work and help the company reorganise the workforce as well as help implement systems and processes until such time.

The power equations between unions and management have also shifted post liberalisation given the shifts in the global economy, the absence of ideology-based unions and the government taking a pro-industry view. Unions are struggling to find meaning and identity in what they stand for and finding it extremely difficult to garner membership. The presence of a huge contingent workforce has also resulted in splitting the interests of unions and their advocacy remains for the permanent workforce (which is generally their members) at the expense of the contingent workforce. Thus, this category of employees has been completely neglected and unrepresented, and this has resulted in violence and fatalities when things have gone out of hand.

Recognising this limitation, unions have modified their approach to becoming more 'reasonable' in their approach to employee issues. This has resulted in reskilling of the workforce, improved productivity and continuous restructuring of teams as per business requirements.

Alongside this, the growth of the IT, ITeS, financial services, telecom and retail sectors has hugely changed the profile of the workforce. These employees come from more educated backgrounds and their proclivity to collectivise or unionise has been much less. Being members of unions is not seen as being socially desirable. This has further eroded union membership. Several attempts to form unions in the IT sector did not quite take off. Only when there was a scare of mass retrenchment did these employees look for some collective action but that too has been limited and scattered and of a transient nature.

Significantly, all these changes have also led to the erosion of skills in managing any form of collective action, industrial strife, disputes and differences. The employee relations profession which gained a lot of significance given its ability to deal with and manage unions has lost its place of pride in many ways. For organisations in remote locations that do need good employee relations professionals, the challenges of hiring good ones are enormous.

The other extreme of the changing power equation is the very transactional nature of relationships that employees have with their organisations and the power that individual employees derive from a vibrant labour market.

Easy mobility and the social acceptance of short tenures has completely shifted the power balance for an entire class of employees with the right skills and has put organisations at their mercy.

Governance Boundary

One other critical dimension of the boundary has been around governance of any kind.

When organisations dealt with a workforce with low maturity levels, it needed to enforce discipline quite strongly. There were strong punitive measures for tardiness, absence, negligence at the work place, bad behaviour, theft, violence, work negligence and so on.

Such enforcement was never easy and posed severe challenges to the relationship. The dismissal of a single employee was often enough reason for workmen to strike work.

Over a period of time, with changes in the social setting and the entry of a more skilled and educated workforce, the boundary of discipline has changed. It became more purposeful.

However, the large-scale hiring in the IT and other service businesses has led to the subject of discipline being revisited.

Organisations are today grappling with much more serious issues of discipline including sexual harassment, cybercrimes, falsification of credentials, large-scale fraud and of course threats of terrorist infiltration into the workforce. More and more organisations which are in extremely competitive businesses have a zero tolerance policy on issues of ethical violations. Also, the adoption of global quality standards and processes has led to the task of standardisation becoming more implicit and enforced through training and acculturation rather than through discipline.

On the other hand, more and more organisations realise that the boundaries between work and home are crumbling. This is leading to organisation revisiting issues such as working hours, punctuality and so on.

The entry of a large percentage of women and the challenges of living and commuting in our cities with inadequate infrastructure and of course spiralling real estate costs is leading organisations to look at policies to encourage working from home.

Similarly, the advent of a large number of front-line service businesses has also resulted in the growing maturity of the workforce which understands that serving the customer with professionalism is not negotiable.

In summary, task standardisation and internal controls have become an integral part of the entire business process rather than remaining just an HR process and on the balance seems to work much better today.

Social Boundary

The social boundary of the organisation does not end at the work-place. It now extends to the community within which the organisation does business. Environmental concerns, the mandatory need to engage in corporate social responsibility (CSR) projects and the presence of an overactive media have resulted in the social boundaries being redrawn.

Therefore, companies are being called upon to hold themselves accountable not only for the quality and reliability of their products and services but also for the positive impact that they need to create in the communities that they work in.

Communities also believe that companies cannot work within their narrow confines and are in some cases arm-twisting them to get what they want. The stress in the relationship therefore has become more visible, forcing the need for collaboration and shared progress. In some cases unfortunately, it has also led to some tensions where things have not worked out.

Again, take the case of Uber and the backlash created because of its troubled relationship with its drivers or the public outcry that the BPO industry faced when it had underestimated the challenges to women's safety en route to work and back.

Rivigo, a technology-enabled logistics company, disrupted the industry by putting at the heart of its business an innovative 'driver relay' model which ensures that its pilots (not drivers) live a life of dignity, fulfilment and respect. They ensure that their pilots are able to relay shift and return home every evening and avoid staying away.

Finally, organisations are beginning to have a social identity, thanks to the advent of social media. This also makes them more visible in the public space and makes them open to public scrutiny like never before. So I may not work for your company but may still have a strong point of view about everything that you do or don't do and will feel free to air those views or contribute to propagating news about all the good or bad things that you do.

Closing Reflections

The more we look at the changes in the boundaries of the relationship between employers and employees, the more we are convinced that economics will strongly influence.

A good development is that organisations with a sound value orientation and a philosophical outlook will proactively shape the relationship around those values and make it transparent and fair. There is a looming fear too that all disputes and differences will be up for public scrutiny.

At another level, employees will take their own actions to fight for their rights and privileges and will not wait for legislations.

Finally, function will matter more than form when it comes to the boundaries of the relationship. That will make the relationship easy to engage with or even easy to disengage from.

22
What Really Matters

Some years ago, we overheard a conversation outside a cake shop in one of our metros:

'Hi what's up? What are you buying?' This person asked his friend.

'Well, I am just redeeming this coupon for my birthday cake', replied his friend.

'Coupon for cake?' asked the former.

'Well, you see, earlier we used to cut cakes and celebrate birthdays in our department. Now that we have grown large, HR has put a process. So I get these coupons for my birthday. I can come and select the cake I want and then go home and celebrate!'

Another employee-engagement initiative bites the dust, isn't it?

While more and more organisations are desperate to get started and make some progress in the area of employee engagement, many of their measures seem desperate, half-hearted and amateurish. In the bargain, many organisations have ended up trivialising employee engagement.

This leads us to ask the question, 'Is employee engagement a department, a role, a set of activities or a state of being?'

Engaged employees are seen to be 'productive members of an organisation who are psychologically committed to a role in the organisation in which they use their talents'. 'They are supposed to speak positively about the organisation to co-workers, potential employees and customers, demonstrate an intense desire to be part of the organisation and exert extra efforts and take on work that contributes to employer success'. It is supposed to be 'a state of emotional and intellectual involvement that workers have in an organisation'.

The key ingredients of an engaged employee seems to be tenure with the organisation, the display of emotional involvement in what one does, doing more than what is expected and displaying pride in the place one works in.

It seems a welcome development that more and more organisations at least recognise that engaged employees are productive employees and it makes good business sense to ensure that the drivers of engagement are present in the workplace. So what is wrong with the current approach of organisations in securing employee engagement?

Many organisations are doing what they find easy to execute or just doing something to tick the boxes. They are failing to pay attention to things that really matter.

Learning from Abraham Maslow

A Theory of Human Motivation[1] published by A. H. Maslow in 1943 (also known as the Hierarchy of Needs Theory) is a good place to start our journey of understanding our current approach to engagement and also discover what really matters.

Maslow had said back in 1943:

> Human needs arrange themselves in hierarchies of pre-potency. That is to say, the appearance of one need usually rests on the prior satisfaction of another, more pre-potent need. Man is a perpetually wanting animal. Also no need or

---

[1] A. H. Maslow. 1943. 'A Theory of Human Motivation'. Originally published in *Psychological Review* 50, no. 4 (1943): 370–396.

drive can be treated as if it were isolated or discrete; every drive is related to the state of satisfaction or dissatisfaction of other drives.

Safety Is Still Supreme

Maslow has said:

> Just as a sated man no longer feels hungry, a safe man no longer feels endangered.... In between these extremes, we can perceive the expressions of safety needs only in such phenomena as, for instance, the common preference for a job with tenure and protection, the desire for a savings account, and for insurance of various kinds (medical, dental, unemployment, disability, old age).

Many of today's young employees aspire to work for 'Big Brands' and this is seen as a recent phenomenon. We think this is completely in line with the 'safety needs' that Maslow spoke about so succinctly in his Hierarchy of Needs Theory. Decades ago, a job with the government was considered 'secure'. Years later, a job with a public sector undertaking or a bank was considered secure. Today, an organisation with a strong brand gives employees the same security they are looking for. Brands seem to signify 'safety', 'reliability' and 'credibility'. In fact, the desire to belong to a big brand is so high that people who are unable to join a big brand from campus keep changing jobs until they get a big brand on their CV.

Similarly, the pursuit of 'money' may be seen as an ill among today's workforce, even as a sign of greed. Our research tells us that employees seek money as a compensation and protection against the risk that they are now subject to, given the new employment arrangements that are emerging. No different from the safety needs Maslow spoke about!

Unfortunately, after centuries of business and industrial progress, organisations are still struggling to offer its employees the sense of safety that is clearly considered important.

Organisations continue to be under a huge amount of pressure to make their workplace safe. This need has become very high with more and more women entering the workforce. It is not just their physical safety when they come to the workplace and get back but also their psychological safety at the workplace. While legislations are in place, it appears that a single legislation is woefully inadequate to make our workplaces safe for women.

How can organisations make managers more sensitive to the safety needs of employees? How can HR professionals create policies that promote safety and how can they ensure that safety concerns are reviewed at the highest levels? A safe workplace is also one where the weakest employee's voice can be heard.

The ability of organisations to respect the safety rights of employees and provide for fair and open grievance redressing processes will be critical.

Addressing this need fairly and squarely is a clear prerequisite for engagement.

How Well Have We Understood Love and Belonging Needs

Maslow maintained that when physiological needs and safety needs are, by and large, taken care of, one begins to feel the need for friends, a partner, children, affectionate relationships in general and even a sense of community. Looked at negatively, he maintained, one becomes increasingly susceptible to loneliness and social anxieties.

Organisations that promote a sense of community are able to provide for some of these needs to be met. On the other hand, in organisations that promote a workplace that is cold and clinical and devoid of any human connect, these needs are seldom met and in fact creates a sense of alienation.

In the interest of promoting this sense of community and connect, sometime they go overboard on so-called engagement activities such as events, shows, sports activities, parties and so on. When done as an activity and a tick in the box, they seldom achieve the intended purpose of promoting a warm and empathetic workplace.

This confusion in the minds of HR professionals between 'engaging' with employees and 'engagement' is concerning. Engaging with employees is about establishing a connect, a relationship and a bond. This is essentially an *employee relations* process. A lot of what large organisations are struggling with is to do with just trying to 'connect' or 'engage' with their employees, leave alone achieve 'engagement', which is the much more complex process of securing commitment and dedication.

The pursuit of scale and expansion has led organisations to automate and outsource the delivery of many of the services that HR traditionally provided to employees. In such an environment where physical touchpoints with employees seem understandably difficult to maintain, the question is whether technology can compensate. One important question in this context is whether it is possible to achieve engagement without having a real connect or engagement with employees? The proponents of technology seem to believe that it is possible. The other important question is whether undertaking hordes of activities that merely secure 'connect' will lead to real employee engagement.

The Impact of Managerial Styles on the Need for Esteem

The need for esteem that Maslow spoke about is again so clearly visible in today's organisations. The fact that employees who join an organisation based on its ability to fulfil their safety and belonging needs end up leaving because they could not work with their managers whose style did not meet their esteem needs is all so familiar.

Similarly, the same young employees who seek out big brands on campus seem to seek out smaller organisations a few years later with the hope that they will get the respect and recognition, dignity and appreciation they crave for at that stage of their career. Many of the recent employee-engagement models have reinforced this belief by highlighting the role of managers in promoting engagement. Unfortunately, not many have found answers.

A large number of managers are thrust into people management roles with little preparation. They just do not know how to manage people. Making matters worse is the fact that their ever-growing task demands rob them of the opportunity to connect with their teams at a human level.

Finally, the role of managers in evaluating and determining rewards prevents employees from displaying their vulnerability or trusting their managers with their real problems.

Many HR professionals are not addressing these very significant problems and hence their organisations keep struggling with manager-caused disengagement.

The Importance of Understanding Deficit Needs (Homeostasis)

Organisations in India today go to great lengths to provide a 'great work environment'—convenient transport facilities, great cafeterias, state of the art recreation facilities, on-site child-care facilities, regular employee surveys and periodic get-togethers to promote bonding and so on—all with the hope that it will create a great motivating environment. Alas, the cribs continue as if *it all means nothing at all*. This is exactly why Maslow described these as *deficit needs*—if you don't have enough of them you have a deficit— you feel the need and if you get all you need, *you feel nothing at all!* In other words, they cease to be motivating. Companies which do not have it work hard to make it available and those who have it lament about its effect fading away!

It appears that safety and security, love and belonging are all deficit needs. Organisations which are able to offer them in an acceptable measure are able to ensure that deficit needs don't exist. Organisations which continue to have challenges in one or more of these areas cannot compensate for them by any other means.

The business model of an organisation or its business realities, its financial constraints or its lack of deliberate attention to the areas can all contribute to deficit needs remaining. For example, a highly reputed global organisation may be forced to reduce head-count or pull back on some of its benefits causing certain deficit needs to surface. These are inevitable developments and lead to employee stress. So while, in certain situations, there will be challenges we find organisations facing the issue head on by supporting employees deal with the stress.

Supporting Employees Under Stress

In his research, Maslow had mentioned that under stressful conditions, or when survival is threatened, we can 'regress' to a lower-need level. When there are threats of job losses, nothing seems more important than holding on to the job, even if one were to deal with a bad boss.

Young employees are experiencing a lot more stress than any of the earlier generations. Be it the problems of living or the problems of working, all of them seem to cause enormous stress.

While stress is likely to continue to be a reality in the years to come, what matters is our ability to enhance the maturity of our young employees so that they are able to experience control over their destinies and take charge of it. In other words, they need life skills. Mature employees are more likely to be engaged with their work and their organisations.

The World Health Organization (WHO) has defined life skills as 'abilities for adaptive and positive behaviour that enable individuals to deal effectively with the demands and challenges of everyday life.' WHO's definition of life skills includes a comprehensive collection of cognitive, personal and interpersonal abilities that help people make informed decisions, solve problems, think critically and creatively, communicate effectively, build healthy relationships, empathise with others and cope with and manage their lives in a healthy and productive manner.

In an article titled 'Understanding Life Skills', Madhu Singh of UNESCO Institute for Education, Hamburg says, 'The importance of skills with broader development of personal potential becomes significant when the future is uncertain'.[2] She quotes the Delors Commission (1996)[3] as saying, 'human being's further progress depends less upon continued economic growth than upon an increase in a broader "personal development" and empowerment that people need to steer overall developments in a sensible way'.

This single need for life skills in many ways is often behind other needs that employees experience and is in that sense, very pervasive. It is in this area that employees need the most help.

Organisations often attempt to organise training programmes to impart all or some of these skills to their employees at various stages of their career. While this is certainly welcome, it is too little and often too late. Given the crucial influence of the role of society, culture, family and upbringing on the presence or absence of these skills, developmental efforts need to start very early in life.

If employees do indeed enter the workplace with significant deficits in these areas, which is often the case, it is still possible to make up for lost time and develop the skills as long as the development process is integrated into the employees' work life. Sensitive supervisors or managers can help their employees develop these skills through their everyday workplace interactions. Similarly, when organisations are community oriented in the way they operate, they end up creating the climate for employees to be, to know and to live together.

This is where well-designed employee assistance programmes or professional employee assistance are very effective.

Our research into the current state of evolution of Professional Employee Assistance clearly points out that the biggest roadblock is the stigma attached to seeking professional assistance. With primary sources vanishing and tertiary sources still not socially

---

[2] Madhu Singh. 'Understanding Life Skills'. (Hamburg: UNESCO Institute for Education, 2003).

[3] J. Delors and Mayer, F. presented the report of the International Commission on Education for the 21st Century 'Learning: The Treasure Within.' (Paris: UNESCO Headquarters, April 1996).

acceptable, employees end up suffering but not seeking help until it reaches breaking point. Very few realise that early intervention has great benefits.

While employees are victims of stereotypes and stigmas, organisations are victims of poor commitment when it comes to professional employee assistance. Organisations which have experienced the direct impact of employee distress in the form of one or more suicides, work place violence or visible psychiatric emergencies tend to more readily see the benefit of professional employee assistance.

On the other hand, organisations which have not experienced any visible problems or seen some of the warning signs find it much harder to either set up such services or sustain them.

Above all, there is no system for measuring the psychological health of employees in organisations. Without measurement, there is no incentive to change. Organisations are also avoiding engaging in any form of action research and publication about the issues of psychological health among their workforce.

The Need for Meaning, Purpose and Achievement

Maslow pointed out about the needs that people have for the respect of others, the need for status, fame, glory, recognition, attention, reputation, appreciation, dignity, even dominance. He also talks about the need for self-respect, including such feelings as confidence, competence, achievement, mastery, independence, and freedom.

Finally, he talks about the need that people have for meaning, a sense of being connected to a larger purpose and of course the desire to be and become all that they can and want to be.

It takes a lot of will and wisdom for organisations to transcend their preoccupation with fulfilling the deficit needs to start paying attention to these higher-order needs of employees. This is about ensuring that the job itself is engaging, that the voice of the employee can be heard, that the employee is able to associate with the larger purpose of the organisation and that the person can see his or her unique skills being utilised and the opportunity to realise one's potential.

Of course, it will also call for the ability to be realistic enough to know that these higher order needs will not even appear in the radar, until some of the more basic needs are taken care of.

What Really Matters

The last several decades have seen the emergence of several models of employee engagement. All of these in many ways attempt to articulate what really matters to employees. However, in trying to be different from one another, these models may not help articulate the science behind the thinking and that is what has been attempted in this chapter.

Stated very simply, here is what really matters to employees:

1. Employees need to feel safe and secure in the work they do, people they work with and the organisations they work for.
2. Employees need to feel a sense of connect, belonging and community at the workplace because this can be the greatest source of psychological support and sense of well-being.
3. Employees must feel good, valued, appreciated and be respected.
4. Above all, employees would like to be connected to a larger purpose, experience meaning and a sense of fulfilment in what they do and what their organisation does.

As has been stated several times in the book, fulfilling these four needs may constantly be threatened by external pressures and demands. This is where value-based organisations and matured HR professionals are able to make a difference. They do this by putting the employee at the heart of their efforts. When they do this consistently, the genuineness and authenticity comes through and employees are able to understand, accept and live with the inevitable vicissitudes of business.

Closing Reflections

While more and more organisations embrace one or more of the popular employee-engagement models to measure and manage engagements, it is apparent that the scientific drivers of motivation as established decades ago continue to remain relevant. While more and more organisations seem to be preoccupied with the transactional and hygiene dimensions of engagement, we see more and more employees calling to attention gaps in the way higher-order needs are being addressed. When it comes to motivation, separating the noise from the signal and focussing on what matters is most crucial.

Organisational Experiences

Beroe: Engaging Millennials at Work

As Beroe operates in the knowledge industry, employees play a very critical role in the success of the business. The ability to hire, develop and retain employees determines how the future of the business will shape up. Back in 2014, Beroe undertook a study on how to engage its employees— 80 per cent of these employees were millennials.

Beroe realised that one of the most important aspects of engaging millennials was to ensure that the engagement for employees was around work and how they can enable employees to attain mastery in their respective fields and bring their whole self to work.

Focus on Continuous Learning

Beroe's core proposition to its clients was centred around continuous competitive advantage through procurement intelligence. The focus on learning was a critical contributing factor to ensure that Beroe's analysts were able to translate their knowledge of the industry and deliver actionable insights to the procurement teams leading to significant cost savings and process improvements.

For employees, the focus on learning translated to mastery in their respective fields and the ability to influence and advise leading MNCs on their sourcing and procurement strategies.

The first step towards creating a culture of learning within Beroe started with a training and development assessment for analysts across Beroe. The next step was to restructure the organisation to create rewarding career paths for individual contributors and people managers. Beroe also initiated 'career conversations' with every analyst to understand their aspirations, provide guidance and draw out a roadmap to excel in their respective fields. All these efforts took shape in form of Beroe University—a platform to consolidate and disseminate continuous learning within the organisation.

The platform enabled Beroe to formalise learning as part of the growth path of every analyst. It also helped to completely revamp the onboarding and induction process at Beroe.

Launch and roll-out of the Beroe University resulted in increased scores for both employee and client satisfaction.

To further inculcate the learning culture amongst employees and enable them to pursue their passions outside of work, employees were offered to pick up courses based on their interest, for which Beroe would fully reimburse the course fee. Employees could pick whatever they wanted to pursue—be it psychology, certification in digital marketing or a study on the history of rock music.

Improving Work–Life Balance

At Beroe, policy-making has always been employee-centric and collaborative. Beroe has been consistently introducing initiatives which focus on employee well-being and enhancing their experience at the workplace.

Four-day workweek: In the year 2017, Beroe introduced the four-day workweek as against the industry practice of either a five or six-day workweek. The objective of this initiative was to ensure a better work–life balance and to improve productivity and creativity in employees.

The four-day workweek allowed employees to pursue their passion outside of work, while ensuring that they are fresh and recharged when they come to work every Monday.

As the initiative had a direct impact on client deliverables, Beroe made all efforts to onboard clients with communication around the initiative and ways of working during the process. To measure the organisation's productivity during the four-day workweek, Beroe launched the Beroe Performance Index. The index measured the organisation's performance across two key parameters—client feedback and deliverables—on a month-on-month basis, and it was shared with the entire organisation to track the progress.

The results from the Beroe Performance Index have been extremely positive. Employees not only embraced the four-day workweek wholeheartedly, the results from the initiative have been outstanding—with improvement in employee productivity and increased customer-satisfaction levels.

One-year maternity leave: Beroe's one-year maternity leave policy is a further testament to the organisation's focus on employee's well-being and creating a workplace that truly believes in enhancing work–life balance. In addition to the six-month maternity leave mandated by the Indian government, the one-year maternity leave at Beroe allows women employees to avail six additional months of paid leave which includes a three-month 'extended work from home' option.

Welcoming a newborn into the world is a life-changing event and such moments are far and few. Beroe strongly believes that employees should get the opportunity to make the best of such moments.

bringHERback: Beroe's unique return-to-work programme was conceptualised to enable and empower recent mothers explore the freedom to be independent, to define life on their own terms, to experiment and seek professional fulfilment. *bringHerback* programme offered a wide spectrum of roles across the organisation to mothers wishing to explore a return to professional life—in core research, HR and marketing, reiterating its commitment to let employees explore the freedom of their individual ambitions without having to make a choice between their personal and professional selves.

Work from anywhere policy: With a workforce that is geographically dispersed, Beroe introduced the work from anywhere policy that allows employees to work from the most remote of locations. The flexibility to work from anywhere allows employees to design their own workday while improving productivity and creativity with uninterrupted time. Location is no longer an impediment to hire prospective employees for Beroe, as employees can be based out of any location and still contribute in a very effective manner for the organisation.

For Beroe, employees are the most valuable asset and the organisation continues to invest in them to ensure they are able to excel—both on the professional and the personal fronts.

23

Towards Progressive Employee Relations

Not too long ago, we embarked on a research project to see if progressive and differentiated employee relations practices, specifically in the manufacturing sector, led to sustainable results and of course peaceful coexistence.

Our research on this subject was triggered by the interest that one specific organisation had in understanding how organisations across the country were proactively shaping their employee relations (ER) strategy. The project was undertaken at a time when the country was seeing a series of ER conflicts which had turned quite violent.

Our hypothesis was that while business realities and pressures were understandable, organisations with a certain value fabric had a *differentiated* way to address these challenges that set them apart.

As the ER practice and philosophy undergoes rapid change, paying attention to and learning from progressive practices might be invaluable. In this chapter, we would like to share these research-based insights on what we consider progressive practices in ER.

These were seven valuable insights that we gleaned from organisations that had a progressive ER orientation and track record:

1. They had a well-articulated or well-understood ER philosophy, strategy and structure.

2. They invested in building a trusting and collaborative relationship.
3. They encouraged autonomous work groups and self-managed teams.
4. Their wage philosophy was fair, performance oriented and sustainable.
5. They invested in the skills and career development of their employees.
6. They instilled and nurtured a culture of cost orientation.
7. Their social and environmental agenda was embedded in their ER philosophy.

Let's now explore each of these seven insights in some detail.

A Well-articulated or Well-understood ER Philosophy, Strategy and Structure

Organisations with differentiated ER practices have either an explicit ER philosophy or an implicit but well-understood philosophy ingrained in their DNA.

The philosophy is personally driven by the CEO and his or her team across the organisation and it influences everything that governs workmen at the workplace and outside. The philosophy then becomes non-negotiable and is consistently practised at all times including the testing times and extreme catastrophes. The CEO clarifies and articulates the ER approach across the organisation and uses this as the basis for policy-making and reviewing its effective implementation.

Organisations have a formal process of capturing learnings from critical incidents of the past and for creating practical insights for the future. This is also used to create ER renewal strategies periodically.

The task of building trust-based relationships with employees is a long-term process and calls for significant investment of time and taking of many affirmative actions with no direct links to immediate gains.

In fact, large employers even in technology and financial services companies are beginning to recognise the need for such a long-term approach more than anyone else and are appointing seasoned ER professionals in their organisations to steer such initiatives.

ER strategies are not a one-time fix. Progressive organisations revisit their ER strategies regularly, as much as they revisit their marketing and manufacturing strategies. Many do it every year and not just when they have trouble.

They also distil learnings from past actions, build a knowledge repository and shape future policies on that basis.

Asian Paints has an annual meet with all manufacturing leaders to review their ER strategy and leverages this forum for sharing best practices of transformational ER initiatives.

Elgi Equipments Ltd believes in a philosophy of transparency and continuous, two-way communication. They put the employee first and speak up for those with the weakest voice. Elgi started its journey from 1993 with a 90 crores turnover. End of year 2000 they went into a deep financial crisis and they had to restructure the company. The company did not want to hurt its workmen. Many workmen were shifted to their sister concerns and others were given a VRS option and the money was put in a bank where the returns were equivalent to their monthly take-home salary. Many workmen were encouraged to start their own business. From 800 workmen they reduced the count to 300 and increased the productivity five-fold.

The ITC Group having businesses in several sectors invests significantly in the capability development of the new-generation HR managers. They ensure the new-generation HR managers are trained in change management and salient aspects of ER.

Earlier HR managers (present/retired/senior professionals from other organisations) are called to do a story-telling on how an incident happened, what went wrong and what the learning was. A lot of emphasis is placed on case study analysis as well.

Indian Hotels Ltd has an employee-centric philosophy and even in times of catastrophes it put their employees first and is ready to break the rules to ensure employee safety.

Organisations such as Asian Paints and the Tata Group also overtly communicate their employee-centric philosophy. More than communication, it is woven into their people practices and cultural fabric.

HUL has an ER philosophy of 'Nurturing Relations and Partnering Progress'. The execution of this is managed through their ER Strategy Wheel and Delivery Model. ER Strategy Wheel is a conceptual snapshot of the function handling ER. The wheel moves from tactical transactions related to basic healthy environment through productivity and development initiatives to strategic ER thought leadership.

Invested in Building a Trusting and Collaborative Relationship

While organisations continue to engage employees in welfare, recreation and other motivational activities, they have now taken the participation and engagement to a higher plane. The engagement is now built on trusting relationships with employees sharing with them information on critical business matters and transformational changes, while inviting them to shape the future course of action with the management.

Workmen today cocreate the vision and the value systems in the organisation. This is a bottom-up approach. Organisations are evolving an extensive tiered approach to workmen participation in management starting from basic welfare amenities to business processes transformation, quality and customer centricity. Organisations are also investing in building the leadership capabilities of the trade union members for their meaningful engagement in the management of the company.

The ER philosophy of a large public sector company is very well articulated in the short tagline of 'Partner in Progress'. The ER structure is a pyramidal structure with different platforms for workforce representation at different levels. At the shop-floor level, the company has participative professional and welfare forums that discuss and tackle issues about basic amenities such as canteen, welfare, housing and the like. All these issues are discussed at this level along with their immediate supervisors. These forums meet on a weekly/monthly basis. They are also rewarded for meeting a business goal or solving a key problem.

The next level is at the business level where the representatives of all unions meet with the unit head (equivalent to a GM) every quarter. This covers any issues related to business goals and requirements for that quarter. There is a half-yearly forum for the regional communication meeting that includes heads of regions in HR, supply chain and finance with the union representatives of those regions.

Encourage Autonomous Work Groups and Self-managed Teams as Characteristic of the Future

Organisations are looking at autonomous work groups/self-managed teams (SMT) as a long-term transformational journey and make this as a part of their long-term vision and business strategy. Organisations invite participation of workmen in this transformational journey thereby ensuring total buy-in.

Organisations go the extra mile in their investments by providing time off for skill and capability development rather than making it a point of bargain. They forge relationships with institutions that provide customised learning.

Organisations have started to reap high rewards from this transformation in terms of world-class productivity and quality and an empowered workforce taking ownership of the customer from the shop floor.

Elgi has a full-fledged SMT in place. Their foray into SMT was a six-year-long journey that involved extensive training and understanding the usage of SMT tools. Every SMT has three stars among the workmen who will each lead a department [production star, quality star, *theni* star (honey bee)]. Each star gets four months to perform and lead his team. The stars are responsible for day-to-day operations, productivity, quality and customer demand. The supervising engineers don't monitor these stars. They spend their time on innovations.

Wage Philosophy Which Is Fair, Performance Oriented and Sustainable

Profit sharing is becoming a more equitable and uniform practice across these organisations. Workmen earn a share of the profits based on set parameters of business performance being achieved apart from the statutory bonus (where applicable).

The representatives of employees and the management jointly study the real increase in cost of living based on the relevant basket of needs annually and arrive at market relevant salary increases. Common principles are applied in salary-increase programmes and market positioning across all the levels.

From a time when all ER energies were invested in signing a good settlement with the hope that it would help bring peace and serve to govern the relationship for a reasonable period ahead, the wage settlement has now become a small part of the overall ER strategy.

Given the complexities of doing business and the economic cycles, much seems to happen in the intervening three- or four-year period. This therefore calls for continuous efforts to engage the workforce and not rest on the laurels of a good settlement.

Many organisations have signed three-year settlements with increases of more than ₹9,000 in cash benefits. There is no variable component in these increases. Other benefits are not costed into these settlements. Thermax aims to keep their operators compensation in the top quartile of the region and industry.

Organisations such as Thermax, Titan, Tata Group and Asian Paints have a philosophy of transparency and equitable treatment ingrained in their culture. They ensure common benefits and facilities are provided across levels and roles.

The basic compensation philosophy of Titan is that is 'If the company is prospering, share the prosperity with all'. The unit goes to the local market and determines the cost of expenses which a shop-floor employee will incur and study the neighbouring organisations and decide the quantum of increase. Apart from that, the normal dearness-allowance increase happens every six months. The long-term settlement is for a three-year period. The organisation looks at three parameters: (a) 75th market percentile, (b) productivity linkage and (c) prosperity sharing. The increase agreed to has two components—a flat increase and an annual lump sum. The annual lump sum varies depending on company's target achievement of earnings before interest and taxes (EBIT). Communication is transparent on one's wages. In a particular year, after discussions with the union, no increase was given and this was accepted by all with hardly any conflict.

In case an employee dies (not necessarily on duty), the company either gives employment to a family member or the surviving family is given a protected monthly income amount equivalent to the employee's bonusable salary till the time of notional retirement. An alternate to this is a lump sum which is a multiplier of the employee's cost to the company.

Employees who retire from the company and their dependent spouse continue to be covered for life under a group insurance hospitalisation scheme.

Investment in Skills and Career Development

There is a shift in the way workmen can grow in today's times. Career progression plans of workmen go beyond the highly skilled and supervisory roles to managerial roles even beyond production functions.

Organisations are investing in the enhancement of skills through in-house capability building programmes or through tie-ups with external institutions that customise learning programmes and these help in speedy progression.

Organisations such as Thermax and Turbo Energy invest in building the skills and competencies of their workmen by providing them developmental experiences. Thermax has a tradition of sending all blue-collared employees to MRA Panchgani (now called the Initiatives of Change). The company has almost completed nominating all its workmen for the above programme. It has resulted in bringing a sense of belongingness and respect for others' viewpoints. It has created a feeling of true moral responsibility amongst the participants and a sense of empowerment. It gives them the feeling that 'I have a voice and I will be heard'.

At Thermax workmen also get direct exposure to the customers to understand their requirements and demands. This experience is a part of a series of workman education programmes.

'Stepping into One' programme is a well-structured process at HUL to identify HIPO workmen and build their capability to make them ready for future white-collar roles proactively. 'Sparkle' (a capability-building tool) enables the linkage of skills training to operational performance at a factory and product level. By targeting the right skills, the company maximises personal skill development and career progression for the factory workforce. The company has conceptualised a Blue Collar Academy and White Collar Academy to enable it to develop skills and potential of employees to make them future ready.

Instilling a Culture of Cost Orientation

Investment in skills and capabilities, a culture of trust, collaboration, autonomy and empowerment at work are critical ingredients of building a cost culture in organisations.

Organisations are now sharing business-critical information as part of employee communication programmes in a manner those employees feel their contribution has an important part in the success of the organisation. Workmen also get direct exposure to customers and their issues.

At Turbo Energy, the employee-suggestion scheme is highly appreciated by the employees and attracts amazing participation and contribution from them. Employees are encouraged to submit their suggestions for continuous improvement in the unit. All such suggestions are evaluated on their implementability and cost impact. All implementable suggestions are appreciated and rewarded with cash prizes. Two functions are organised every year to appreciate and reward all good suggestions. All suggestions are converted into cost value. The amount of cash award depends on the amount of savings or extent of value addition. This scheme has enabled Turbo Energy Limited to win many internal and external Kaizen Competitions and it has also helped the organisation to imbibe a culture of continuous improvement and people involvement.

Thermax has a culture of cost orientation ingrained in the organisation's culture. The entire charter of demands is costed and communicated. Monthly and quarterly shop-floor meetings are organised where all costs are shared with the union and workmen. Information on orders obtained as well as orders lost and the associated financial implications are discussed. All financial results are also shared in a transparent manner. This has resulted in reducing overtime work and payments significantly.

The Social and Environmental Agenda is Embedded in the ER Philosophy

Organisations focus on maintaining a harmonious relationship with the community. The focus is greater in remote and the economically weaker areas. Organisations involve and contribute to the society by investing in the health and infrastructure of the community.

Creating a greener environment and self-sustaining communities are part of the culture, values and DNA of organisations. Organisations are creating employment opportunities by reaching out for talent from remote parts of the country. They invest in their development including absorption into the new society and enriching their families. The social and environmental agenda is not always equated with the return on investment (ROI).

It is evident that as businesses grow, expand geographically and employ more people, their workforce begins to reflect a slice of the local social setting and consequently start to mirror all local social issues and challenges.

Progressive organisations are recognising these social agendas and taking affirmative actions to address these social needs through their ER policies and programmes. While mental health, stress, lifestyle ailments, diversity and safety are social issues that knowledge-oriented businesses are grappling with, education, employability, community development, environment, health and sanitation are issues that manufacturing-oriented businesses are paying attention to.

As a global company, Tata Motors has invested in Community Development Centres (CDCs) to create a generation of scientific, skilled and educated young women and men who will play an important role in empowering their communities. These communities are not only a source of get-togethers but a platform wherein community members can identify and build better solutions for hyperlocal problems and develop sustainable solutions that positively impact the whole community. The facilities provided for members at CDCs range from sports, gym to medical facilities and libraries. Apart from this, Tata Motors have also formed clubs such as Kalasagar, photography club and adventure club for employees and their families. The important point to note here is that all the clubs are managed by the employees and mentored by the senior leaders of the company.

Tata Motors' Grihini Udyog aims at providing sustainable livelihoods and economic independence to the wives of the blue-collar workmen. This trust manages four cooperative societies wherein spouses and close relatives of workmen find employment as per their skills and educational qualifications. Being a true epitome of a cooperative welfare society, a profit-sharing philosophy and collective decision-making are followed. The arms of Grihini Udyog extend far into the local community of women in Pune. The employees don't just get the benefits of a basic salary but enjoy work–life balance as well as various employee benefits. Under the stable leadership and support of Tata Motors, today Grihini has transformed from manufacturing household consumer products to intricate wiring and hi-tech automotive electronic products. Grihini has four major lines of business—ranging from electronics, cable harness, tailoring to food products; it presently gives employment to 550 women and has an annual turnover of more than ₹8.5 crores. Tata Motors procures finished goods such as food items, uniforms and the like from Grihini, and it also provides avenues for Grihini Udyog to explore business opportunities within Tata Motors and Tata Group's ecosystem.

Titan has adopted a village to provide drinking water, community health and education to increase employability. They educate the villagers on necessity of improvement of the well-being of girl child through the Titan Kanya Scheme. Titan also maintains a lake near their factory to maintain the ecological balance of the locality.

HUL partners with NGOs to implement health and hygiene, water conservation and livelihood initiatives in rural areas around its factories. The programme 'Prabhat'—a community intervention—comprises of community-centric developmental initiatives aimed at enhancing livelihood, conserving water and promoting health and personal hygiene. Through Prabhat, HUL aims to impact the lives of one million people. The key themes are enabling livelihood, water conservation and hygiene through active participation of their employees.

Some Larger Lessons

As we met these organisations and listened to their experiences, we were able to draw certain larger lessons about what goes into making ER practices progressive:

- First, it was clear that company leadership had a great role to play in shaping good ER practices.
- Second, ER philosophy is long-term oriented but calls for constant renewal.
- Third, these organisations were fully alive to the changing sociocultural shifts.
- Fourth, they recognise that the long-term settlement is no longer a panacea for peace and engagement.
- Finally, the contingent workforce is a given and managing it with respect and dignity is what matters.

Closing Reflections

Organisations which transcend the temptation to surrender to pure market-orientated practices and take a value-based approach, interestingly, end up being able to make transformational changes in partnership with their workforce. It is a myth that being value based and having a philosophy runs contrary to making money. It can rather aid moneymaking and of course make it sustainable.

It must also be pointed out that these insights are of equal value to manufacturing and service businesses.

The authors thank all the organisations (quoted in this chapter) that readily shared their differentiated ER practices with us and also granted us permission to publish the same. Their contribution has enriched this chapter and brought alive invaluable lessons in progressive ER.

Organisational Experiences

Proactive Industrial Relations at Tata AutoComp Systems

Being proactive is so crucial in managing industrial relations (IR) effectively. At Tata AutoComp Systems (TACO), effective IR is so critical given its large spread of 7 business units and 33 manufacturing plants. Effective communication has been the bedrock of good IR and has helped the workforce contribute with high performance and enhanced productivity improvement. A strong bond with the union has also led to an uplift in employee morale and positive atmosphere on the shop floor.

The following initiatives have helped TACO in achieving harmonious IR:

- Engagement initiatives that involve employees and their families
- Transparent and open communication by business unit leadership through open forums
- Active participation of employees in all the 10 plant committees
- Reward and recognition at plant level
- Prompt resolution of payroll-related issues through HR help desk
- Strategic workforce composition

How TACO Did It

The business units of TACO have faced lot of turbulence in IR during the 2012–2014 period which prompted TACO to reinvigorate its IR strategy with focus on proactive employee engagement. TACO introduced the following initiatives to revamp its IR policy:

- Standardisation of manpower composition in various categories and monitoring of its effective implementation
- Revised selection criteria of students for traineeship, training period, assessment process during training period and introduction of semester system
- Creating an HR help desk on the shop floor to address issues of blue-collar employees
- Starting a monthly open forum for all employees to ensure effective and transparent communication. In this forum, business updates, business challenges and customer issues are discussed with all employees
- The following reward and recognition initiatives were also launched:

  - 'Abhinandan'—on-the-spot recognition scheme
  - Recognition at open forum
  - Employee of the month award
  - Competition related to Kaizen, 5S, quality circle, safety and so on

- There was monthly feedback from operators stationed at customers end
- Launch of enabling and collaborative improvement platforms such as plant committees wherein those potential opinion makers can participate and help the organisation to improve various areas which affects the lifecycle/existence of employees and engagement, through joint participation
- The practice of starting negotiation meetings well in advance between the management and the union was initiated to enhance understanding and arrive at an amicable wage settlement before due date

- An outbound programme aiming at breaking the ice, setting the norms and building the trust was conducted for each unit before the negotiations started, involving the union-office bearers, opinion leaders and key plant management staff.

To ensure effective execution of the aforementioned, the group IR head reviews IR management information system (MIS) received from the business unit HR heads in the monthly meetings.

What Benefits Were Delivered

All these engagement efforts help to build strong rapport not only with unions but also with individual workmen at large. Following these initiatives, TACO could amicably resolve wage settlement at its Automotive Stampings and Assemblies Limited (ASAL) Bhosari, ASAL Chakan, TACO Hendrickson Suspensions Pvt Ltd (THSL) Chakan and plants at Pantnagar location.

The wage settlements were signed before expiry of earlier settlement, without any unrest or loss of production.

In the subsequent wage-settlement cycle, ASAL Bhosari was the first company due for wage settlement, whose union leaders came forward and communicated to the management by their letter as follows:

During the existing wage settlement period, Management has developed transparent culture by implementing good systems and practices; hence we have decided not to submit charter of demands (COD), because relationship based on expectations is not the true relationship. We do agree that, we made number of mistake in the past and we have full realisation of the same. We assure you that during our discussion on proposed settlement, we will not use any coercion, violence, slow-down, strike and abusive language etc. To make this successful, we also look forward for Managements cooperation.

If our wage settlement is signed successfully on time with this approach, it will set an example in the industry located at Chakan and nearby Chakan area, as well as this will set the company and its workmen to build the positive image.[1]

Further the union also submitted the list of various improvement projects to be undertaken with a view achieve higher productivity and will demonstrate their wholehearted participation in its implementation to make this a self-funded settlement.

This initiative of ASAL Bhosari union was welcomed by the management, and wage settlement was amicably concluded on time. The said practice adopted by ASAL Bhosari union was very positively received by many other unions in TACO, and they also decided to sign the wage settlement without submitting formal COD to the management and have signed wage settlement amicably on time.

Following are the salient features of the wage settlement:

1. The wage settlement signed for a period of *four years* against normal industry trend of *three years*.
2. Signed the wage settlement averagely for ₹8,000 for four years against industry trend which is approximately 28 per cent lesser than industry for three years wage settlement.

---

[1] Extracted from the letter dated 25 June 2015 by the ASAL Kamgar Sanghatana Union Leadership addressed to management.

3. The variable dearness allowance (VDA): To have predictable outflow, TACO has done away with the concept of VDA in many business units (BUs), whereas, few BUs have demonstrated downward trend on VDA.

4. Block closure of *30 days*, against previous practice of around 10 days and industry practice ranging from 6 to 10 days, to deal with business contingencies.

5. The benefits under the settlement are based on productivity improvement. If the base level productivity is not achieved, the wage increase is liable to be withdrawn partially or fully.

6. Discontinued the present practice of salary, festival and other loans and advances and given option to form employees credit cooperative society with seed capital. Now the credit cooperative society takes care of financial need of the employees.

In fact, the IR practices in ASAL have won it recognition and its HR leaders have been invited by others to share their experiences.

The Unique Wage Settlement at Thermax in 2015

Thermax has a history of signing long-term settlements in a peaceful manner every three years. Thermax workmen are perhaps the highest paid in Chinchwad Industrial Area. The average CTC (all costs included) is ₹72,000 per month. The factory has been in existence for around 40 years.

This story is about the settlement that expired in May 2013.

The negotiations on the settlement commenced and at a point of time, as it happens in many protracted settlement negotiations, it reached a point of deadlock. The management and the union were on the negotiation table for almost two years. The CTC at that point of time was ₹50,000 per month and the last offer of the company was of an increase of ₹10,000 per month that would have taken the CTC to ₹60,000 per month. The union committee was firm on accepting nothing less than a ₹12,000 per month increase over ₹50,000.

The negotiating team for settlement at Thermax is led by the ER head along with a factory manager and two senior managers from manufacturing area. They are vested with all the powers to take decisions once the framework is agreed to with all stakeholders. The committee tried its best and ultimately they offered the union to take the matter to Conciliation as the parties could not reach a mutually agreed settlement. The union in the meanwhile gave a notice of strike. As a last resort, the MD and the HR head came to the factory to meet the union committee and appeal to them not to resort to strike and hinted that a small adjustment could be possible and that the negotiating team is empowered to do it, though the offer of ₹10,000 per month was reasonable and it had stretched the limits of affordability from a cost point of view for the factory.

The union committee maintained that nothing less than ₹12,000 per month was acceptable. It was a bit of a surprise as the union had an image of being progressive and understood manufacturing economics well. The HR head had the support of his business heads even if it meant disruption in manufacturing. The options were to face a strike and probably it would have been settled somewhere in between or take it to the end where it either results in workers feeling lost or it results in a lockout.

Many a times in IR the union committee becomes the central focus and we tend to forget that the workmen on the shop floor are the real constituency of the management. The HR head requested the MD that they jointly address the workmen and explain to them the facts and how what has been offered is reasonable. The decision was not to succumb to the union demand.

In this charged atmosphere of strike notice, they decided to address all the workmen in the factory. As expected, the union gave a call to the workmen not to attend the meeting and instead they announced a parallel meeting just outside the factory at the same time, obviously to ensure workmen don't attend the meeting called by the HR head and the MD. The venue of the meeting called by the management was in a makeshift arrangement actually near the gate.

The move was successful and about 75 per cent of the workmen attended the meeting. After hearing the MD and HR head, even before they could be told to ask questions, there was a spontaneous signal from the workers that they did not want a strike!

They went to the extent of asking the management to tell them the break-up of their offer and that they were ready to look at it.

Immediately after the meeting, a notice giving the break-up was displayed and the workers started streaming in to the time office the next day stating in their individual capacity that they are ready to accept the management offer. The voice from the shop floor was 'we trust the management', 'we will not be shortchanged'.

The difficulty was how to pay? The union committee was nowhere to be seen and the advice was to go for a Section 2(p) settlement under the Industrial Disputes Act. But in reality it was a moment to write a new chapter in IR and the management decided to pay without a settlement on the basis of an affidavit by the workmen that they are accepting the offer without going into legal complications. It meant a risk to the management as it could be opened again later by the union committee saying that it was not a settlement. But such was the trust level between workers and management that arrears for almost two years and the settlement benefits were given based on individual affidavits and all workmen except the 11 committee members gave the affidavit.

Later, after about four months, a new committee was chosen by the workmen who formalised this process through a settlement. Thereafter one more settlement was signed in 2016 in 58 days of negotiating time! The increase given incidentally was of ₹12,401 per month!

HR
HERE
AND
NOW

THE MAKING OF THE QUINTESSENTIAL
PEOPLE CHAMPION

PART 7

The Making of the
Quintessential People
Champion

24
Advancing in HR

How would one define true career advancement for an HR professional? Should it be their ability to move multiple pay grades with rapidity? Should it be a function of their mobility?

The pace of growth of an HR professional is often a function of the industry in which she or he works in, the business environment, the personal investment that the person has made for professional development and of course the maturity of the function in the organisation(s) that she or he has worked in.

During times of high growth, many HR professionals got several easy breaks and advanced rapidly; whereas during times of slowdown, many professionals seem to be staying where they are for a long time.

The true yardstick of advancing in HR cannot be the pay grade or job title. If HR were to be truly considered a profession, then the true yardstick of career advancement would be the achievement of professional mastery at each stage of one's career, much the same way you would measure the success of a doctor, a surgeon or any other professional. So what are the markers of professional mastery?

HR professionals progress through *three professional development stages* in their entire career journey. Each stage demands and provides a certain level of mastery in a collection of competencies and arising out of that is their capability to play roles with a certain level of impact and contribution.

When professionals gain such mastery and move from one stage of development to the other, they demonstrate the ability to perform increasingly complex functions with aplomb by constantly acquiring and demonstrating relevant professional competencies.

The competencies for each professional development stage vary depending on the career track that the HR professional is in. While some of them are common, others are unique to a certain career track. In fact, the problem with today's HR function is that there is an overemphasis on developing track-specific competencies rather than holistic stage-specific competencies. When HR professionals develop holistic stage-specific competencies their scope for mobility is likely to be enhanced.

The following diagram shows the three stages of professional development as defined by us.

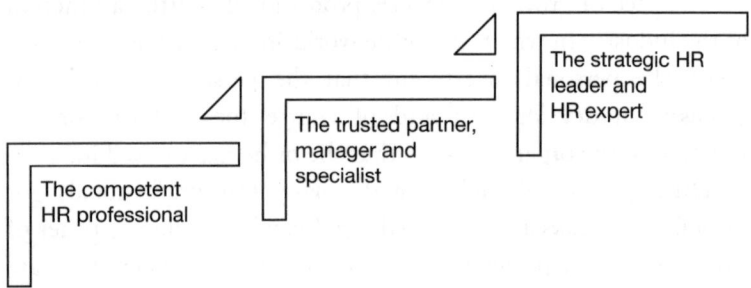

The strategic HR leader and HR expert

The trusted partner, manager and specialist

The competent HR professional

In each of these stages of professional development, we attempt to articulate the milestones of mastery, the typical developmental needs and the experiences that will shape mastery. Let's examine each of these in detail.

The First Stage of Professional Development: The Competent HR Professional

The goal of the first stage of professional development is to achieve foundational competence as an HR professional. Specifically, by the time an HR professional exits this stage, he or she should be able to manage oneself effectively, engage with others, understand and internalise the professional standards and acquire competence in the fundamentals of the function across all specialisations.

What Signifies Mastery in This Stage?

Those who achieve mastery in this stage demonstrate the ability to:

1. Be self-aware
2. Engage with employees and other stakeholders in an effective manner
3. Master routine and transactional pressures and deliver consistently
4. Understand and articulate the basics of how things work across all specialisations in HR including the rules, policies and processes
5. Uphold the professional standards of the function
6. Shape one's role proactively
7. Analyse people data and draw meaningful insights to support decisions

Typical Developmental Needs

Some of the typical development needs that young HR professionals have in this developmental stage are:

1. Good life skills required to plan, organise, solve problems, take decisions, cope with stress or even assert oneself
2. Mastering routine workload
3. Working with an ambiguous role brief
4. Upholding the ethical boundaries of the profession
5. Understanding HR from first principles
6. Understanding the business purpose, its constituent parts and their way of working

Experiences to Shape Mastery in the First Stage

Working in at least two of the following four functional special-
izations contributes to gaining mastery:

1. Staffing, recruitment and selection
2. HR operations
3. Employee relations
4. Learning and development

In addition, a stint as a generalist or people partner responsible for
a group of employees would also help.

The Second Stage of Professional Development: The Trusted Partner, Manager and Specialist

The goal of the second stage of professional development is to
achieve maturity in engaging with line managers to support them
in implementing people processes. This includes the ability to
evaluate existing functional processes and suggest improvements
and changes, the ability to develop depth in one or more functional
areas and the ability to manage other professionals in the team.

What Signifies Mastery in This Stage?

Those who achieve mastery in this stage demonstrate the ability to:

1. Influence business decisions with confidence
2. Define and solve HR problems in the business
3. Demonstrate a systemic view of the entire function
4. Devise systems, processes and add new knowledge in one or
   more functional areas
5. Manage a work unit and its people
6. Engage with business leaders and line managers with
   confidence
7. Appreciate the context and work challenges of other
   functions

Typical Developmental Needs

Some of the typical development needs that experienced HR professionals have in this developmental stage are:

1. Engaging in an assertive relationship and hold one's own
2. Building and nurturing relationships with line managers
3. Functional expertise in more than one area
4. Influencing with success
5. Self-confidence and self-esteem to take up ownership
6. Adding value to the function and to the business unit beyond the routine

Experiences to Shape Mastery in the Second Stage

Working with specialists (as part of special projects/regular process) in at least two of the following five functional specialisations they are not directly responsible for and do not have earlier experience in would be valuable.

1. HR operations
2. Employee relations
3. Management and leadership development
4. Organisation development and change
5. Compensation and benefits

In addition to rounding off their specialist stint in a few of these core areas, the opportunity to partner with line managers for creating significant business impact would be useful.

The opportunity to work in an operational role in business (cross-functional stint) or in a new business or country (cross-cultural) at this stage would be of great value.

In our view, this is the stage at which many HR professionals come to be stuck. They might move to higher pay grades or may even be hired by other companies but not everyone achieves true mastery of this stage.

The Third Stage of Professional Development: The Strategic HR Leader and HR Expert

The goal of the third stage of professional development is to achieve mastery in making the organisation effective by aligning the function to the business goals. They achieve such mastery by building a competent HR team, by bringing expertise in one or more functional areas and by being available to the CEO as a trusted advisor on matters of people and organisation.

What Signifies Mastery in This Stage?

Those who achieve mastery in this stage demonstrate the ability to:

1. Create and drive a compelling HR agenda.
2. Build an effective HR organisation to deliver on the agenda.
3. Champion and lead change. Be able to leverage networks.
4. Bring insight, advice and guidance to the CEO and the leadership team on matters relating to people and organisation.
5. Leverage the function to deliver business value and help the business choose the right interventions that enhance value.
6. Build leaders and enhance the leadership processes.

Typical Developmental Needs

Some of the typical development needs among HR leaders in this developmental stage are:

1. Understanding business nuances and strategic business choices
2. Being strategic in their thinking and action
3. Moving out of transactional work to conceptual and strategic work
4. Providing leadership to the function

5. Inspiring others to have trust and confidence in one's abilities
6. Forming influential networks

Experiences to Shape Mastery in the Third Stage

To gain mastery in this stage, HR professionals must have played the role of an HRBP for an entire business or independent business division or geography.

In addition, they must have led or managed at least two or three large organisation effectiveness initiatives. They should also have participated in a few mission-critical cross-functional initiatives.

Closing Reflections

It will take the interest and commitment of the CHRO to make meaningful career development happen for the team.

As a first step, HR professionals need support to discover their strengths, preferences. The leader will need to promote a culture of planned internal mobility. Young HR professionals who are given the opportunity to move every two years in the first five or six years are likely to develop into very well-rounded HR professionals. This will also take away the boredom that often sets into many of the front-line HR roles.

Having established career tracks can of course make a huge difference.

Finally, a functional competence development programme that is linked to a planned approach to building a strong cadre of HR professionals who can systematically progress across the three career-development stages will make a huge difference.

Beyond all this, of course, is the motivation of individuals to pay deliberate attention to their professional development and their career choices to become true people champions.

The HR profession holds huge opportunities for advancement. It is however often a maze and not easy to navigate. Planned actions by leaders combined with motivated individuals can make a difference.

25

The Young HR Professional's Readiness to Serve

How and when does a reputed hotel decide if its young front-office employees, cashiers or order takers can actually begin to handle guests? When are wealth management professionals permitted to start engaging with clients to give them information or guide them with their wealth management decisions? For that matter, when does a pilot get to fly the plane or a surgeon begin to perform surgeries?

One of the most important moments of truth for any professional is when he or she gets to go live and perform a task, offer a service or deal with real customers. This is a big moment and the manner in which it is handled can make a lot of difference, not just to the recipients of the service but also to the professional himself or herself. When managed well, the professional grows in confidence, stature and of course competence. Or else the professional can make mistakes, cause huge risks to the recipients and harm to the reputation of the function or profession and of course end up feeling completely demotivated.

HR professionals are no different.

Have we not seen many a new HR professional starting off his or her career facing customers (employees and people managers) without due training and preparation and as a consequence suffer humiliation, loss of confidence and of course add ammunition to the perennial criticism about the function?

In fact, a large number of the so-called HRBPs who were hoping to do strategic stuff end up spending a lot of their time solving operational problems or troubleshooting mostly because somewhere some young, new and mostly untrained HR professional who was the first port of call did not do what was meant to be done in an error-free manner.

So when can we say an HR professional is ready to be put in front of our stakeholders? Given that the young HR professional is in many ways the focus of this book, we dedicate this chapter to their readiness. There are at least four clear areas in which the person needs to acquire a base level of proficiency before being cleared to engage with internal customers.

Understand the Organisation's Published Policies, Products and Programmes

Every new HR professional must be completely familiar with all the published HR products, programmes, processes and polices of the organisation. This familiarity should help them answer basic questions and explain how they work, why they are the way they are, how one can avail of them or comply with them. The HR professional must be fully familiar with anything that is put in the public domain by the function—intranet, bulletin boards and mails—no different from the way business-to-consumer (B2C) businesses keep their customer-facing employees fully briefed about all new products, services and offerings.

Understand How Pay, Benefits and Other Policies Are Actually Administered

It is equally important for the new HR professional to know how the company's payroll actually works, how various benefits are administered, how provident fund gets remitted or withdrawn, how some of the basic employee welfare services such as cafeteria, transport and so on work, how things such as attendance and leave are recorded and computed, how new employees are onboarded, how HR service providers are paid, how tax is computed, how the final settlement works and so on.

This unfortunately is easier said than done. With most HR functions at least in large organisations moving towards shared services, there is a worrying trend. There seems to be an entire generation of young HR professionals who are completely disconnected from the role of aiding policy implementation. They are growing up believing that they can leapfrog into business partnering and leave this seemingly inconsequential stuff to shared services.

Young HR professionals would do well to spend at least a few months working mandatorily in shared services. This way they will understand how the basics work and also experience the moments of truth as faced by employees.

Young HR professionals must also get proficient in case work—solving some of the most common problems, issues, complaints or grievances that are raised by employees and their managers. By learning to analyse these problems under due guidance, they will also figure out what typically goes wrong and how they can fix it with a spirit of service orientation.

Training in Customer Engagement and Service Skills

New HR professionals must be trained in the basics of service skills so that they can present a very professional image of themselves and their functions. They must know how to greet and professionally answer the phone which rings at their desk. They must know how to respond to mails with clarity and accuracy and know that a mail is different from a text message.

They must know how to handle an irate employee. They must be able to listen with empathy and respond with understanding to an employee or a manager who has an issue and is looking for a solution or just wants to be heard.

They must know how to handle a complaint without becoming defensive and also how to recover when there is a service failure. They must know how not to take the employees' anger towards company policies and processes personally.

Grooming

They must, above all, be well groomed. It may be fine for a young employee to wear faded jeans to work. But an HR professional who is supposed to be the custodian of critical people processes and represents the organisation to the outside and inside world should be groomed professionally.

Role Clarity

The new HR professional must not only be clear about his or her role but also about how he or she impacts the larger functional responsibility and its overall service-quality levels. When faced with an employee query or issue, the professional should readily offer to help and not say it is not his or her job—just the way a well-trained hotel staff will make every effort to help a guest with any problem in a seamless manner no matter which department he or she belongs.

Once a young HR professional qualifies across these four basic dimensions, at least to an acceptable level, we might say that the person is service ready. He or she can now be safely put in front of employees or managers with the assurance that the person will do what is right for the person as well as the organisation and profession, and through those actions grow in confidence and professional stature. On this carefully built foundation, the person will of course need to keep adding higher and higher levels of competence on a continuous basis.

Until that is achieved, it is best that he or she wears an *HR trainee* badge and merely shadows a trained senior.

Commitment Towards Professional Excellence in HR

Beyond these four areas, young HR professionals must know that by upholding certain standards, they can demonstrate true professional excellence. Here are five standards that are considered foundational for professional excellence and form the bedrock of HR as a profession.

Demonstrate Fairness

Fairness needs to be present in every aspect of an HR professional's action including selection, pay, rewards, access to opportunities, career progression decisions, policy implementation, transparency in communication and respect for differences.

Ensure Safety and Well-being

Ensuring safety and well-being includes ensuring that the company's overall business strategy and actions are consistent with all applicable laws and regulations that govern the workplace environment as well as the welfare of employees. It also includes adherence in spirit to the guidelines issued by various agencies including the judiciary [The Sexual Harassment of Women at Workplace (Prevention, Prohibition and Redressal) Act 2013].

Pursue Ethical Business Conduct

Demonstrating prudent judgement, professionalism, trust and integrity in the way one conducts one's work including one's own personal conduct within the organisation. It will include handling confidential and proprietary information; avoiding conflict of interest, not accepting favours; demonstrating personal integrity in the use and handling of company property and funds; maintaining acceptable workplace behaviour and avoiding offensive conduct.

Uphold Trust Through Integrity

Trust through integrity includes gaining the confidence of junior-most employees or senior-most leaders through confidentiality and discretion, the credibility earned through the unvarnished truth that one speaks, the consistency of one's actions, the faith that the professional will not expose the organisation to huge risks, the faith that one's counsel has the best interests of the recipient and so on.

Display Diligence

Diligence is called for in almost all the actions of an HR professional. This can include the information they provide to support decisions, the recommendations they make to business to solve problems or make improvements, the interventions they suggest for progress, the people they recommend for hire into various positions, the compensation proposals they make, the diagnostic data they present, the laws and rules they interpret, the policies they frame and the proposals they make to the board or other decision-makers.

Closing Reflections

The formative years of an HR professional can be very impactful in shaping their confidence, capabilities and their attitudes towards the profession and its stakeholders. Helping them launch themselves well is a great way of contributing to their long-term career success.

26

The CEO's Schooling as a People Champion

Every new CEO in today's world will acknowledge that 'people' and therefore human resource management is one of his or her key drivers for business success. Given this conviction, they embark on or champion a series of interventions in this area. The CEOs are therefore rightfully the most vocal people champions.

The manner in which they go about doing this is often influenced by their experiences, views, perspectives and visions about HR as a function or its professionals. In other words, the manner in which they were schooled in people championship in their formative years often influences their thinking and actions.

This question becomes very relevant because very few CEOs are formally trained in or educated about some of the key HR processes, leave alone the larger science and art of HR. As a result, many may even start with the premise that 'Anyone can do HR work', much like star chef Auguste Gusteau's motto (in the movie *Ratatouille*), 'Anyone can cook'.

The Frames of Reference

There are at least five frames of reference that influence the view and approach that CEOs take to people championship.

Understanding this might help us support the schooling process more deliberately and effectively.

Conceptual Frame

Many CEOs approach HR with a certain conceptual frame of reference. The organisational behaviour course they studied in B-Schools, some of the bestsellers they have read about some of the global corporations' cutting-edge HR strategies, a master class they attended as part of an executive education programme, a TED Talk they saw or an article they read can all add to their conceptual frames of reference.

Their exposure to some of the popular HR models and frameworks, thanks to the consultants they worked with, can also contribute to their developing a strong conceptual appreciation of the function.

More the leaders get exposed to the science of HR the more they tend to develop a healthy respect for HR as a profession and its contribution and tend to take decisions keeping the science in mind.

First-person Experience

This is best explained with a small personal example. In one of the global corporations, it was well known to many that the head of the Asia Pacific region hated HR guys and here is why: When he was a young management trainee and was relocating from one city to another and wanted to ship his only prized possession, his scooter, the HR guy quoted company policy and disallowed it. From that day on, his experience of HR as a bureaucratic bottleneck got so indelibly etched in his mind that liberating employees and line managers from HR's bureaucratic ways became his mission statement.

The view that CEOs take about HR is often influenced by some of their first-hand experiences early in their careers. On this basis, they develop views on what the function should stand for and that also influences how they will treat the function and its functionaries.

When HR manages the moments of truth well, it not only contributes to engaged employees but also shapes future leaders' attitudes and views about HR. It is that powerful!

Partnering Experience

When CEOs were in middle-management positions, many would have had the need to partner with HR professionals to address many of their people management needs and challenges. This could be on issues ranging from large-scale hiring, large-scale downsizing, turbulent union situations, attrition, morale, productivity, capability building and so on.

If they got to work with competent and credible HR professionals who were able to help them solve these pressing people problems and support their success, they tend to develop a very healthy respect for the professionals and the function in general. This sense of respect gets further reinforced if they grew up in organisations which invested in building and implementing robust HR processes to support these professionals.

On the contrary, if they failed to receive such support and had to do things in a manner they know best, they may end up believing that such expertise is just not available or even necessary.

Great HR business partnership is certainly a huge contributor to shaping the view of leaders about HR.

Industry and Organisational Culture

The kind of industry one grew up in or the kind of organisations one worked in also shapes one's frames of reference about HR. Certain industries and organisations may be more market oriented and exigent in their approaches as we have seen. Others tend to be a lot more value driven. Depending on where the CEO spent his or her formative years, a certain kind of HR schooling is likely to have taken place.

Personality

Beyond all this, one's personality including one's beliefs, preferences, character strengths and values plays a huge role in shaping one's orientation to HR.

What Helps

Mature HR leaders recognise that they have a role to play in educating their business leaders and managers about HR and through that help them develop a balanced view of the function and functionaries. To this end, they adopt an extremely inclusive style involving these business leaders and managers in shaping policies and programmes. HR leaders also recognise that positive experiences create a virtuous cycle—good moments of truth and good partnership support lead to positive experiences and therefore a healthy respect for the function and, most importantly, an educative experience.

The ultimate contribution that any HR leader makes to his line colleague is to make each interaction a hugely educative experience. When the line manager or leader feels educated or richer by the interaction, one can be assured that the schooling process has been positive.

Closing Reflections

Business founders and CEOs are getting younger by the year. While they have many great strengths, they may not have had the opportunity to learn about HR. Like the CFO, the CHRO has the opportunity and responsibility to enrich the leader with teachable points of view and make each interaction educative and valuable to the CEO and to the organisation.

Epilogue

O ne of the common jokes that employees and line managers make about HR professionals is this: When you ask HR folks a question, they never answer you straight. They always say, 'It depends'.

Well, we must say that we agree with that observation but not the allegation!

The work that HR professionals do is almost always contingent upon a whole lot of dynamic contextual factors. So, when the person says it depends, he or she is right.

As the three of us got together to author this book, we realised that even the three of us ourselves did not see many of the issues that we raised in the book in the same way. We had varied views, perspectives and approaches to the same issue. As we engaged with each other in the spirit of true listening and understanding, we realised that there was huge merit in the diversity of the varied points of view. It was apparent to us that each of these points of view was based on our own individual experiences set in different contexts. We soon realised that the diversity in views amongst us represented the reality of the diversity in the real world.

Equally, we also seemed to agree on the few foundational professional principles and values.

This is what led us to recognise that HR is in part a science and in part an art form.

There are some things which easily lend themselves to logic, reason and a scientific rigour, while there are other parts of a function and profession which are open to multiple interpretations and approaches. It equally calls for grace and humility in accepting that there isn't just one way of doing HR work and that our way is not always the right way.

The more we explored the possibilities, issues and dilemmas, more the wisdom of this realisation dawned on us. We also recognised that we could certainly not claim to have clear-cut and definitive answers for all the questions that were raised.

If you recollect, we started this book by articulating the significance of context in shaping HR work. As we finished writing the book, we were even more convinced that *it depends*.

This brings us to an all-important question: What are the things that the future of HR work depends on? In other words, what are some of the potential external developments that are likely to influence what we in HR do and how we do it?

The Immediate Context

As we look at the immediate national context, three things emerge as being significant in terms of their impact on HR work.

Economic growth: How much will our economy and some of its critical constituents grow? To what extent will this growth lead to the creation of meaningful, quality jobs? Will the demographic advantage that we were so proud of really get leveraged to achieve this growth, or will the emerging demographics and insufficient growth create large-scale mismatches and challenges?

Workforce orientations: What will be the values, attitudes and orientations of the workforce today and tomorrow? How will they view corporations, leaders, managers and work itself? What will be their dreams, aspirations, motives and expectations? What is the extent to which organisations will be able to positively influence and shape these orientations, or will the divide widen?

Governance: Who will lead our nation and our states in the coming years? Will there be stability and will they do enough to improve the overall standard of life for the average citizen? As rapid urbanization continues, will we see enough being done for our cities, for our infrastructure and for our overall safety and security?

The Larger Context

As we look at the larger global context, six trends and possibilities strike as significant in terms of their impact on HR work.

Artificial intelligence in our lives: The disruptive advances in the field of artificial intelligence that we are witnessing seem to hold more fear than hope for the future. Very few of us know the true implications of robotisation and its impact on human lives and the future of work.

The geo-political landscape: After several years of globalisation and living in the belief that the world is flat, we are now beginning to realise that the world is not flat but walled. Growing barriers to trade and commerce seem to be making it hard for anyone and anything built on global aspirations. Can the aspirations of a nation be fulfilled within its borders? Will nations build more walls or is all this a storm in a teacup and things will get back to where they were some time ago?

The emerging social fabric: What more and more researchers are telling us is that what concerns our employees more are the problems of living and not the problems of working. How will some of the challenges fuelled by social–cultural changes, such as relationships, parenting, personal health, the health of the elderly, finances, domestic migration, lack of support for emotional and physical needs, and lack of skills to cope with these challenges, impact the social fabric and the ability of employees to give their best?

How will social disparities play out in the coming days? Will they get worse? Will social strife flow onto the streets? Is there the possibility of a revolution? Will there be a breakdown of law and order?

There is an ever-growing fear that we live in an unsafe world with threats of safety and security from multiple sources. We certainly know that not feeling safe does not augur well for a healthy and productive life at work and at home. Will these fears grow or diminish?

Breakthroughs in science and technology: We are seeing significant breakthroughs in science and technology that hold the promise of a better life every single day. Be it health or conveniences or energy or communications, there is hope that on the balance, we are seeing progress. What are the new frontiers that science and technology will open up and in what ways will it positively impact our work and our lives remains to be answered.

The dreams and aspirations of future generations: What will the future generations aspire to accomplish? What will be their orientation to life and work? What is the nature of choices they will make in terms of the way they would like to live and work? What will matter to them more and what will not? What will be their motivational hot buttons?

Mother earth: How will we treat mother Earth and how will she respond? What will the global environment look and feel like? Will the heightened awareness and some of the breakthrough ideas help heal mother Earth, or will the ecological disasters that we are witnessing only increase in the days to come?

The HR Response

While many of the potential trends we have outlined seem ominous and others uncertain at best, it is our belief that the right people will end up coming together to engage, understand and find solutions.

As in the past, the field of Human Resources will turn to other allied fields as well as its own scientific origins for insights and wisdom, and will come up with new and different solutions.

If the larger goal of all HR work is to help individuals and organisations realise their potential, then we do know for sure that such work will get done somewhere in some manner and under some name.

If you were to ask us what titles the future generations of HR professionals will carry or how they will be organised or where they will come from or which part of it will be human-driven and which part automated, we can only say that *it depends*!

About the Authors

Ganesh Chella has, in a career spanning over three decades, come to be acknowledged for his contributions as a practitioner and thought leader in the field of Organisation Development, Human Resources and Executive Coaching.

After a successful corporate career in Human Resources for 16 years, Ganesh founded totus consulting, a strategic HR consulting firm; Coaching Foundation India Limited, a pioneering institution for coaching and leadership development and totus HR School, an HR capability-building institute.

He has authored the book *Creating a Helping Organisation: 5 Engaging Ways to Promote Employee Performance, Growth & Well-being* and co-authored the book *Are You Ready for the Corner Office?* He has a very large body of published articles and blogs to his credit.

Ganesh is an alumnus of XLRI, Jamshedpur, a professional member of the India Society for Applied Behavioural Science and trained and certified as a Coach by Dr Skiffington, Australia and Coaching Foundation India.

Harish Devarajan is a Leadership Coach and Consultant. He is known for his vivacious, inspiring style of engaging with people and lives by his personal credo—'committed to making a positive difference'.

An alumnus of XLRI, Jamshedpur, Harish was the Chief Human Resources Officer (CHRO) in Hindustan Unilever. In this role, he led the HR transformation journey for Unilever across 40 countries in Asia, Africa and Australia. He then founded 'People Unlimited', a consulting practice that focuses on Organisational and Leadership Effectiveness.

Harish has been accredited by the International Coach Federation, USA as a Master Certified Coach (MCC). He has also been honoured with numerous recognitions for his leadership and professional accomplishments. As President of the National HRD Network, Bangalore Chapter and the convenor of the XV National HRD Conference, he has made meaningful contributions to the HR fraternity.

Currently, he is an Independent Director on the board of Bank of India and also serves on the advisory board of other companies.

V. J. Rao, an alumnus of the Tata Institute of Social Sciences, Mumbai, has been an operational HR professional for 40 years with experience in a wide range of industries such as engineering, projects, FMCG, IT and ITeS.

He was Head of HR of GE's joint venture in India, Godrej GE Appliances Ltd and later Head of HR of India's largest IT Company, TCS. He helped TCS obtain a PCMM level-4 rating in 2001, which was a first in the world. He was the Director of the Tata Management Training Centre, headed Tata Administrative Services (TAS) and senior-level recruitment in the Tata Group and was responsible for several initiatives in leadership development in the group.

V. J. Rao was a Member of the Board of Tata Auto Plastics and also Country Head, HR and Head, Global Talent Management at Suzlon Energy. He is currently a Leadership Coach and an Executive Director of the totus HR School.

The authors have collaborated on several in-company HR capability-building programmes and HR research projects over the past several years. These efforts have served as the inspiration for the book.

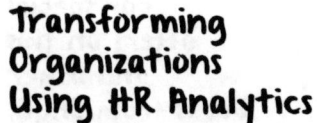

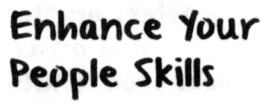